Universal Hidden Insight
Presents:

The Self Beyond
A Field Guide to Personal Activation.

Navigational and instructional insight for your journey toward self-discovery, deeper healing, and soul awakening.

The Self Beyond

Contents

FORWARD 13
THE LEGEND 19
   THE COMPASS 19
   THE QUEST 20
   THE DIAMOND 20
   THE SLEEPERS 21
Chapter 1: Aligning and Emerging 23
THE OBSERVER 23
EDUCATION 25
   PREREQUISITE 26
   GOOD WORK 29
   THE HURT 31
   THE DOORWAY 33
   RESISTANCE 34
INNER WORK 36
   TOUGH LOVE 38
   METAMORPHOSIS 40
   DEPTH 42
THE LIGHT 44
   IMAGINE 44
   GOING WITHIN 46
   LETTING GO 49
   CLEANING HOUSE 51
   INNER TEMPLE 52
   MAKING TIME 53
MEETING THE ONE 55
   CLIMB 57
   THE LOVER'S 58

- IMMERSION 59
- Chapter 2: Rising and Learning 61
- AVOIDING THE TRAP 61
  - OPEN MIND, OPEN WAY 62
  - JUST EXIST 64
  - ALL IS ONE 66
  - BEING "SPIRITUAL" 67
  - THE FOUNTAIN 69
- ACTIVE SPIRITUALITY 70
  - BEING POSITIVE 71
  - UNCONDITIONAL LOVE 74
  - FOCUS AND AWARENESS 76
- THE CENTER 78
  - BELONGING 79
  - THE MOUNTAIN 79
  - VIBRATION SEED 80
- THE BLUEPRINT 83
  - ENERGY 90
  - SPACESUIT 91
  - ELEMENTS 92
- ALIGNMENT 93
  - THE HEART 98
  - TUNING IN 100
  - SENSE 102
- PRACTICE 104
  - SILENCE 105
  - CREATIVE EXPRESSION 106
  - WALKING IN NATURE 106

REFLECTION 108
MEDITATION 109
MOVEMENT 114
GRATITUDE 116

Chapter 3: Vision and Mental Clarity 121
SET AND SETTING 121
THE QUANTUM SELF 125
   CHANGING YOUR MIND 128
   COHESIVE HEART 130
   NO LIMITS 132
   "TIME TRAVEL" 132
   ACTIVATION 135
SECONDARY CONSCIOUSNESS 136
SOUND AND MUSIC 138
STAR BEING 145
   POLARIS 147
   BLESSING 148
   THE WALK 149
CONNECTING TO THE HIGHER SELF 149
   MANY WORLDS 152
THE ART OF WATER 154
   LOST & FOUND 156
   MANY FACES 157
   DON'T WAIT 162
NATURE MESSAGES 163
   TREE OF LIFE 166
   THE CAVE 168
   THE SUN 173

Chapter 4: Healing the Whole Self 175

HEALING FROM THE INSIDE OUT	175
MY HEALING JOURNEY	177
WHAT DO YOU SAY	181
NEW PROGRAM	183
THE INNER CHILD	184
WILLINGNESS TO CHANGE	185
FORGIVENESS IS FREEDOM	186
ACCEPTANCE AND SELF-EMPOWERMENT	188
CHOOSE HEALING	191
FOCUS AND ACTION	192
HEALING ALL BODIES	194
ENERGY BODY	197
THE POWER OF BELIEF	201
PATTERNS	202
THE PROCESS	202
SOUL CONTRACTS	204
OLD AND NEW SOULS	206
THE SIZE OF THE SOUL	208
SOUL PURPOSE	209
THE DEPTH	211
Chapter 5: Opening the Heart	213
LOVE IS	213
IN RELATION	214
LIMBIC RESONANCE	216
MISUSED CONNECTION	216
BREAK OPEN	221
INFINITE LOVE	231
LOVE LANGUAGE	233

SENSITIVITY AND STRENGTH	234
GENTLE WARRIORS	234
THE SONGLINES	235
INTERVAL	237
THE CIRCLE	238
THE MICROCOSM	238
THE CUP	239
MAGIC	240
BECOMING LUCID	241
TRAINING	244
BALANCE	246
HEART OPENING	249
LIVING TEMPLE	250
TAPESTRY	252
THE FROG	253
SCULPTOR	254
THE PATH	255
LOVE BEYOND	259
PEACE	260
FOLLOW YOUR HEART	261
LIGHTHOUSE	262
Chapter 6: Beyond the Self	265
THE PLUNGE	265
THE INNER OUTER	267
DUAL-MIND	269
THE DARK SIDE	271
SERVICE TO OTHERS	274
HOME WORK	275
EARTH	276

The Self Beyond

THE VEINS OF OUR PLANET 281
THE LUNGS OF OUR PLANET 283
HOW TO BE A CLIMATE WARRIOR 286
CHANGES THAT MATTER 288
THE HUMAN RACE 291
    THE THEATRE 292
    WORLD ISSUES 294
    THE ORDER 300
    WAKING UP 303
THE RE-EVOLUTION 304
    GLOBAL COMMUNITY 305
    ALL WAYS 307
    UNCERTAINTY 312
THE PARADOX OF THIS PARADIGM 313
    THE LIGHT SIDE 316
THE CHOICE 319
    THE GARDEN 320
    THE ROOT 320

Chapter 7: Activation and Ascension 323
ALCHEMY 323
    THE CRUX 324
    DRIVING FORCE 326
    YOUR CALLING 327
    ATLAS 328
    ACTIVATE 329
CROSSING OVER 330
THE UNCONQUERED 332
    Affirmations for a New Beginning 335
        To Help Others: 337

The Self Beyond

> A single event can awaken within us a stranger
> totally unknown to us.
> To live is to be slowly born.
> ~Antoine de Saint-Exupéry

The Self Beyond

FORWARD

In the early summer of 2017, upon watching the wonderful and terrible momentum of events transpiring on the world stage, I sat in dread and awe. Can this be real? Careless world leaders sending nations into a nightmare scenario, threats of nuclear annihilation, massive floods, record breaking hurricanes, large scale earthquakes, civil unrest, and great division has all come out of the shadows, now at our doorstep in such a way it leaves little room for denial. Most people became terrified crying, "The world is ending!" Some citing Revelations and preparing for the worst. Yet, perhaps this is not an ending, but a beginning.

Something else is happening too. Something more subtle, yet pervasive. Divinely inspired and courageous visionaries, healers, lovers, and artists alike stood up and said, "No," moving up to meet these dark events like breakers meet the storm waves as they crash toward shore—shattered waves infusing the sands representing sparkling hope, compassion, love, and great care for the heart and soul of our collective family. This countering energy is a movement, a revolution, an awakening. One in which we are each participating through our consciousness, our energy, and our very being. There were those who recognized this for what it is; an opportunity for collective ascension; and a chance, however small, to change for the better.

The Self Beyond was born of a very basic understanding that people need healing, not just superficial healing, but deep self-healing. This work was inspired by the simple concept that we can find our own answers if we can connect from within, which most of us have forgotten how to do. The many issues we are seeing in the world are due to millions of individuals stumbling around unable to see the bigger picture. We have been incapable of drawing on the source of Love from within so we spend all we have chasing it, at the cost of who we are. People, by and large, need repurposing in a world that has only offered shallow and unfulfilling meaning. We need a shift in our core priorities to infuse our lives with something real that can bring us back to life and balance.

As this flood of overwhelming urgency came over me, I began writing this book. It poured out of me, thousands of words in just a few hours. Every day more came to the surface having been neatly collected in the files of my mind just waiting for the appropriate moment in history to be read. We each are being called to share our gifts: to speak, to act, to write, to sing, and to go deep within. All to contribute to the greatest healing and transformation of our time which is happening *right now*. We just need to be able to tap in and know it.

Through this darkness coming to the surface we have been given a choice. What will we choose to align with: the chaos of impending doom or the courageous co-creation of a better world and a better us within it? There is no bypassing this now. We are up against the decision of our time. What we do now will not only shape the course and destiny of our individual lives, but those of many potential generations which follow us. We are making the choice in every moment, every thought, every feeling, and every action.

Realize, the world is not in crisis, *we are*. This is not a battle of forces of light and dark over the soul of the world, it is a battle of the light and dark within *us*. A battle of the spirit of humankind. Reality as we know it is truly shifting. Many of the rules and limitations we have believed no longer apply. It matters more than ever that we become aware of ourselves in a new way. If we wish to heal the world, we have to first heal ourselves. From my standpoint, there is nothing more necessary right now than individual healing on a global level.

We affect the whole and the whole affects us, just as if one part of our body is out of balance, it can create imbalance in other areas. Addressing this perpetual feedback loop requires attention on our *intention*, mastering both our emotional and mental states to become a calm within the storm. We are each creating the world we see and our individual contributions are as relevant as whether you use salt or sugar to make a cake. A hammer can be a tool or a weapon. We are the same. We are utterly and inextricably linked to each other and all life on this rare blue dot in the ocean of galaxies, just as your fingers are connected to your hand.

For my part I realized that we already know the answers to these larger problems in our lives and the world. Our problem is we have forgotten how to connect from within and heal ourselves as we once could. The purpose of this book is to support you in reconnecting with that which you already know, to help you access what you already have inside but whose path has long been lost. This book is meant to bring you back into your greater self-awareness, to facilitate self-healing and initiate a self-sustaining alignment with your most natural state of Being.

Understand, this work will *not* outline my path or how I got to where I did. There is no cheat sheet to the tests of life. This will not list out steps that you can check off a checklist on your spiritual journey. No one can do that for you. A great teacher or sage may have an answer, a method which works for them. Maybe many others find that particular method also resonates for them as helpful guidance. It is still only a piece of a map, not the road itself. It might be the compass that points you in a certain direction, but you are the one who must find the way. This work will not offer an ultimate answer. This is meant to provide you with the questions. The answer is hidden within.

The answer must come from within *you*. The trail is yours to chart. You have already begun. Since the day of your birth you have navigated your own path. The path has now drawn you to this text, *this moment*, and for that my truest intention is there will be a message here that will change your life, *not your path*.

Your path is your own. Bless it always in faith that within you is the compass, the map and the key. Deep within you, you have always known the way. There is no wrong route. The journey is not about finding anything, but discovering for ourselves—our Truth.

Our minds open new layers of awareness as various concepts are introduced. This text is multidimensional in that it may read one way, one day, and a different way the next. There are many levels of meaning. Some concepts you may already be familiar with, but there are always new ways to look and revisit. Some ideas will be repeated as a main facet of the thesis and intended as the primary takeaways.

Think of this book as a field guide. Like the little pamphlets they hand out to you when you go to a National Park, for instance. A little guide to get you started, to outline what you can access, and some beautiful places you might want to stop and check out. This is meant to assist you in aligning with your own higher self and soul purpose; to provide you road marks to access the infinite data bank of cosmic information already stored within you waiting to be unlocked; to activate the journey already within you.

I will offer here a modifiable prototype for deeper healing, inner work, and personal transformation. We will explore the Universe and Divine Design, nature and all her brilliant metaphors, the quantum connections and your non-linear self, the practical aspects of applying spiritual wisdom, and unveil a more panoramic awareness through examining some global issues. This text cuts through the ideology to make what is essential accessible to you.

Of course, not everyone believes themselves to be spiritual. And misappropriations of words often happen, associations we relate to words can skew the context of meaning. But if you believe in something, anything at all, then that is spiritual and there is a way to take that deeper. Whether it is Love, a higher power, humanity, the earth, or a universal law of chaos or design. That is still very spiritual and it is in that context I appeal to that system of consciousness within you.

Understand, here there is some knowledge that cannot be put into words. It exists beyond the lexicon of our language as a feeling: a Knowing. Like the messages in the clouds, the essence of the unspoken. This vast resource of Loving Intelligence which cannot be intellectualized, only felt as a presence within, as a connection with something much greater. I do recommend to read this slowly. Sit on a paragraph, a section, a sentence, absorb it. Let it do its work. It will unfold in layers, like a flower opening petal by petal, each layer building on the last.

I do add a few disclaimers: much of what I write does not feel like "mine." I have simply cultivated my attunement to the higher universal consciousness. This allows the field of cosmic information to easily flow through me. (Anyone can do this, and I hope to help you do this as well.) I spend a lot of time in the solitude of nature and often I receive my insights during this time. It comes in many voices and threads. Due to this, many tones come across. Various thought streams will be introduced in this text. Some will repeat and reaffirm universal principles you are already aware of. Many will be introduced from a brand new perspective, with a new flavor. Some will seem revolutionary, visionary or perhaps even idealistic, but each of the topics and perspectives discussed here are significant on this great journey back to our truest self.

The message of spirit has many voices, but tapping into the universal language of Loving awareness, with an open heart and mind, allows these insights to flow through like an endless river of conscious intelligence. Love is the highest message. If a message speaks of pure Love then within that knowledge there is true wisdom. *Love is the voice of the soul.*

Here I am going to ignore the seeming juxtaposition of various belief systems. It matters not your religion or lack of one. It matters not if you consider yourself atheist, intellectual, existentialist or any shade in between. Being of any specific philosophy does not bar you from the relevance of this text, and it is also not a prerequisite of it as this goes beyond all those confines into what I will ubiquitously call spirituality with no strings attached. That term is meant to have whatever significance and implication most resonates to you on your personal journey, excluding none and welcoming all. Love is the epicenter of all pursuit toward Spirit.

For many, it is not just about being spiritual, but exploratory; to seek intellectually, or rather philosophically; dissecting the deepest truths to reach the core of all cores. In being spiritual I know that core to be Love. Love rests unchanged and unchallenged for all time as the reigning champion. It is the sole monolithic Truth. That is the starting point, then the venture to expose every pathway between here and there begins; between the mind and heart, between us and our true nature; to bridge that gap and integrate the ultimate connection at the center.

I have been a seeker my whole life. I don't remember a time when I felt I was satisfied with the superficial. I have always been drawn to the depths of discovery, the elusive, the existential point of this bizarre enchanting and complex life. For over two decades I have studied, written and researched on a vast array of subjects related to consciousness, philosophy, spirituality, quantum physics, self-discovery, inner healing, world issues, and cosmology. After all these years I have found this to be a ceaseless search. There is no end in sight. That may extinguish the flame of passion in some, but it has only fueled mine. This is for *you*, another endless seeker. Wherever you seek Love, you will find it.

The Self Beyond

THE LEGEND

A long time ago, in a place where time does not exist, Spirit, the Great Intelligence, wondered how far it's Love could stretch. How could it embody the most primal of forms from its most sacred state without losing the essence of Divine Consciousness? With the greatest of Love, the Source of all things would splinter itself off and create fractals of itself into infinity. Every fractal contained the Whole, a Whole of the Whole, though not knowing its wholeness. (This may confuse some, but will come together soon). With compassion and faith this was meticulously charted as the Destiny of the Eternal Existence. Many of these fractals forgot what they once were, a Light of the Light in a place filled with pain. Subtly the voice of the Spirit speaks whenever there is silence, reminding of the immense and Infinite Love. Still many confused in their confusion, lost sight of the connection to the Cosmic Soul of All that Is, and likewise, lost connection to the Source within themselves. So came the time when these fragments began to stir into waking. They were sent visions and insights, profound feelings of synchronicity in daytime and dreams. That was the beginning of humanity's greatest journey, the commencement of the time of the Great Remembering.

THE COMPASS

When the Loving Intelligence in Infinite Wisdom designed this great journey back to itself some fundamental guidelines were written, a Deep Magic within the human design. In this Great Experience the brave souls that would come, would forget that which we are: as One Cosmic Soul. Forgetting where we came from as Flames of the Light was part of the experience, but where would be the clues to guide us back to the One?

The golden keys of wisdom could not be made too easy to find, or the whole point of the experience would be missed. So they were hidden to allow for the Divine Process to unfold within the Spirit of humankind. Many have sought in various places; in teachers, in preachers, in lovers and books still the answer evades. It requires reaching, it requires seeking, it requires the test of the

Will of the Heart. Till then they in silence, in the stillness of surrender, through heartbreak or loss, or deep self-reflection may stumble into their first glimpse. The Intelligent Love was All knowing and placed the golden key in the one place we cannot lose—and so it is *within us*. Within you is the compass, the map and the doorway. Within your heart the key to unlock the Great Mystery. Seek there the answers to all of your questions. Seek there the healing, the Light and the Way. The Truth of all the Infinite Wisdom is always awaiting our homecoming back to the most sacred state of Being.

THE QUEST

So began the lifelong journey for the many souls who sought to increase their remembering. (This life is as going into a room and forgetting what you went in there for). The quest to recover the awareness we lost is the greatest journey back to the Truth of our Self. The secret cosmic irony is we spend all our time trying to get back to that Love, while Love spends all time trying to show us it has never left us. Always right there, though perceived as beyond us through some ill-defined barrier that does not exist, there is an intersection, a Gateway within us, which has never yet been severed, only in the minds and hearts that have closed their doors. But to the open and humble the connection is recalled and the Loving Intelligence once more can flow through.

THE DIAMOND

Through pressure, through darkness, through pain and through breaking, we crack through the shell that veils *all we are*. Through chiseling away all that is not us, the worry, the fear, the false identities, we begin to uncover the Diamond at the Center of the heart. *Deep at the Center* is the key to all knowing. Go to where Love lives and you have entered the most ancient Kingdom. Live from the heart space and you will conquer the darkness. There is the Light that illuminates the Sun from within.

THE SLEEPERS

Some had waited for many eons for the sleepers to awaken. Watching from beyond they exclaimed with great ecstatic joy upon seeing this Awakening take root. "A wave of change is coming!" they said to those that could hear through the Silence. "Carry only Love; infinite Love, purposeful Love, intentional, glorious, overflowing, radiant, righteous, unparalleled Love!"

What is there to do once you've awakened to a world that seems still sleeping? Coming out of a kind of cryogenic frozen state of the illusion of separation and fear, there is work to be done on space ship earth. That is the focus of this text: how to recover, replenish, reconnect, and revive the Soul of the Utmost within you and the world we share. This is the moment, the pinnacle of all epochs, and you are here to share in the Event of all events.

The Self Beyond

Chapter 1: Aligning and Emerging

THE OBSERVER

When I was a very young child I lived in the northernmost part of New York State. Potsdam is about as close as you can get before you're in Canada. It's incredibly cold there and just the right conditions for the northern lights. Sometimes at night while driving my parents would say, "Look can you see the northern lights?" And I would strain my eyes through the car windows but all I could see was the reflection of the street lights. I wasn't looking through the glass at the light beyond, but at the light on the window. I didn't understand how to look. Life is exactly the same way. There is something magical just beyond us, outside our own window, if we could stop being distracted by the reflection.

Imagine yourself on a city street like Time Square. People bustle by on their various trajectories; shopping, working, going many ways intently. Some may float effortlessly. Others may barge their way through. Imagine the faces, the sounds, the smells,

The Self Beyond

and the feeling. Now imagine where you stand within that busy street center. Where are you and what does that bring into your awareness?

Good. Now take a step *outside* of yourself. This is hard for some to conceptualize. Do your best. Imagine you are taking a break, sitting on a bench watching your "You" in this midst of this street. Instead of standing knee deep in this fray of energies you have the ability to now simply observe it. What is the self that you see thinking and feeling? What is the self you see doing in the midst of the buzz of life that surrounds them? What do you now experience in a state beyond doing, in a state of Being?

Becoming self-aware is becoming the observer. The pinnacle of consciousness is to witness your own existence. That ability is what separates us from a computer or soulless object: to have the ability to self-reflect. Reflecting in a way which brings one to non-linear consciousness. Becoming aware of the fact that you are not only *in* your body, but all around it. Your body does not contain the Spirit, but rather the Spirit contains the small vessel which we think of as the body. This one epiphany alone causes a chain reaction within you of expansion.

Bringing all inner and outer aspects to awareness allows us to transcend the linear mind. It allows us to go beyond what was once conscious and subconscious to marry them into a superconscious state of awareness. Be aware of your thoughts and emotions. Be conscious of your tone and your energy. Be observant of how what you *do* makes you feel, and how what you do or don't do affects others.

Being is the dynamic energy state of our heritage. Existing as a wave (potential) not a particle (actual). Do not be nervous about these terms. I will help you understand if you do not already. A particle is the actualized manifestation: its journey is complete. The wave is the infinite possibilities that exist eternally. That is quantum physics. We are likewise imbued with infinite possibilities in which we can choose our direction. We have a choice in every micro-moment during our ride here on the plane of learning.

EDUCATION

We make a shift thousands of times a day without realizing. Moving from being into doing and back again. Both forms are necessary for different reasons. Being is a place from which we can recharge, recalibrate, reconnect and revitalize ourselves. It is the existential state. Doing is the place in which we continue to learn and grow. It is the experiential state. It is important to be capable of witnessing yourself without becoming attached to your own thoughts or feelings. This teaches us to release. It is equally important to have experiences which generate those thoughts and feelings. This teaches us to allow. Both states of Being cultivate our self-development.

Part of the purpose of this human experience is to be *in* it: all in, fully and completely present. Not to bypass or deny the many facets of the human experience, but to embrace them, is central. Some of the popular new age doctrines push people away from this kind of immersion, and instead promote a total detachment. That does have its own purpose but can become a form of escapism. None of this work is to teach you how to escape yourself or your life. That is counterproductive. Anyone can forsake society and live in a bubble of self-created bliss. This book is meant to realign you with the reality of your own presence and assist you in self-actualization, which is the opposite of escape.

It is through the journey of our life that we come back to our self. All Love and loss, all passion and pain, all hurt and healing is teaching us something about our own meaning. Everything that comes to you, everything you draw to your life, is there to bring you closer to total healing and deeper understanding. We are sent people and situations to remind us about what we now need to look at and study within ourselves. We are here as both students and teachers. We grow through the many stages of a lifelong education. The great lesson is in remembering the Love that we are. The supreme message comes by being aware that *all of this*: every beautiful, painful, and wonderful moment, is a lesson in Love, and that lesson brings us back to our true self.

The Self Beyond

Here in the very beginning, I invite you to commit something to yourself. We thrive best and grow best in a relationship which does not place expectations upon us for what we need to be or do. We do best when we are not met with the obligation of conditions which can become limitations. This is true in our own relationship with our self as well. Try not to set expectations or conditions on yourself in this, instead allow your own process to *become* in its own way. This will happen in your own perceived time, in your own perceived space. Just allow.

PREREQUISITE

I am going to make a presumption, however primitive this may seem, its relevance will be revealed in time. I am going to imagine that you, yourself, are very special, that you have many talents and insights which you may or may not give yourself credit for. I assume the very nature of your spirit is to care deeply about the human condition. Perhaps you have a heart full of passion and caring that few can truly honor. Perhaps you have spent many years of your life feeling misunderstood or unheard, underappreciated or even alone in many ways. These are hallmarks of the deep seeker, the sensitive nature of those who walk just beyond the comfortable, carved out pathways of the masses. If you relate, you may in fact be a creative, powerful, and courageous healer.

What we need for you to know now is this: *you* are a good person and we need you here. When I say "we" this comes from the Universal We to which we are each inseparably connected. You are Loved and accepted. You are supported and guided. You are absolutely essential in all your glorious imperfection exactly as you are in this world. Your unique experiences and perspective, which no one else on earth has ever, or will ever, replicate in its exact form or measure is necessary and profoundly valuable.

To become aware of your worth, even just in theory, in and of itself causes a proliferation of positive energy in our lives and maybe even the universe as a whole. So many of us, the best and the brightest of us, the most Loving and sincere among us, have been holding onto this hurt, a deep hurt, for so very long. I greatly relate to that hurt. The hurt of a lifetime of others not understanding, of not being appreciated for the beautiful being

The Self Beyond

that you are, of being neglected and often abandoned after giving so much of our Love. Here in the beginning, I hope you will find some comfort in knowing you are not alone. You are not going crazy. There is nothing wrong with you. You are perfect as you are. Any expression of your truth is valid. Any emotion is allowed and accepted. It takes a great deal of courage to be real in a world that is so often defined by the artifice of the disingenuous.

Make no mistake your very existence, and all you are, is changing the world. Planting Love may seem fruitless at times. So many cold hearts that have not yet met themselves. Yet, even for those who seem unaffected, you have planted a seed that will inevitably grow. You are planting the best of things: Love and understanding. Here, I invite you beyond the limiting boundaries and definitions society has created that do not support the rich spectrum of the expression of life, but instead stifle and suppress it. I invite you to set those precincts on fire and break free!

A large part of this text will address how to access the higher wisdom within you even during the moments when you feel most lost in the dark. Remember, the dark is not a bad thing. There are no "bad" things. Darkness has its purpose too. We have to feel it so that we can heal it. The transformations we go through often do not happen in the Light, but in the darkness; in isolation and profound loneliness, in discomfort, even in great agony at times.

You're might feel like a mess. But if you really want to do a deep clean in your house, you basically have to get into everything; all the drawers and closets and boxes that you haven't dealt with in forever. Then you go through all that crap. You throw it all in a pile in the middle of the floor so you can look at what you want to keep, and what you want to throw away. At first you might think, "Damn... I made things worse. There is a bigger mess now than ever!" But as you start to itemize everything, and start getting rid of the deep clutter that's been sitting in the back of your mind, you will feel new again; brighter, lifted, and a whole new space opens up for you. That is what is happening. Stay with it, the mess is a blessing, it means you're doing the work.

If you can, allow yourself to get very still and start with the breath. Just focus on your inhale, then your slow exhale. Take nice deep breathes a few times and then allow yourself to fall into a comfortable breathing pattern. This is always the fundamental place to start. Inhale cool fresh cleansing air. Exhale hot tense air and release anything you have been carrying right here. Let the noise of the thoughts within your mind work through but do not hold onto them. Try not to feed the bear (so to speak). The point is to help us get to the quiet place where our own higher voice can speak to us.

Do not force anything. Just organically bring your attention to the vantage point within you where you can observe the traffic of thoughts in your mind; without judgement, with compassion. Without attaching yourself to them, or identifying with them. Just allow yourself to become more and more still, more and more silent. Be wherever you are now. Give yourself permission to be comfortable. Get yourself very centered. You can intend to. Intend your energy centers to balance and align within you. Intend yourself to allow a release of any unhealthy thought patterns or feelings that are not serving your well-being and growth.

Through these little conscious efforts you will begin to hear a deep wisdom come through from within you. You already know that voice. It is the voice you were born with. When you connect with this aspect of higher awareness within you, you can ask yourself questions and get very clear answers. You can also flow with profound insight. The more you can enter a deeper stillness, the more you will become adept at allowing yourself to tap into that infinite well of Love and Wisdom. The more you will be able to give yourself the advice you would give to another that you care for deeply. The more you will be able to constantly support yourself with compassion, the way you would for someone that you truly Love.

Know that you are brilliant. What you are personally going through I cannot pretend to understand exactly, but there is a theme we all touch on in the human experience which is shared. A shared heartache. A shared connection. I can empathize greatly in the many times I have dealt with feelings of utter loss, grief, and the painful processes of growth. When we are in the middle, it is hard to remember. Sometimes it takes months, or even years, to discover that there is a reason.

Be ready to accept that the journey is not always a blissful, rainbow ride. It can be scary, with emotional and mental obstacles that may seem impenetrable. For so many, sometimes, it all feels like too much. But that is where your deep healing is hidden. Sometimes growth feels like loneliness, discomfort, pain, and loss of things you held dear. Transformation is not always about comfort or light filled bubbles of paradise. It is at times an inwardly violent revolution, a liberation of the soul. If discomfort arises, as it often will during healing, do not be fooled into thinking you have made a mistake. If you can have courage and faith, you will find what you seek. You are on the path and your heart will guide you home. On the other side of suffering, I promise you it will have been worth it for the person it is all shaping you into. We shed layers of ourselves throughout our lives, and that progression is an emotional one. It can feel like we are not doing anything that even resembles growing, when in fact that is when we are growing the most. Pain is not a hindrance to healing, it is a prerequisite.

Know that you are deeply Loved from across the universe. Imagine (if it helps) a group of great ascended masters of Light watching you and sending you Love every moment, supporting you for all that your unique path can bring in. Consider just how very much you have to offer. Yours is a critical role in a world which is also hurting. We are the bridge builders and the healers. We have this ability because *we* have been so deeply hurt. And we have great work to do. But first we begin with *you*.

GOOD WORK

The first point is: do not be obsessed with progress. The concept of progress, like love, has been corrupted. Sometimes "progress" means pavement over a once beautiful field. Progress can be a very sad thing indeed. Instead be satisfied with the untamed fields and wild pastures of your own growth. Marvel in the beauty of what is ageless and ancient within you. You are already the evolution of eons, be still.

What then do we need to do? How do we meet in the middle of existence and experience? Gaining access to your truth, your wholeness, your healing, and your true Self takes patience, practice, persistence and a constant compassionate allowance of the *process*.

The process is simple. Where are you? You are here. There is nowhere else you need to be. You need to be with yourself

The Self Beyond

and within yourself. What time is it? It is now. It is always a never-ending and eternal now moment and that is where all your true power lies. Every answer, every insight, every key and doorway to your dreams is within you right now. Accessing that is easier said than done. We will talk about connecting within many times throughout this text, don't you worry. We cannot rush anything. Everything must happen organically.

Right now we all have one main job: Love and expand. That is the only "work" for us to do. It is the Good Work. Feel Love, breathe Love, *be* Love, radiate Love like the sun radiates celestial Light. Speak Love, show Love, align every aspect of yourself with Love. There is a powerful new world awaiting, filled with endless possibilities beyond all limitations. Receive it. Allow it. See it. *Believe* it. Infinite and immeasurable Love was always available to us, within and all around us. Right now it just so happens to be incredibly easy to connect with. Right now is the most important moment, we will never be here again.

> "*Can you imagine what it would feel like to become aware of an omnipresent ocean of wild divine love that has always been a secret to you in the same way that the sea is invisible to a fish?*" ~Rob Brezsny.

To connect with this well of Love within you, you may find many routes here in time, but to begin I suggest focusing on your breath as you inhale. And then again as you exhale. Did you anticipate something more profound? I hope I have not disappointed here in something so basic, but again and again we will come back to the breath. I do wish we could satisfy the intellectual ego by making it more complicated but this is our anchor. The breath and the center. We have to walk before we can fly.

So we breathe. Focus only on that exquisite action which comes so naturally. Do a body scan. Do you have pain somewhere? Your back? Your stomach? Perhaps behind your eyes? Wherever it is that you feel that pain, know that we will address the root of it later but for now just send it some Loving awareness and healing energy. Love is healing. Do you believe that is true? Place your hands there if it helps your visualization. Charge this energy with your intention to disperse any dis-ease within your system. Allow your body to begin to relax, starting with your limbs to your core, to your muscles, then your bones. Just be there with yourself. Sit comfortably, or lay down. Position does not matter. Alignment from within yourself is the key.

Right now you are accessing a powerful state of consciousness within you. Sit here long enough in a peaceful relaxed state and your brainwave patterns will begin to shift. From beta to alpha, to theta and for the very skilled meditators—gamma (at which point you will have dropped my dear book). We will discuss the brainwaves more in detail later. Again, for now just practice accessing this place within you. It does not matter where you are, whether you are in a peaceful field, or a crowded mall. You can tune out or tune in as much as you like. You are the navigator. It works just like the volume control on your television. Yes, you have that much influence over your own experience. *Will* can overcome many things.

Do you, here, begin to feel a subtle or even physical sensation? Some may feel it on the crown of the head. Some may feel it in the spine, going up the center of the body. Some may feel it on their arms, or neck. Bring your attention to your own heart. Not the muscular heart which pumps blood, but the etheric heart from which you feel yourself falling in Love. Imagine the sensation of falling in Love. That is what this Love feels like once cultivated to its fullest activation. The only difference is this Love does not require an outside stimulant. It does not rely on anyone to give it. It flows freely from the Source. Can you begin to sense that?

It is ok if you are not there yet, we have many more exercises to go through. Take some time this week to practice this, the more you do this, the deeper you will go, the more you will access, and you will begin to feel your heart open like a flower. Petal by petal, your higher heart will emerge radiating Love throughout your being. Do not worry about the simplicity of this method. We are starting with just being, peacefully and purposefully, within our own body.

THE HURT

Moving beyond the pain is one of the most difficult obstacles of self-emergence. Many on this journey have been scared to awaken due to already feeling so much so deeply. They are those who felt everything, saw everything, heard every unsaid word and it all broke their heart. These broken hearted lovers are the empaths, the understanders. They are the bridge between this world and the next. And, perhaps, one lives in you.

To those that struggle daily to stay afloat in the depths of emotional tides this world carries, you are not alone. You are seen, you are felt, you are held in the highest Light. To you the gentle voice of Spirit consoles with great compassion saying, "You are hurting. Hurting deeply. A lifetime of hurt. You need validation. You have it. You have it. You have suffered. We see that. We see through into your heart and know your pain as if it is our own pain. We cry with you. We hold you closely, always in our Light."

You have to forgive this deep pain. Realize the pain shows you where the damage is, and where healing is needed. It is a marker, not a life-sentence. Allow yourself to recognize this and then release it. Allow yourself to learn what it needed to teach you and show you, and be free. Thank the lesson. Hold the message, but let go of the hurt. You are not alone. Thousands, millions, of souls are making this shift. The shift to heal, the movement back to wholeness and Love. It is time. You feel it, don't you? Are you tired of being tired? Tired of pretending to be ok? Can you look at the face of your shadow and see it is a part of you, but not your whole. *You* are the Light within. You are the Light of the Light.

Can you let go of this attachment to the wound that drives you? Like an old pair of jeans that give you comfort but they no longer fit. Your nature is the state of Unconditional Love. Be. Just exist in your own sweet existence. You have been waiting for permission your entire life. You have it. You have it. Allow yourself to know it is ok. You are ok. You are deeply Loved. You are a beautiful expression of the Divine Experience that moves through worlds. You are the breath of cosmic creation inhaling and exhaling. Just breathe and Love the whole Self that you are. As you find yourself and remember, this presence of You is exactly who you were always meant to be. You are not your pain. You are the Love that has conquered it.

THE DOORWAY

Perception is the doorway, a kind of keyhole, through which we view our world. What we *see* is based (nearly completely) on how we are looking at it. The viewpoint we create will be reflected back to us in our experiences and all we see. This works two ways: in our reflection outward and the outward reflecting back to us. An outward reflection to us would be if someone says something that feels like an insult, it may hurt our feelings, but we may recognize that our feelings are hurt only when we perceive it as something personal. If we can see it rather as a reflection of that person, not ourselves, that hurt can be relieved. In this case the reflection is of their own inner state.

In the case of our reflection outward we might look out at the world and perceive mainly a cruel and uncaring world, and that is what we will then see, any goodness will be diluted and even filtered out by our bleak perception. But if we perceive the world as mostly a good and caring place, we will see the cruelty diluted and start to fade. Our perception can amplify or diffuse what we experience.

Our perception is the key to most of our suffering and trouble. This gives us some power because perceptions can change, and *we* can change them. We can change the way we look at our lives, others, and even the world. We can influence our own perception by introducing thoughtful questions to ask ourselves honestly such as, "Is this really personal?" or, "Am I feeling overly emotional due to this being a repeated situation in my life?" The more questions we ask, the more we open up that keyhole for a larger viewpoint to emerge.

As we broaden our perspective this will greatly affect what we see and experience from our new perception. Think of how much more scenery a wider lens can capture. Think about how much more light a diamond with many facets can reflect on. If we only come from one angle, one side, we may miss a lot of the truth. Greater perception means more awareness, and greater awareness means more truth. The doorway of your own perception can be opened at your command.

The Self Beyond

"If the doors of perception were cleansed every thing would appear to man as it is, Infinite. For man has closed himself up, till he sees all things thro' narrow chinks of his cavern." ~William Blake

RESISTANCE

There is a constant resistance with which we have been conditioned. We have been trained to oppose our most natural state of being which is oneness, connection, and a high resonance of Love. We have full on resistance to what *is*; what is coming, what has been, what is within others or within ourselves. Pause

---

[1] Obtained from Pexels under Creative Commons Zero (CC0) license

for this moment. Be silent within. Do you hear how all the thoughts are rushing through like a train? Allow yourself to let those remnant thoughts conclude and stop fueling the engine. Allow the noise of these thoughts to come to a slow halt. Is there still resistance? It is ok. You are not your thoughts, or your mind. You are the Loving intelligence beyond the mind. Allow yourself to tap into the part of you that can simply behold it all. Stop fighting it. Don't hold on. Don't let go. Just *surrender*. Allow yourself to be.

Do not chastise yourself if it is difficult to come into silence. Make no mistake, except for skilled practitioners in Zen and meditation, it *is* difficult. It is not, however, anything that some practice cannot overcome. This is a tool to assist you in the beginning. We are now learning to *allow* our own resistance, in order to transcend it.

In this moment Love yourself exactly as it is that you are. No exceptions. You do not need to try to change yourself as you are. Only accept the whole of you. The shadows and the Light, the wounds and the strengths, the emptiness and the fullness, the frantic overwhelming compulsions and the calm stillness. Healing comes once you accept yourself completely. And through that we can begin to accept all others with unconditional Love. Radical self-acceptance is key to overcoming resistance. To realize, there is no part of you that is "bad" or "wrong." All is welcomed but nothing becomes your personal identity. Let it come and let it go.

> "*I detach myself from preconceived outcomes and trust that all is well. Being myself allows the wholeness of my unique magnificence to draw me in those directions most beneficial to me and to all others. This is really the only thing I have to do. And within that framework, everything that is truly mine comes into my life effortlessly, in the most magical and unexpected ways imaginable, demonstrating every day the power and love of who I truly am.*" ~Anita Moorjani

INNER WORK

We won't get anywhere, not anywhere meaningful at least, without doing inner work. Inner work entails many aspects which can be broken down into five categories: addressing the past, taking responsibility for where you are and your life, acceptance of all you are (good and bad), releasing all that is no longer beneficial for your growth, and aligning yourself with your heart. I am going to go into each of these aspects more deeply throughout this book, but would like to do an overview here early on.

Reviewing our past is the most uncomfortable piece for most people. Even the thought may create physical resistance, grief, denial, or even rage. I understand this with a *deep empathy* and want each reader to know as you have you own experience in reading these words, you are supported in Love and you are *not* alone. [2] Some may find it is helpful to work through their journey with a support system of family, friends, or even counselors in place. Others may be capable of doing this work on their own. Choose the healthiest way for you. Only you know what you need.

Many of us have buried our past so deep within us under so many layers of issues that we don't notice it until it comes up to haunt us. Perhaps in an overreaction to our children's innocent request for attention, or excessively emotional response to a partner or loved one. Some of us may push people away, or hold them too closely. Some of us feel overwhelmed by daily mundane tasks, we may be much too careful, or find ourselves reckless and have no regard for our own wellbeing. All of these are traits of damage done early on, and please know that there is nearly no one who has escaped the past unscathed. There are no small wounds. Understand that each person's unique wounds are their own personal level of challenging, no matter the "size." It is their

---

[2] For those with particularly traumatic deep seated wounds, I would always recommend seeking a professional counselor to do more one on one work with you as you journey towards healing.

The Self Beyond

individual worst and we have to have great respect for one another in that.

We may tell ourselves it doesn't matter, we are adults now and it's behind us. That is true once we have properly healed. However, if it is premature, it only creates denial, exaggerates the root of the issue, and prevents proper healing. Our upbringing drastically sculpted our inner narrative, and that program perpetuates what we create in our present day life. In order to rewrite our scripts, we have to be willing to go back there to understand the source.

As we come into a mature understanding of how where we came from has affected who we are now, we can have many realizations. We may find a more compassionate understanding about why we have been so angry as an adult, or why relationships have failed us. We may identify the event which caused us to be so hard on ourselves, to never feel worthy, or to feel as if we could never do enough. This is a powerful time which can illuminate many aspects of your psyche to allow for a lasting and profound level of healing.

Forgiveness is the mastership of the work we have done in looking to our past. This is something you must make a choice to do for yourself. Forgiving the neglect, the abuse, the absence, the betrayal, whatever it is. It is fundamental to inner work to forgive the root of your pain and those who caused it. This has nothing to do with those that have hurt us. Nothing at all. This is about *you* and what *you* need to live to your maximum potential. As we forgive we can allow ourselves to let go of the patterns we have subconsciously preserved. Forgiveness allows you to set yourself free. Free to create a new narrative, one of strength, healing, insight, power, compassion, and heart based wisdom.

Whatever it is that happened to us as children, or even as adults, we are under no obligation to continue to maintain those same patterns any longer. Give yourself permission to be free from any outdated patterns, any negative images of yourself or your life, that have prevented you from thriving. We are here to evolve. Constant evolution is the active state of self-awareness, to be aware that we are meant to change many times throughout our lives. To shed old skin, to shift into wiser and more versatile versions of ourselves. To break the patterns of our past is to *heal the roots*. This is part of how we come back into self-Love. If we can understand ourselves more deeply, we can Love ourselves more deeply.

TOUGH LOVE

We are not victims or bystanders of circumstance. We are powerful beings and must recognize the responsibility of that. Accepting our responsibility for who we are, where we are, and what we have created in our life is key. If we continue to blame everyone else, all the factors beyond our control, then we are giving away our power. Why would we want to do that to ourselves? Make ourselves subservient to circumstance?

Empower yourself to accept that you alone have chosen who you are, the place you are in, and what you have created. This is a choice you have to make for yourself. You decide either, "No I do not take responsibility. This is not my fault." or, "Yes, I accept that I, alone, am in control of my life, my situation, and who I am within it." Do not misunderstand, what happened when we were younger and less capable of choosing was not our fault. What happened in our past is no longer within our reach and we can, once we have dealt with that, let it go. What heals is to take responsibility for where we are *now*, based on the choices we can control today. We make it emotional and get political with ourselves but it only harms us and disempowers us further.

In a universe designed with the edict of free will, it has only listened to your inner commands. Look at the evidence of this truth in your life. If you say, "No one loves me." The universe says, "I will show you what you wish to see." If you say, "I'll never make it, I'm not good enough, no one cares, I'm all alone." The universe says, "Your wish is my command." We see this evidence every day, with every thought and every echo of circumstance as it relays back to us. Yet we are stubborn. We make it personal when it is not.

Just as a test, a little homework assignment, try saying, "I am surrounded by Love. Life is full of miracles. I am good enough as I am. My life is a reflection of the abundance I have within me. I am blessed. I am so very blessed and grateful." Say this every morning as you wake, and every evening before you sleep. Smile as you say this. Then over the next week just pay attention to see what that begins to create in your life.

The Self Beyond

The suggestion that we are responsible for our own lives may create anger and cries that, "You don't understand!" I know this feeling. I sympathize greatly on this point. I felt it too when it was first submitted that my life was my own doing. How could they blame me, the victim, for abuse, for heartbreak and loss, for chronic illness, for everyone I had ever loved leaving me, for so much pain? All this had reaffirmed an old program I had been running since childhood; that I will be misunderstood and abandoned, that I am not truly Loved for who I am, that I do not fit, that I am not worthy of Love and compassion. Yet upon less defensive reflection I realized, in quite an epiphany, *I* was the one running that program. I was not under gunpoint. No one was telling me I wasn't good enough, only me. In my defense, my life had showed me these statements were true, but my continuing to believe them only propagated their truth.

After days, even weeks, of resisting, the seed of this thought began to unravel the protective mechanism of my reality I had so tightly held onto. There was an undeniable connection between these subtle background programs that I did not think were doing any harm. But no matter how much self-work I had done as an adult, my true healing did not begin until I was willing to accept this simple truth: *we create our life*.

All our relationships, our situations, our grievances and our blessings, we call them all to us through our thoughts and emotions. We continually project onto our reality the filter of whatever we focus on. If we have inner turmoil, we will see turmoil. If we believe we will never have Love, then we will chase it away. If we believe the world is cold and dark, we will see that. But this seemingly harsh truth has a treasure hidden on the flip side. If we can focus on creating inner peace in our thoughts and emotions, we will begin to have peace. If we believe the world is good and beautiful, we will see that too.

Here, perhaps, you can begin to see this is true in your life as well. We will sit with this thought seed for a little bit before going further. You don't have to accept it yet, but I ask that you allow it as a consideration. Sample it as you would a new wine. Perhaps you don't like red wine, but now you are willing to give it a swish. If resistance is clearly present, see it for what it is. It is not full on rejection, it is an automatic reaction to our perception being challenged. The same way our knee jerks when tapped with a rubber mallet. Remember that this is where growth lives, just beyond our comfort zone. If we truly want change in our lives, we have to also be willing to change.

METAMORPHOSIS

Accepting that change is inevitable, and necessary, is a mark of a maturing psyche. It is healthy to seek to better ourselves but also tremendously important not to reject who we now are. We are transforming through healing but the essence remains the same: accept yourself as you are now, *all* of who you are. No part of you is good or bad. You cannot dissect out parts to discard. It is all connected. You are one whole and complete being. Nothing you are doing is correct or incorrect. Think of it rather as what is benefiting your life and what may no longer be benefiting your life.

What is beneficial to you may change throughout your life. You may have times in which you get a great deal out of being social, for instance, then other times when you may learn a great deal about yourself by being in solitude. You may have times where you feel happy for months on end, and times where you feel deeply sensitive and distraught. Don't make the mistake of thinking that anger or sadness are automatically unhealthy. They are not. They are natural human emotions. They only become unhealthy when left unexpressed, or expressed in an unhealthy way such as fighting, or blaming yourself or another. You have to find within you a deep compassion for both your Light and your darkness, your healing and your pain. Pain is a part of life and guides you back to Love. Pain does not mean you are not healing, pain comes with the process of healing.

Discomfort, loss, and sorrow each teach us something about our true Self. Accept them gratefully as teachers. Love the lessons that they bring up within you to teach you something you did not yet know about yourself. Every flower came up through the dirt. Sometimes when we think we are being cut down, we are actually being pruned. Pruning off the dead overgrowth allows for healthy growth. That is a true tending of the garden. We just have to make sure we water the seeds, not the weeds. We flourish wherever we shine the Light of our attention. We cannot ignore what we don't want. It must be acknowledged to be dealt with and settled, but we cannot dwell there, either.

Every strength has a weakness and every weakness has a strength. The trick is to nurture the strength in the weakness, and to recognize the weakness in the strength. An example is being very strong willed. That is a great strength to have. Many would admire this trait, up until the point where the strength turns into stubbornness or rigidity which can be a kind of weakness: a lack of the ability to adapt. You may believe you have a fatal flaw in a weakness such as being "too sensitive," yet think about how often that serves you and others who may need someone with emotional depth who can understand and empathize. This is a characteristic which can be cultivated into a genuine strength: to be strong enough to feel.

Here is a simple exercise to create some equilibrium within you. Write a list with four columns. Above the first column write "Strength" and then above the third write "Weakness." List out your greatest strengths and weaknesses and do this without bias and without judgment. This is not meant to make you feel bad in any way. This is meant to help you have greater self-awareness.

Now, in the second column, next to each strength you listed, write the characteristic tendency of that strength when it becomes too strong. This is the over-activity of the strength, or the weakness in that strength.

1) Strength   **2) Over-active Strength**
_____   _____
_____   _____
_____   _____

3) Weakness   **4) Active Strength**
_____   _____
_____   _____
_____   _____

This is simply to help you become more conscious of these areas which will help you become more intentional and calibrated. For example, if you wrote "Loving" under strength, but wrote "easily hurt" next to it. This can help you to know when it is time to draw on this strength (as a strength) without it becoming an unintentional weakness. Now write out in the fourth column the active strength in every weakness you mentioned. This is so important because it allows you to recognize how empowered you are in your perceived weaknesses. Now you can see the hidden strength within them, and use it when needed.

You do not have to change who you are. That is not the point. This is about becoming aware of who you are, so you can appreciate your own unique gifts—and use them more wisely. This, in itself, is a great transformation. Not every change happens outside of us. Some of the most meaningful changes occur from within.

Do know that change is constant. Do not be scared of them. Stay with those changes. Know that at the center, the heart within you is not changed, only uncovered. Metamorphosis is not changing what we are, but discovering what we are capable of being. It is not removing the "you-ness" of you, but removing that which has attached itself to you that is not you. Some of these things we have held onto as parts of us, but they never were. Stay fluid, adaptable and remember you cannot lose who you are, only who you are not.

DEPTH

Now we begin the deeper work. This is a lifelong process which is never fully complete. We begin to release that which is no longer beneficial to us, and allow ourselves to receive what comes, gratefully. Many things need to be released; negative affirmations we have reinforced, illusions of a false self, outdated beliefs about ourselves, the world, and reality (as a whole), ideas like separation, notions, like blame. We are not separate. We are all connected. I am connected to you through these words. You are connected to me as you read them. You are connected to your family through blood, to your community through shared space, to your environment through your effect on it, and its effect on you in return. We are each connected to the whole of earth and every living being.

Even our own bodies are communities of billions of microorganisms which maintain our biological system. Everything is connected, and everything we experience is part of our journey. Part of our lesson. All of this is a mirror, reflecting

The Self Beyond

back to us pieces of ourselves we need to deal with, learn from, and use. Nothing in this life is here to hurt us, it is all meant to heal us and help us remember.

There is no one to blame or reprimand. When others act with poor behavior or have poor attitudes, they are living in deep sadness and disconnection from their own spirit. When someone does not value the sacredness of life, or takes for granted the blessings and beauty, the miracles surrounding them, they are still lost. They need guidance, they need compassion, they need Love, not blame. Try to understand if we wish to be Loved and accepted for all that we are, we must also Love and accept others in the fullest expression of their truth as well. Even if that truth does not match ours.

There is no right way. There are many roads to destiny. There are many paths up the mountain. We each make our way in our own perceived time, in our own perceived space. As you align yourself each day with your higher self, with an open heart, you will attract more and more beauty, more and more to be grateful for in abundance and Love. Pay attention. Notice the beauty. Notice the abundance, the gifts, the blessings. They can be invisible. They can be silent. They can come in disguise. We may think something "bad" is happening, when in fact it is the best possible thing for us. Trust the Universe and the Universe within you (whatever that Universal Source means to you). Your heart knows the way. Be there with it.

To align with your higher self, you only need to connect with yourself from within. This may mean different things to different people: meditation, prayer, or silent devotion (for those who find this a little too sentimental, understand this is the way of the Samurai. Do not discount the warrior strength within this). You might try various spiritual practices such as yoga, tai chi, gardening or even cooking. The *way* is imbued within every facet of life. It is a matter of tapping into it. Find the vein that carries you back to yourself. There is a great energy flowing through everything, every moment and every breath. Only with an open heart and in a state of mindful awareness can we receive it and flow with it. *A heart that is healed is opened. A heart that is opened is healed.* You become aware simply through intention. Just intend to be aware, mindful and present and you will be. Tap into the peaceful warrior within.

THE LIGHT

It is not about becoming anything, it is about reconnecting with what is already within you. The truth has always been within you. It has only been shrouded, hidden by the layers of insecurities we drape to cover its brilliance. Our false identity of ego, the deceptions of the outer world, all these attachments become shades which dim the Light within us. Material desire in an immaterial realm. We only see solid matter to train us to remember, nothing is solid, everything flows. All you think you see are waves of infinite possibility. Everything around you, everything within you is Light and resonance. We will talk about the scientific reality of this soon. Do not hide your radiant self. Let your brilliance shine through, unrestricted. Your *you*-ness is your superpower. The Light that enlightens from within.

Not so far away, at all, those that support and guide us on our journey send us messages. They share the Unconditional Love and compassion of the Spirit to which we each belong. They say, "Make of yourself a Light within, a flame so magnificent that it overcomes all else. A Master of Light knows the way is Love. Love is the heart of your Truth."

I am not telling you a story. I am not telling you anything new. This is nothing you do not already know. Search yourself. You already know all the answers. This is simply a map back into your own Soul's Truth.

IMAGINE

Could you imagine the highest vision of yourself? The person you want yourself to become? All the confidant vivacity that person embodies. Paint that picture with as much detail as you like. Understand, it is important to celebrate where you are right now without being hard on yourself about where you think you should be. You are exactly where you need to be. It is also healthy to continue to challenge the potential you have within you to grow and transform. If you could imagine this optimal self, what do you need to let go of to become that? What do you need to cultivate

The Self Beyond

within you, using the capabilities you have already? What do you need to heal and forgive to get there? This is the beginning of a personal spiritual to-do list.

Spiritual To-Do List

Who do I see when I envision my best self?
_____
_____

What do I need to let go of to be my best self?
_____
_____

What or who do I need to forgive?
_____
_____

What do I need to focus on cultivating within me?
_____
_____

What do I need to heal?
_____
_____

What steps do I need to take and what better choices can I make?
_____
_____
_____
_____

How can I Love myself better?
_____
_____
_____
_____

GOING WITHIN

Meditation is the act of going within. While this sounds straightforward enough, it remains an elusive practice for many people. We have been so ingrained to keep our minds busy, filled, and we are inundated with distractions. Nearly everything in our world is designed to take our focus outside, to make us aware of what we are without, instead of all we already are *within*. This is the goal of meditation. To go deep inside yourself which paradoxically takes you much farther beyond the self.

Many people do not understand the goal, or the point of meditation. There are several layers to the practice of meditating, first quieting the mind, finding stillness and silence. That is challenging enough! Perhaps you are someone who has made many attempts, sitting, adopting some version of poses you have seen in pictures, and closing your eyes only to find your mind is racing. You might think, "I don't understand why this isn't working. Everyone else in the pictures looks so happy!" You are thinking of a million things; what to make for dinner, bills you need to pay, some issue at work, something you forgot to get at the store, wounds from past lovers, something someone said that has irked you. All of it is loudly apparent now. This is enough to chase most people away. These mindless thoughts persist; your leg is falling asleep, your face itches, you are thirsty, you have to pee. Now that you think about it you have a *ton* of things to do. *You must be patient*. This is your first test and passing through this begins a journey of personal perfection. A perfection of your inner self.

Once you navigate beyond this initial intense surge (which is, literally, just the boisterous ego's last defense of itself) you realize surrender is the only tool of survival here. Now you may begin to relinquish the sense of control over your mind and the next layer sets in. The key is not to quiet these thoughts. The key is to allow them and observe them, without feeding into them. Your mind will settle on its own if you do not continue to fuel the train. If a thought comes in observe it and let it go, in the front door and out the back. Do not let your thoughts overtake or overpower you. You have the power. The higher mind above all of this is the master and the captain, not the everyday grocery list mind or the leg falling asleep body. You are beyond these aspects

The Self Beyond

of yourself. They are merely extensions; expressions of your outer projections of your inner self.

How to go beyond this? Discipline. No one likes that word. It sounds harsh. It sounds cold, perhaps. It sounds like detention at school. But compassionate and dedicated self-discipline over your own mind is required. Your mind is a tool, not a weapon. Realize that your mind wants to focus on something, anything! Desperately it is constantly seeking some new obsession. Instead of feeding it the junk food of recycled thoughts, patterns and worries, just breathe. Focus on the breath. Start there. It should always come back into the breath, the current of life. Now listen. Hear the ceiling fan, the birds, any background noises going on. Observe them. Take note, but do not attach to them. [3]

[4]

Now move your attention to the body. Start with the toes, the fingers. Allow yourself to feel them relax. You can intend them to. Give your body permission to release any tension you have been holding. Move through your hands, your feet, your legs and arms, your thighs and core. Let your stomach and butt relax

---

[3] This technique may work well for overwhelming moments, panic or anxiety. There is more help at sites like this as well, The Anxiety Centre, http://www.anxietycentre.com/anxiety-tips/stop-anxiety-attacks.shtml

[4] Obtained from Pexels under CC0 creative commons licence

as you sit comfortably. Let the muscles of your back relax. Continue upward. Let your shoulder blades and shoulders relax. Relax your chest, your throat. Relax your neck and your ears. Relax your jaw and your mouth. Relax your cheeks and your eyelids. Feel the comforting weight of gravity holding you in your space. Relax your forehead and now your crown. Melt into yourself. Simply be aware of this feeling of being in your body, grounded and comfortably aware.

Visualization or guided meditation can assist beginners. Even practiced meditators use these tools. For now, try to visualize a calm serene environment. Perhaps a beach with the golden sun shining down, and the turquoise waters surrounding the white sands. Imagine the waves peacefully coming in, and rolling back out, like a pulse. Breathe with this natural rhythm. Allow the tranquility of this space to envelope your consciousness. Nothing exists but this beach, the blue sky, the billowing clouds, the dancing green leaves of the trees behind you, and those gorgeous calming waves. Be aware of this space which goes beyond your physical body. This is also an extension of you, is it not? You have created it from within you. An entire world spontaneously emerging from your very consciousness. That is the power of your mind unleashed.

Now imagine feeling a beam of golden white Light coming down into the crown of your head. It gently comes through, radiating down, filling your mind with warm and calming Light. Bathing every thought in golden blissful serenity. It continues down to your throat, then filling your chest and emanating inwardly as a deep feeling of Love, serenity, and wholeness. This wondrous ray of Light continues through the core of your body to your very roots. Really add some color to this visualization. Allow it not to just be a fantasy. Remember that *you create your reality*, which means this is just as real and valid an experience as walking the dog, cooking dinner or listening to a beautiful song. If you are present in this experience, then it is important. It is valuable for you, and it is your own reality within.

Feel now the earth beneath your body. The vibration of the entire planet which is our home. Feel her mountains, valleys, oceans, and woods. Send her Love for any pains she is dealing with (the earth hurts too). Feel the movement of all the life which travels on with its various daily tasks; the birds in the sky, the great whales, the wild horses, the little bees, the ants, the squirrels and the great elephants. Become aware of their existence in this shared world. Look around within you and notice the trees, so graciously offering their shade, their leaves drinking in the sunlight. See the vivid colors. Breathe in the scents and the sounds of nature and life. Connect deeply into this universal rhythm. The harmonics of the tapestry of this world. This vibration is the energy flow of the entire cosmos. And you are also made of this fundamental vibration, every molecule and cell of you. Aligning with this current of life can allow you tap into your own true nature, which is peaceful, which is whole, which is in complete balance always.

Imagine that the earth sends up a rainbow violet flame which comes up through your body like the roots and branches of a tree. It begins in a crisp apple red, then quickly shifts to sunset orange. A delicious yellow radiates into a neon lime, then into a deep emerald green. A gentle turquoise turning to sapphire blue, then a violet purple emerges, ending in a glorious fuchsia like a wildflower. This warm Light extends until it meets together with the golden ray of Light from above. Just bask here for any length of time you feel is appropriate, among the sunshine, the waves, the trees, and golden Light pouring through you. From this place, simply be present and breathe. You have cleared your mind of its own mindlessness. You have silenced all the unnecessary chatter. This is the beginning of a communion with your true self.

> *"Go deeper past your thoughts into silence…*
> *Past silence into stillness..*
> *Past stillness into the heart..*
> *Let Love consume all that is left of you."* ~Rumi

LETTING GO

Letting go is one of the most difficult things to ask a human to do. Many other species and lifeforms have this innate ability to let go. Not us. We want to have control. It is through trying to control that we lose grasp of the very thing we wish to direct most: our self. Let go of the desire to control. Surrender to a higher power within you. I do not mean to speak of God, but this can be taken in that sense if that resonates with you. Whether you believe that Source to be coming from beyond you or within you

The Self Beyond

is not so much important. What is important is the self-realization that when we let go, we allow life, and our own energies within life, to Flow.

We block the flow when we constantly micromanage what we should be doing, thinking, or feeling, where we should be, the specific results we want. There is a huge difference between beginning to manifest the life you want, and trying to manipulate it. You cannot control it. You can co-create. You cannot *make* something happen, you can allow it. You can leave yourself open to receiving it by letting go.

We attach ourselves to so much that is not us, then we wonder why we feel so off balance, so weighed down, so restricted. Consider a person who has kept every old trinket and article of clothing from everyone who has hurt them. They carry it on their back day after day. Consider a person who has constantly kept with them every paper filed, every deadline, every call they made and email sent. They carry it with them, even when business hours have long past. What about someone who carries every worry of the future, or someone who spends endless hours ruminating about one emotional encounter or relationship issue? Can you imagine a person who has realized they no longer need to carry the articles of those who have hurt them, or their worries of the future, or their issues from the past, and the weight released as they let go? This is the person who has become lifted and liberated. This is the power of letting go.

Letting go of all that is not you might sound simple, but this is the longest leg of the path back to your true self. The issue is we have defined and built our identities with the very things which limit us from moving forward, or growing. We identify ourselves with our jobs, our relationships, our hurts, our illnesses, and even our personality flaws (which are not truly flaws). Through all these outer aspects, we draw a picture of who we believe we are, what we have become accustomed to, which we assume defines us and, therefore, our worth. Yet none of these outer aspects define us at the most fundamental level. How do we get in front of that deeply ingrained misperception of ourselves and begin to strip this all away?

Start with a basic question: who am I? *Ask yourself*: am I my possessions, my career, my partner or my family? Am I the hobbies I have? Am I the things I like? Am I my personality? Am

The Self Beyond

I my beliefs, my passions? Am I my past, my present, or my future? Am I the thoughts I think, or the feelings I feel? Realize here: you are none of that at all, not really. It is not the "Am I" that defines you, but the "I Am" that defines you, and how you complete that sentence is what creates who you are in your world.

All of the outer can be lost. It can all change. The external definitions are transient and unreliable. You, my Beloved, from the soul at the core of your being, are eternal. Anything that can be stripped away was never truly who you are. It was only a part of you, a part which you do not need to identify with. The whole of you is beyond all of this. This is both, perhaps, troubling and emancipating, terrifying and amazing. That is why the process takes so long. It is one thing to have a concept make sense. It is quite another to live it, to become it. This is how we get to the center of the center: by releasing, by surrendering into the abyss of the unknown until it becomes the known. We must do this until we come back to the self, beyond all that is not self.

CLEANING HOUSE

To create a state of peace and a sacred space within us, it helps if we can create a simple quiet place in our own homes. Think of your house as your mind. If it is cluttered, messy, unorganized, then so too will be your mind. If you cannot find what you are looking for when you need it, if you are tripping over piles of stuff, if you throw things instead of place them, then this is a good indicator of the need for organization. Do not feel offended. Many brilliant people have been less than particular about housekeeping while still being greatly successful. Understand that minimalism and organization creates coherence. If you hold onto useless things that bring you no joy and serve no purpose, then you are likewise holding onto old energies that need to be cleared out. If you are carless with your space, you may be unintentionally careless in other, more important, areas of your life. This is an exercise in restoring that kind of care.

Cleaning does not have to be a chore. It is a meditation of the mind. Clean with joy. Infuse your space, your home, or your apartment with happy new clear energy. Pick up pillows and blankets, give them a few good pats, and shake them off. This breaks up stale energy and allows new energies to come in. Play music while you clean. Make this an event: a cleaning party! Get the whole family involved, or roommate, or even your pets if you have them. If you live alone, even better. This means you can be in total management of this project to clear out the old and brighten up, not only the space, but the energy of the space.

Your space is like a metaphor for your mind. Keep, there, only what brings you joy. Do not overfill it, or there will be no room for anything new. It just creates blockages and disorder. At least every couple weeks, give your dwelling a good dusting, vacuuming, sweeping. Take care of the cobwebs, and declutter. Give old clothes you have not worn for months or years, away to homeless shelters, church groups helping the needy, or charities. Get rid of items that serve no purpose, except for those that inspire your spirit, such as art or sentimental ornaments. What is no longer needed can be paid forward to a companion who could use it.

Cleaning is important because it encourages us to take responsibility for our own mess. Cleaning reinvigorates and recharges the space which makes up the environment in which you spend much of your free time. This is a worthwhile investment. A clean home supports a clean mind.

INNER TEMPLE

Treat your body as sacred. Build a temple within yourself. This requires being ultra-conscious of the toxins we ingest willingly. Processed foods are damaging to you and the planet. GMO's (genetically modified or engineered foods), chemicals, heavy metals in many foods, and preservatives are all harmful to our body. They fog up our minds, and they slow down the body's natural ability to fight off disease. Our body is already designed to heal itself. Our amazing body is capable of defending itself and cleansing itself from any harmful invaders like viruses or bacteria. We have an immune system which does the fighting for us, if we keep it healthy and strong.

Make organic raw food choices whenever it is possible. Decline taking medications unless absolutely necessary or life-saving. Filter the fluoride, heavy metals, chlorine and bleaches from your water. Choose pure water over soda. Make infused water instead of drinking juice full of sugar. Sugar is a leading contributor to poor health, illness and even cancer. Avoid or

The Self Beyond

abstain from animal products that the body cannot digest well, and lowers your vibration. The amount of antibiotics and additives that are in dairy and meat are highly unhealthy for a human body.

Move your body daily. We are meant to use our muscles and move. This keeps joints lubricated and prevents many aches and pains. Try to exercise 2-3 times a week, or supplement this by making the most of all movements. When playing with your children, try to initiate more physical activities that involve the whole body; kickball, hide and seek, tag etc. Don't forget to stretch! Use the times you are walking to work your leg muscles, your back and your gluts. When you bring focus to a muscle group you can intentionally work them.

Strengthen your core. The core of your body is the center that holds everything else together. Yoga can be great for this and all other muscle groups. A simple core boosting exercise you can do right from the comfort of your own home is a "plank." This is done from a push up position but while propped on your forearms, looking forward, and holding it here for a few minutes (very simple). Jogging or brisk walking both help keep your body in optimal condition. Please do not feel bad if this is something that is not now a part of your life. Many people have neglected this type of light workout. It is never too late to begin. It will help in your other healing work to have a body that feels better.

Pamper yourself when you can. Take relaxing and restorative baths with Epsom salts, baking soda, and organic oils (such as lavender or eucalyptus). This combination helps draw out toxins in your system, and, also, just feels really nice. These are just a few little ways to honor the temple which houses your spirit. Treat this space as you would an actual temple. Bring your body offerings to restore the life within it every day. If you do not Love your body, how will you Love yourself within it? Your body is sacred. Every part of you should be treated with great care.

MAKING TIME

For many, you may feel you do not have time to devote to meaningful moments on a daily basis. Allow me to explain how this is not so. You do not have to set aside special time to have meaningful time. Every moment can be injected with significance if we change our presence in the moment. Turn things you *have* to do, into meaningful, or even spiritual, practices. This is as easy as transforming your morning shower into a cleansing ceremony, for instance. You can enjoy your shower, instead of rushing through it. Let the water wash away any residual energies from the previous day. Use this as a time to renew, realign, and release. Many of our visualizations can happen right here. Use this time as a talk up time. Do some positive pep talking to yourself before the day begins. Think of yourself as your own personal spirit-coach. This infuses your entire day with good energy and an invigorated attitude. Changing your attitude, alone, will move mountains.

You can change how you think about your time spent driving to do errands by savoring it instead of resenting it. Use it as a chance to look around, to take in the understated beauty of the city you live in, the landscape and the community. Notice the clouds, the trees, and the history. Notice the abandoned places, even the spaces that need Love, and appreciate them too. Extend your attention to the meaning within those spaces. Try not to overlook what you do not want to see. Those who need help, notice them. Have compassion, suspend judgment, share what you can. What is more meaningful than that? If you travel with your children make them a part of this. Ask them what beautiful things they see. Make it a game. Be creative with it. Have them point out any birds they see, or flowers, or acts of kindness.

Take chores of all kinds and look for ways to fill them with meaning. When folding laundry, when vacuuming, when mowing the lawn, consider all you have to be grateful for. Use these jobs as tools. They can be moving meditations. Insight comes during the most menial tasks, *if you are present*. Create your own meaning. Create your own rituals and devotional practices. These are the practices most filled with meaning because they are personal and relevant to you. I have created my own little sacred times and they fill mundane moments with purpose and joy.

We spend so much of our time doing things we *have* to do. We take that time for granted. We try to bypass it. We begrudge it and detach from it. We waste so much of our own precious life in waiting for a more meaningful moment to enjoy. We resent our time at work, when we know we will be dealing with people, for instance. But we have a real opportunity to use that time to make a meaningful connection, to make the work we do make a difference. Try to change your mind about these moments. Don't dread them. Look forward to them. There is a purpose behind every person we interact with. We are meant to connect with them for a reason. Don't miss out on that. Use these times to challenge yourself and see what meaning you can bring into them. I don't care if you make sandwiches or if you are the CEO. We have chances to connect with people no matter what we do and every time we connect with people, we have an opportunity to change the world for that person, and allow them to change ours.

You do not need to do "spiritual things" to have a meaningful life. Everything we do can be meaningful. Look for ways to imbue your life with purpose that is significant to you. It is not in what you do, so much as it is in how you do it, how you perceive it. Recognize that purpose is imbedded in every part of your life, and life has no spare parts. Walk with purpose, move with purpose, speak and act with purpose. When I am saying "purpose" it is from an understanding that all we do has purpose, whether or not we are aware. All this is really saying is fully be in your Being. Be fully present. Be fully authentic. Walking, moving and acting in your own sacred truth, wherever you are, is the deepest meaning of all.

MEETING THE ONE

Many of us have been conditioned to obsess over romantic relationships. We do not feel complete without the "other half of our whole." This has been a very self-deteriorating and even divisive mistake we have perpetuated in our time. Seeking someone else to complete us, seeking another to "make us happy," seeking Love, validation, acceptance from any source outside of us can lead to a lot of disappointment and unfulfilled expectations. Often, the relationship most negatively impacted by these undeveloped connections is the one we are meant to have with our self.

We cannot truly Love someone before we rightly Love ourselves. We cannot be in any kind of healthy relationship, without first having one with ourselves. We have to first become whole. We have to make ourselves happy. We have to enjoy our own company in solitude before we can be any good to someone else.

You might say, "Well I love myself." But think very hard on this. Do you still seek validation from others? Do you allow people to cross your boundaries? Do you find yourself saying, "Yes" when you want to say, "No?" Do you have trouble letting someone in? Do you feel you *need* someone there, and feel uncomfortable when you are alone? That is the problem. We aren't comfortable with ourselves, in our own company. Think about that.

Consider how important is it that we are capable of being with ourselves, having fun by ourselves, and creating meaning in our own lives that does not revolve around another. I do not mean being able to lay curled up in a blanket binging on movies by yourself, either. I mean taking yourself out, going on an adventure by yourself, going to dinner, going dancing, really living vibrant experiences and enjoying them, by yourself. It is fundamental to have self-Love, to *be* with yourself, and find wholeness and fulfillment there first.

We spend much of our lives searching for "the one," when, really, the task is to *become* the One, to realize the One is within you. You are your own perfect match. You are the Love of your own life. Romance is important, along with all the things we can learn from the mirror of a relationship. But romance is not compulsory, like Loving yourself is. No relationship should supersede the relationship you create with your own heart and spirit. That relationship you build with yourself is meant to be the epic Love story of your life.

Meeting yourself for the first time can be surprisingly uncomfortable. To begin, go to a mirror. Look at yourself. What do you see? Don't judge yourself. This is not about vanity. What do you see in that person's eyes; Love, compassion, hurt, loneliness? What do you see in your own heart? Do you see how hard you try? Do you see all the Love you have to offer? Do you see the pure divine beauty within this person who looks back at you now? He or she needs you, *more than any other person you will ever meet*. He or she has been waiting for you to be there with them, to care as much about them as you have everyone else, to

The Self Beyond

make them a priority, to listen, to acknowledge, to validate without judgment. He or she has felt those inner judgements you have made on yourself. All the times you told yourself you aren't good enough, all the times you told yourself you were ugly, or stupid, or too much, or too little. You have been saying that to this beautiful person before you, looking back at you now.

Do two things right now as you do this mirror work: forgive yourself, and accept yourself. See the perfection and allow it to eclipse any notion of imperfection. See yourself the way you would see someone you care for deeply. Love this person who looks back at you. Love the whole of who you are gently, fiercely, and completely. See how strong you are, how wise, how much you have overcome. Realize how much you deserve. Give yourself permission to say, "I Love myself! I accept my whole self! I accept the truest expression of who I am! I am worthy of Love! I am worthy of compassion! I am beautiful! I am here for myself!"

Getting to know yourself in this way can take time and practice. Do not discount the power this has to heal and transform you. Befriend yourself. Become a lover of yourself, and rise in Love more each day. Fall in Love with the beauty within you, the unique insight, your passion, your creativity. Spend time each week and each day, if possible, being there with yourself to listen to what you have to say. Realize that investing in yourself is the most important investment you will ever make. *You* are the One. You are the Love you seek. You are the only one who can make yourself happy. It all begins within you.

CLIMB

If you are a climber, then you must climb the mountain that most terrifies you. If you are a dreamer, then you must create the visions of your dreams. If you are a counselor, then you must listen more than you talk. If you are spiritual, then you must open your heart and be still in wholeness and peace. If you are an adventurer, then you must be willing to get lost. If you are a writer, then you must know what broken feels like, and healing too. If you are a friend of humanity, then you must be conscious beyond yourself; patient, consistent, and have a strong sense of who you are. If you are a thinker, then you must reflect. And if you are a Lover, then you must do all of this.

The Self Beyond

THE LOVER'S

Open hearted, full of passion, full of art and pain and healing, full of Love—we are Lovers! I believe in Love with my whole heart. I believe in the way Love changes people, transforms us from the inside out. Connecting with another deeply and intimately in Love is the mirror that reflects back to us everything within ourselves, so it can come to the surface to be acknowledged, healed, and transformed. We grow through that kind of higher Love. It is a quintessential part of spirituality to share in the connection of Love. To Love all that you are through Loving all of another. And somewhere in the worlds between us, there is Art. There is union. There is resonance. It is there, beyond the illusion of separation, that we experience the truest state of being. That is the divine connection of Love.

Love (in this brief soliloquy I speak of romantic love) doesn't always happen how you planned. It collides like galaxies, like stars in fusion. It grabs you with both hands and compels you to take a good hard look at your own reflection. It calls you beautiful even when you feel like a mess. Love overpowers every other force. It has its own gravity, its own magnetism. It is the emotional equivalent of being struck by lightning, or finding a

---

[5] Obtained from Pexels under CC0 creative commons licence

pearl, depending on how you view it. Love's journey weaves through your life like a stream. Suddenly turning a corner at times. But the secret thing you didn't know, is that just around that unknown corner is the landscape of your dreams. Back to the ocean, the Source. Good Love, real Love, will *always* point you back into yourself. It will take you Home. Remember that golden nugget of truth in any romantic pursuit. Love yourself enough to take a moment, and step back.

IMMERSION

It is important to understand the art of being the Beholder. So much profound insight and depth comes from quiet observation. However, to truly understand something you must also get involved with it, intimately. Do not blush at this: you must experience it. Touch it. Get in contact with it. Taste it, smell it, feel it. Let it get into you. Let yourself get into it. Share an exchange of energies. That is where the real apex of transformation lives, in the immersion—in the immersion of a moment, a connection, a place, an experience. One cannot truly Love and appreciate something unless we engross ourselves nearly completely in it, understanding the way it moves and breathes, becoming one with it. That goes for the water, the earth, the sky, the fire, and every heart you meet.

How do you immerse yourself? This becomes a kind of out-of-body experience in some ways. You will have to commit yourself deeply. Take yourself out this week; to a coffee shop, to a music event, to the forest, or wherever you will personally be able to come undone. While you are there challenge yourself to experience it more fully than you have before. Embody yourself fully. Be present and nowhere else in your mind. If it is hard for you to be present, here is a trick. Run through a checklist. What beautiful sights do you see? Maybe you see some intriguing art, maybe a sweet couple clearly in Love, maybe the sunlight through the trees. What sounds do you hear? Perhaps you hear a song that calls your spirit, a conversation that makes you laugh, the sound of the breeze rustling the leaves. What scents do you pick up? You might smell the scent of the coffee, vanilla and cinnamon, the aroma of incense or another's perfume, the lovely smell of wildflowers wafting through the air. What do you feel? Do you feel comfortable, content, and blissful? These are all very good indicators of a deep dive immersion.

Allow yourself to be within this experience, this moment, within your Self. Enjoy the peace, the celebration, the stillness and the movement. Wherever it is that you are, *this*, right now, is *yours*. This scene has been both painted for you and, in many ways, by your awareness of it. Not one other person on earth is experiencing this exactly as you are. This is a Universe unto itself. You can play with this co-creation. You can observe it or you can interact. There is no wrong thing. Follow what you most feel led to do. This is yours alone, and one of the most grateful acts is to enjoy these blessings whenever they occur.

You have done well, and you should be very proud of yourself for the progress you are making. Remember to celebrate where you are now. Do not focus so much on where you believe you should be. You will get there. For this moment, celebrate what you can already do and how far you have come.

> "*Gradually I began to recognize how feeble and transitory the thoughts and emotions that had troubled me for years actually were, and how fixating on small problems had turned them into big ones. Just by sitting quietly and observing how rapidly, and in many ways illogically, my thoughts and emotions came and went, I began to recognize in a direct way that they weren't nearly as solid or real as they appeared to be. And once I began to let go of my belief in the story they seemed to tell, I began to see the 'author' behind them - the infinitely vast, infinitely open awareness that is the nature of mind.*"
> ~Mingyur Rinpoche

Chapter 2: Rising and Learning

AVOIDING THE TRAP

It is my most genuine intent not to simply regurgitate what has already been said by countless others without forming a new outlook on some of the most universally held beliefs. I have followed many of these beliefs such as "We are all One," "Everything you need is within you," "Love and Light," etc. However, there is a danger in any ideology when it becomes just a theory and not a practice. If there is not a practical way to apply it along with independent thinking, without context, then some of these mantras can hinder spiritual growth and personal activation, however well-meaning they are.

Many people who veered away from religion of various sorts, left because they felt limited by the dogma of it. It became words, not actions. Beliefs but not a state of being. That is what we do not want to replicate in our personal spirituality. This is not to, in any way, say religion does not work for anyone. There are many deeply spiritual religious followers who are capable of living the Love at the heart of the message. Then, for others, it simply may not resonate with their path. Just like some people learn better in a group, others learn best independently. Either way is fine. It is about the lesson, not the method of study.

I have found there to be traps within many well intended theories and belief systems. If the practice is not executed with careful consideration and masterful technique these traps may ensnare. I would like to touch on them here before building the framework to our deeper work. I want to address some of the spiritual philosophy that when used in the right context can be illuminating, but when overlaid onto all aspects of life can be detrimental to our independence, our growth, and even cause harm to others by creating complacency. Be careful about attaching yourself too deeply to any identifying label. While some can help you understand or define an aspect of yourself or your beliefs, many can also bind you by deciding for you who you are and what you should believe. The spirit cannot be restricted.

OPEN MIND, OPEN WAY

It is vital to be capable of looking with an open mind from many angles to maintain a balanced perspective. There are many expressions of spirituality, and some may not look like the textbook definition of the "path of the spiritual person." They don't have to. Our journey only needs to make sense to us. We do not owe anyone an explanation of it. We only have to answer to our own higher self. The less your journey looks like anyone else's, the truer it is to your You.

As in anything, we can say and do the "right" things but that does not mean we believe them. We can believe the "right" things but that does not mean we live them. This is key. You are only fooling and cheating yourself if this describes you. So many people become lost in the philosophy that they abandon the purpose.

What is our intention, to actually be more spiritual? What does that mean? Are we trying to evolve ourselves, our consciousness? Are we trying to become more peaceful, more Loving, more compassionate? Anyone can regurgitate sacred wisdom. It is applying it that shows where your heart truly is. It is applying deeper understanding not just while meditating or surrounded by others who vibrate at the same high frequency. It is also applying that same level of deeper compassionate care in all situations, especially when it is inconvenient or more difficult. Such as when you are driving, when you are at the store, when you are confronted with people who may be ignorant or careless. That is the test.

There is a quote that says, "If you think you are enlightened, go home and spend a weekend with your family." I have found this to be an accurate indicator of true progress. I could extend that to say, go spend some time in traffic, or spend some time in a crowded market. There is no secret of the soul that the behavior does not reveal at some point.

In all things, good or bad, irritating or joyful, stressful or calming, ask yourself these questions: Can I be patient *here*? Can I find meaning here? What is life now showing me so that I might learn? Can I see this is also a blessing or gift? Can I find my peace within this?

Spirituality, just like theology, can become oppressive if not applied with great consideration to what we can reasonably expect from ourselves. We should not have to be saints. Most of us are not striving to be nuns or monks. We should not have to necessarily forsake every earthly inclination and resign what makes us, *us*. For many people, we just want to find peace, wholeness, and Love. There has to be room for us to, yes, honor our sacred selves, but also room for our beautiful messy humanness.

Humans are complicated and complex. We are confusing. We are emotional. We are unreasonable, and guess what? That is ok. That does not have to negate or contradict our spirituality. That is just as much a sacred part of us that we should honor, just as the parts within us that are striving toward perfection and mastership.

You do not have to fit in any box. You do not have to eradicate the foundations of who you are. You do not have to stop doing the things you love because the consensus of new age dogma has deemed it "unspiritual." Be who *you* are. Be your bold, raw, unedited self. You do not have to look like anything, do any specific thing, or adopt any rigid guideline for your life except that which resonates with your own soul. This is *your* journey, the path of many paths. There are infinite ways to become enlightened. There are common methods which have assisted a large enough

The Self Beyond

group of people to which communities form in agreement of some shared way, and that can help for those who do not know where to start or what direction to go in. That is fine. Guidance is one thing. It is when it begins to set a boundary that you would not have otherwise drawn which can stunt the growth of your life, instead of improve it.

On the other hand, if you are seeking to fill your life with meaning, to nurture your spirit, and to expand your own appreciation and awareness, then some common spiritual practices that resonate for you, like yoga or drumming, might not be a bad idea. While you are not obligated to eat like a raw vegan, for instance, studies have shown the miraculous positive impact of a plant based diet. You can create the healthiest environment in your body and support your spiritual growth through eating more raw organic fruits and vegetables. It does not mean you have to commit to this hardcore all day, every day. But making a conscious choice to treat your body as a sanctuary for the spirit you hope to nourish, aligns with the intention of greater spiritual health.

All the layers are connected, mind, body and spirit. So what affects one, truly does affect all others. From this understanding, you might appreciate that mental nourishment with healthy engagements such as reading deep spiritual books, watching documentaries on meaningful subjects, and spending time in meditative self-reflective contemplation are vital to a healthy state of being. As is having a night of binge watching your favorite show with piles of junk food, in moderation, of course.

JUST EXIST

There is nothing that you need to do. Nothing that you need to be. Nothing to strive towards, drive towards, struggle for or seek. You are here and that is enough. You are you, and that is all you need to be. Everything you need is already within you. This is a blissful notion and very much true in many universal senses but consider what issues this sentiment might create in the absence of context. This cannot be the cure-all to remedy the stress of every situation, every day. This can create a large group of people who will roll over in laziness, never trying to improve themselves or the world. Perhaps you can appreciate the ironic problems this concept, in itself, may generate.

It is important to recognize that it is ok to just be, just breathe, and just exist. Especially for those who constantly stress themselves out by being so completely driven towards self-improvement they can't even sit still for a moment. But *balance* is key: moderation with this and every other concept. There is a balance point between being able to be and do. A very crucial balance is required to maintain the physical, mental, and spiritual health within us, as well as a balance for our part in this shared world.

Consider how our bodies would atrophy if all we did was lay around every day saying, "All I need to do is just exist." We would blissfully corrode. Muscles would wither and degenerate. We would, literally, lose our ability to stand under our own weight. This is not a healthy outlook to use all day every day.

Life is simultaneously about being happy with our own existence, in this moment, as it already is, along with seeking constant evolution, development, and inner growth for ourselves and for the greater community we are a part of. We are here to experience, to learn, to access the highest levels of our own consciousness in stillness, but also to move, to become better, to evolve. To partake in both ends of this spectrum is as critical to our spiritual health as water is to our physical wellbeing.

I need, here, to make a forthright disclaimer, because anyone who tells you that there is a way to make your life perfect is cheating you. There is no such thing as a seamless life. You cannot bypass having challenges, struggles or hardship. There is no way to completely dodge the awful things which will make their appearance at times in your life. There is no "happily ever after" and it is a fantasy to believe it can be that way. None of this is going to create that for you. This is about building the tools to withstand the storms, not stop them. This is about honesty, an authentic realism which is capable of seeing the good in the bad, and even the bad in the good. Here, we are honing our skills to be able to stay grounded, centered, and aligned with the guiding insight that will help us navigate the hellish curveballs life will inevitably throw. It is an inescapable fact that nothing stays the same. There will always be another wave coming on the horizon. We cannot live in fear or constant anticipation of the next wave.

Our job is to become strong enough to bend at each wave without breaking.

ALL IS ONE

There is so much more to truly evolving than simply realizing "All is One." We are undoubtedly interconnected to every aspect of this world; every creature, every being, every molecule. It is a revolutionary concept sorely needed in a world that is destroying itself. But that can't just be meaningless dogma. It is a way of life, not just an ideology. A method, not just a theory. Being "One" requires deep responsibility. It's important to look within, to genuinely seek your own self-awareness and higher truth. But then you have to come back to earth at some point, deal with relationships, and deal with people who may not have that same level of self-awareness. It is part of the package of buying into oneness to agree that then bonds you to these perceived "others" as parts of your own self. That's the deal.

It's easy to Love an idealized perfection. It's easy to Love in our own little bubble, never extending that Love to all those who truly need it. It's easy to Love unconditionally in *theory*. It's easy not to dive in deep, to stay aloof and detached. It is easier to just reject in another what we don't want to look at in ourselves, no expectations or obligations. But to stay within the froth of our own effervescence, how do we grow? Without the mirror of another, how do we see what we cannot see? If "all is one" then every other is also a part of you, you must examine and self-reflect on.

Spiritual evolution is not just about attaining great heights of cosmic wisdom and all you find for yourself there, it is also about what you bring back to make the world better—and yourself a better person within it. That translates to coming outside of yourself. That requires treating people carefully with deep respect for their feelings and perceptions as you would your own. It means Loving that expression, even if it's messy, misplaced, or clouded with illusion. It means realizing this does not place others below you or above you. Oneness means Loving everything as an expression of the Divine, and seeing the reflection of your own sacred existence in its face.

Oneness is about the whole thing. The world, all life, every expression of emotion and thought is a part of this One in which we all participate. There is a heavenly transcendence within that realization. We are contributors, co-creators. But we also have a responsibility in that. Going beyond your Self, your being, to understand that what hurts another hurts you. What heals another heals you. This works both ways, which is why this book is of such relevant importance. *What heals you heals others*. What you transform in yourself transforms the world.

What I ask, and those supporting us in great communities of Love would ask, is that you take this message in and go out to truly do something with it to be a helper in this world. A beacon to let others know, they are not others, they are a part of you. Be the reason they can still believe in the goodness, the Light, and the power of Love.

BEING "SPIRITUAL"

Do not get hung up on "being spiritual." Those are just words. What we are doing here is beyond words. Words can become limitations and we are trying to break through those barriers within ourselves. The higher levels of consciousness, you will find as you reach them, have no words, none at all. You will feel void of speaking. It would not make sense. The cosmos knows no language but Love. Focus your intention on aligning yourself and connecting from within. Everything else will happen as a chain reaction, organically.

Doing "spiritual things" like yoga, burning sage, or listening to Om chanting doesn't make you spiritual any more than going to church makes you a good person. It's not what we are doing that gives meaning to the experience. What is essential is the meaning you give it. If your intention is to have that true connection, to reach those pure states of being, then you will infuse whatever it is you are doing with the purpose of your soul's evolution and *that* is key. Please remember the legend. We are already Divine Beings. We are already spiritual. We are Spirit. We just need to reconnect with that. There is no map to that except the one that is within your heart.

You do not need to copy and mimic what you think a spiritual person looks like. You don't have to be a pranayama yogi,

The Self Beyond

or meditate all day. You can be a spiritual anything; a spiritual business person, a spiritual mechanic, a spiritual housekeeper. That part isn't important. You can make anything deeply meaningful with your purposeful attention. It's about figuring out how we can honor, cultivate, and nourish the spirit which we *already* are. That's really it.

Sweeping, doing dishes, getting ready for work, playing with your children can all be spiritual practices. Everything has meaning, hidden insight, and secret metaphors if you just look deeper. Every act we do can be a meditation of that act. Everything we experience can be an exercise for the soul. You do not need to emulate an ecstatic condition. Simply finding a sustainable and steady peaceful way is the balance point.

Consider doing dishes. A task many people dread. How can that be spiritual? First of all, it can be a powerful meditation in being grateful. Bless every dish knowing you are lucky to have them. Consider how many do not have such a luxury. Bless every dish that it represents a meal you or your loved ones enjoyed. Consider how many go without food. Bless every drop of water. Be aware of how lucky you are to have easy access to fresh clean water. Go deeper. Every movement is a meditation. Your fingers running the plate through the water. The sponge in your hand. The energy coming from your hands interacting with the water and the dish. The unblemished quality of the dish once it is cleansed.

What metaphors are hidden here? Dishes are used to hold that which nourishes us. Yet they become soiled and must be carefully cleaned. Once they are cleaned they can, again, be used to support our nourishment. They represent a constant cycle. How have you nourished what is essential in you today? How have you carefully cleaned the residue of the day? What are we keeping that will contribute to our soul's growth? What are we letting go down the drain that is no longer necessary?

Every day, every moment, every action is a work of art. It can be sloppy with little thought, or it can be a thoughtful masterpiece. You are the artist of your life. You are the painter and the canvas. The meaning of life is the meaning you give it. If you want to focus on learning something spiritual, learn about *yourself*. Learn about the experiences you are having day to day. Consider how you can make them healthier and more meaningful. Continue to work on making every interaction richer, more

The Self Beyond

peaceful, and more intentional. Focus on aligning with a state of Love, not chanting, not yoga, not meditation. Although each of these can assist you in meeting yourself more deeply, they are *tools*, not the goal. They are guides, not the path itself. The goal is coming back to your Self. The ultimate purpose is coming back into Love. Love is the most spiritual state of existence. Love is the most authentic state of your being. *Only Love will take you Home.*

THE FOUNTAIN

Through endless ages, humankind endured seeking the ever-elusive meaning: the holy grail of existence, as it were, which lay deep within the cavernous heart where even the bravest did not dare expedition. Deep within the hallowed temple beyond the layers of the illusion of self, waited a fountain, a self-spring of wisdom, there for the thirsty of humankind to drink. Being Star Born children, though many have forgotten, the water here activates the Ancient Light stored within. Keys there are to time-space, and transcending awareness. Here is both the gateway and the Spirit that moves through it. This is the overflowing source spring of Loving Wisdom, ready for all who are ready for themselves. Walk into the golden fountain. Stand within the violet flame of the heart. Be opened. There are Diamonds in you waiting

---

[6] Obtained from Pexels under CC0 creative commons licence

to be uncased. You are the Divine Presence. An elegant being in an infinite multiverse.

ACTIVE SPIRITUALITY

I don't believe in passive spirituality. Simply labeling "resistance to what is" as the problem is a quandary, really. *Resist resistance* is what it is saying. I agree, much suffering comes from us trying to control every facet of life instead of allowing, instead of creating and permitting creation to move through us. We can't resist the natural flow. It only creates more turmoil. What doesn't bend will break. However, to use the rule of "no resistance" and apply it to *everything* creates a population of people very easy to control, doesn't it? And that is dangerous, especially in a time like we are in now.

Resistance is absolutely imperative in the face of injustice, oppression, and tyranny, all which do abound in our world. Resistance is what revolutions are built upon and a revolution is sorely needed. A spiritual revolution has already begun, a movement in the conscious transformation of millions of individuals worldwide. But that movement will not survive if it is founded on principles that do not embrace all that must be addressed. It is only through a panoramic awareness that we can recognize there is a time to resist and a time to allow. Trumpeting a universal ideology can be harmful if it does not allow for each personal path and truth to emerge, or if it neglects what must come up to be healed. Otherwise, these mantras can be distorted, turning faith and dedication into rigid rules that do not fit the multifaceted reality we are a part of. The world still needs resistance, just as much as it needs to be centered, healed, and conscious.

We must be critical thinking and selective in what we allow and what we resist. That is an individual and deeply personal decision while (hopefully) taking into consideration the implications for the whole. There is no absolute, it must be carefully considered with the keen awareness that some things are meant to be embraced and *some* things are meant to be withstood. Beyond passive complacency and fear of "rocking the boat" you enter into a kind of active spirituality. You are guided not by dogma but by only that which your heart tells you is right. The world needs more people led by their hearts.

BEING POSITIVE

Being *positive* is *powerful*. It is important to embolden this truth. There is nothing we cannot make better by having a better attitude about it. I, so often, watch others create their own disasters by complaining constantly, by using harsh, negative words to describe relatively mild situations, by dragging out big events and making them ever bigger, or by coming into their own space carrying the luggage of resentment, before something to resent even occurs. Why would we self-sabotage ourselves this way? It is not before we are aware of this pattern that we can change it. We become aware of it by stepping back, coming outside of ourselves and asking, "Is life really making me feel this terrible, or am I?"

Many times, if we can be honest and unbiased, we will find that *we* are the perpetuating factor in our own misery. I will tell you a secret: crappy things will still happen, but you don't have to feel like crap about them. In fact, you don't even have to take them with you everywhere you go. You can let them have their place in time, and keep on moving forward with a good attitude ready for the amazing things which are inevitably on their way, as well.

I have heard often in some spiritual communities that we just need to focus on Love and Light and not think about the "negative stuff." In a quantum sense, when considering the power of the law of attraction, it *is* very important to focus on the positives that we wish to manifest; peace, Love, healing, abundance and joy. However, and this is a *big* however that must accompany it, this can be a stifling restriction to place on ourselves as we go through our own process of healing. How can we heal what is painful if we regard pain as negative, and refuse to acknowledge its presence? Acknowledging the negative is necessary in any true soul work.

It may also be an incredibly irresponsible manifestation of privilege and even ignorance to ignore or deny the many issues which need our attention that some may write off as "negative."

The Self Beyond

Being spiritual *must* mean something deeper. It must mean that we are spiritually strong and wise enough to extend that Love and Light outward to even the darkest places that need it.

We cannot neglect the undesirable realities which need our collective attention. There is profound suffering occurring globally, devastating environmental destruction of the earth, social injustice, systematic oppression, occupation and war, world hunger and millions of people who have been forced to become refugees leaving their homes and once imaginable future behind. There are innocent children, entire families and generations affected, who have never known anything but poverty, struggle, violence, and fear. To deny the existence of these aspects because they make us uncomfortable or because they seem "negative" is a gross misuse of our individual power. These are real things that are happening today. That is the reality of the world we as individuals have collectively created. Those enormous issues need to be looked at, recognized, validated and addressed with compassionate attention.

We cannot ignore what we may consider to be "negative" within ourselves as well. We cannot heal our past wounds unless we are willing to go there, acknowledge them and deal with them. We cannot be our whole authentic self unless we are willing to embrace the "shadow" side of ourselves. Being spiritual is about being authentic and whole—that wholeness includes all sides, the positive and negative. This includes our fears, our guilt, our frustrations, our grief, and even our anger. Ignoring these aspects only serves to empower them. Being whole means accepting and holding space for both the dark and the Light, both the strength and the weakness. It is about being truthful, not living in positive denial.

I realized for myself that when I demonized my anger and grief, it only seemed to make it more out of control. Only by embracing those aspects, with compassion, genuine unconditional Love and acknowledgment of their validity could I calm those savage beasts within me. Those aspects needed my Love, too. I had to pick them up with Love and be there for them. We can say to our anger, or to our deep regret or sadness, "I see you, I am here with you. You do not need to be upset." I had to hold them with non-judgment. Like a raging toddler that just needed to know they were heard. I had to embrace those aspects with Love.

The Self Beyond

It is the same in all beings. We must be compassionate with our rough edges. We cannot abandon or disregard the sides of ourselves we wish we did not have. There is no part of us that is wrong, or bad. There is only the expression of the human condition and that is multifaceted. Love all of you without fragmenting yourself from yourself.

The journey toward enlightenment is not just about being positive. Enlightenment itself is a caustic process which breaks you a hundred times before you open. It is a purging unlike anything you have experienced before in your life. You shed many layers you once identified with which can be a very emotional process. A time more of darkness than Light. You may dissolve into the depths of yourself as you change from the inside out. That is what is required. Many experience loneliness, discomfort, deep emotional pain, and wonder at times if they may have gone crazy.

It is like a caterpillar during metamorphosis. It shrouds itself in a self-made cocoon, shutting out all Light. In that cocoon, it dissolves completely. It, literally, becomes a liquid goo. No more caterpillar as it was previously defined. To the outside world it may appear to have died in a sense. This is what it must do to transform into the delicate butterfly of the soul. This is a great metaphor for what must happen to our identity as the ego, before the Self within us transcends beyond. This, probably, does not sound positive at all, and may scare some people off. Do not be fooled into thinking this is a blissed out psychedelic rainbow bus ride. While at times it might be a heavenly euphoric experience, it is serious business, this journey of the soul. This is not something to do if you cannot handle the negative, or the darkness. You go through hell before you get to heaven. You must master the darkness to reach the Light.

Be assured that the Jewel is there waiting, in the deep shadows of the cave you enter. Know that the journey is still incredibly rewarding and none that have taken it have emerged unchanged. In the end, you will laugh at all of this. That laughter and all-encompassing realization is how you will know you have transcended.

Anyone who has had "an experience," a true moment of transcendental cosmic connection to the Infinite Beyond comes back knowing at least two things: we are all One, and the soul of the whole universe is *Love*. That is awesome! What a life changing epiphany that is! Try to be an asshole after that one. You *can't*, not without being a big hypocrite. I joke here but my point is, does that not likewise beckon a burning moral obligation to one another and all life on this shared planet? My conclusion has always been a resounding yes! We are all connected, and that comes with it heavy responsibility. If I am blessed and provided with my own needs, I cannot overlook another who suffers without.

Look around at the world. It is scary right now. Millions of people are struggling to survive without basic things like water, medicine, and food. Millions of people have been displaced. Victims of war, of political corruption, of religious division, of the endless problems a world that does not realize how it is connected to itself creates. I will discuss these world issues more in detail later but for now please understand there is an urgent need for us to make use of our Love within and extend it outward, to shine our Light on these dark realities and not look away, but to see them, and to *do* something.

There is a revolution of awakened spiritual activists who are collectively refusing to continue to be complacent, apathetic, and submissive. We are saying, "No" instead of "Yes." Being spiritual is not just about affirmation, being happy within ourselves, or living in the Light—but also, just as deeply, about knowing when to say no, remembering that we are a part of something much bigger, and carrying ourselves into the darkness too. There will be many times on this lifetime journey that will not feel "good." There will be times of internal upheaval. And that, my Beloved, is the divine revolution of the soul shaking itself free.

UNCONDITIONAL LOVE

To be a being capable of Unconditional Love is the highest level of active awareness and presence we can reach. To truly create this in our lives is challenging, but many tools will be discussed throughout this book. The most effective method to finding unconditional Love is to come from beyond the perspective of ego, and into your higher awareness. That higher awareness comes from a place of wisdom, not ego, or emotion.

Love is not an emotion, it is a state of being. You do not feel it, you are it. You come from this space when you can Love someone without the "because," when you can Love someone without the "only ifs," when you can Love beyond projections, beyond expectations, with a deep respect for their perceived time and their perceived space; when you can Love another even under their own illusory or false perceptions, when you can Love them even when they are lost or needy, when you can recognize that within them is the same fundamentally perfect imperfection that is within you, that is the highest level of Love we can share.

As you become capable of unconditionally Loving yourself, every part of you, the shadow and the Light, the ups and the downs, you become more capable of extending that same ability with others. That is really the key. We will not be able to Love someone exactly as they are until we Love ourselves *exactly* as we are. Otherwise, we are just Loving what we want someone to be, or do, or say, or feel. Unconditional Love means no conditions, no exceptions, no exclusions, and no restrictions.

Please do not make the mistake of believing that Unconditional Love means you must subject yourself to abuse or mistreatment of any kind. Please do not allow your kindness to become an enabling mechanism for someone to treat you poorly. Do not allow your commitment to Unconditional Love to excuse damaging behavior as another projects their own issues, wounds, and imbalance onto you. Turning a cheek is one thing, but becoming a punching bag is another. You are, by no means, required to allow someone to disrespect the sacred being that you are, just as you would not disrespect them.

One of the foremost tenants of Love is in tough Love. To give yourself prior permission to identify, acknowledge and release those relationships which are not only unhealthy, but harmful. You should honor yourself and Love yourself enough to remove your presence from those who consistently cross your boundaries, who project violence of any kind onto you, or who take your Love for granted. Violence is not always physical, it can be psychological, or even energetic attacks. These can leave us wounded in deep ways, especially those of us who are considered empaths. We have to be very careful about who we share our energy sphere with. We have to keep our own energy high and coming from a place of Love.

I am not saying do not even try to Love someone who is hurting you. People hurt other people because they are hurting. They do need Love, and if you can help them, by all means do so.

That is why we are here doing this painstaking work. But do not become a casualty of that work. When someone is deeply confused, they may need that time on their own to hit rock bottom, and through that, work out their own karma. Sometimes there is a huge life-changing lesson there they need to find. We may learn more in dark valley's than we do on sun kissed mountaintops.

We get hero complexes and want to "save" everyone. We are not meant to save anyone but ourselves, really. We can help someone best by being a beautiful example of what properly Loving yourself looks like. That is what people need to see, self-Love in action. And someone who Loves, cherishes, and honors themselves will walk away in strength when needed. Know when to walk away. Love yourself enough to be brave. Loving another should never contradict Loving yourself. You should not have to sacrifice one for the other. Often, Loving yourself will mean putting your foot down and setting boundaries with another. Do not hesitate to Love yourself that much.

FOCUS AND AWARENESS

There is a difference between focus and awareness. Focus is what we place our attention on, what we put our energy and thought into. Awareness is what we are conscious of but may not spend a lot of time thinking about. We might appreciate that where we place that value can be the difference between something haunting us that does not need to, or something that helps us keep our balance. That can be the difference between something that slips through the cracks that we simply forgot, or something that was kept in check by prioritizing. There is a time to focus on certain things and a time to keep them just in the background, remaining aware of them, but not feeding energy into them. Taxes might be an example. It is good to remember to turn them in on time, to be *aware* of them, but it might not be great for you to *focus* on them all day, every day, as a looming sense of debt hanging over your head.

A more intense example may be that many are now aware of the small, yet powerful, group of individuals who seek through various political agendas, through injecting toxins into food, water, and air, and through mass psychological manipulation, to control the population of the world. In all my research, I have

The Self Beyond

found this not to be a theory, but a true and active collusion. [7] Many of us are aware of that fact and cannot go back to when we did not know such a precarious truth. However, we may also recognize to focus on this every waking moment can embolden the hold and diminish our own growth. (I will talk more later about how we are empowered on this point).

Both focus and awareness have their own place and time, such as in being aware of our own weaknesses. There is nothing wrong with being conscious of where our opportunities for growth are. The damage can occur when we allow that to be a sapping obsessive narrative that undermines our efforts for advancement. Focusing too deeply on things that are better left in the background of awareness can cause imbalance and a tilted spiral downwards. This is true with big things like fears, or smaller things like worries.

Some spiritual people seek to banish fear completely. Fear is not a bad thing, in itself. It is a lower vibration in an energetic sense, yes, but fear is also a survival instinct that helps us react when needed—it doesn't need to be expelled completely, while it does need to be kept in check. Most fear is completely unnecessary and weakening. Worry is the same way. It is ok to be aware you have a big bill coming up that you have to pay, for instance, but fretting about it and focusing on it daily do you no good. That, certainly, doesn't help you pay it. Worry is also almost never beneficial other than being a background awareness of something you want to be conscious of.

We can spend our time imagining all kinds of terrible ways things could go wrong, or we can spend our time visualizing them going right. We have a choice. We can be aware of what is coming and realize all we need to be is *ready*. We can focus on what we can do and beyond that let it go. What is there for you to focus on versus be aware of today?

---

[7] More on this deep dive research in Universal Hidden Insight: The Connection Between Love, Existence and Reality. Or, as always, by doing your own research.

THE CENTER

Nearly all our life is lived outwardly, going and doing. We work, walk, cook, talk, shop, drive, run, move and keep going. Except for those deeply involved in any kind of existential or spiritual journey, we spend very little time focusing inwardly. How can we get back to the core if we constantly drive our energies in every other direction? We are always going *away*, instead of *toward* our self. Nothing urges us to come inward except those few moments in between all the going and doing in which the gentle voice of spirit calls to us. That voice is not commanding. It is tactful and quiet. It whispers.

Stay at the center of the circle, let all things take their course. ~Lao Tsu

We spend so much time rushing in a multitude of activities because there is something we are chasing after, that we feel is not within us already. Is that not so? We see all the flashing lights, and movement, and chaos and it unsettles us so we think we, too, should be moving, in pursuit, and chaotic. The irony is what we pursue is nowhere we can go to, at least not that way. What we need is nothing we can have, at least not that way. The way is inward and all else spirals off of that. We have spent our lives going outward and that may have earned us a nice car, a home, a career, all to which we are now bound. A life spent going inward unbinds you. Time spent going inward gives you what you thought the career, the house, and the car would, but never did—freedom and true fulfillment.

We are whole already. Complete with the deepest Love which the Universe has graciously interwoven into the very fabric of our core. Raise yourself up to the Light like a flower. Light the wick on the candle of your own soul. Come into your heart. Feel the pull of your own gravity. You are safe. Be at peace. Be still from the inside out. Come home. Be with yourself. We are surrounded by Love and compassion. Be so quiet that it can speak to you in the spaces between thoughts and words. It is beyond

The Self Beyond

words, beyond worlds. Love exists perpetually, in infinite expansion, just as you do. What a miracle there is to pluck from the tree inside your own heart!

BELONGING

Nothing belongs to you, and nothing belongs to me. We belong to eternity and in this infinite state within a limitless Universe, we are one: here, we become *all* things and *nothing*. We belong completely. There, we are each other's. There, we are a Galaxy. You do not have to be worthy of anything, and nothing has to be worthy of you. We are Ultimate Love. The truest offering of the highest self we embody within. Our worth is the weight of our heart against a feather, and True Love is weightless.

You do not need to earn this Love, as none must earn yours. This Love has no requirement, no condition, no expiration date or price. Love is not bartering, and is not for beggars. Love is for givers and takers alike. This Love cannot be stolen. It is given freely, endlessly. You cannot miss your chance. You cannot be too early or too late. There is no before or after. There is only one moment, and we are in it.

The Great Spirit, the Loving Intelligence that artfully crafted the existence of All is constantly seeking us with great kindness and *grace*, reminding us that, "Here it will never be said 'where have you been?' You are always right on time. I Am always with you, as You, never coming or going. We have no lines drawn around where you begin or I end. We are in the other unowned. Blossomed like flowers grown from the same bud, forever drinking the same rain, the same Light. Interconnected in a spiraling transformation journey. Growing by the same design." That is where we are each other's. In the flame of our Eternal Beloved, always welcomed and belonging.

THE MOUNTAIN

Have you ever sat on a mountain basking in the shear awe only nature could bestow within the heart of humankind? Perhaps there, as you breathed in deeply you considered many things you had, a few hours prior, thought of as big as they diminish in weight. There in the midst of this glorious symphony of nature, whatever it was now seems relatively inconsequential. Within you a sense of assembly stirs. You begin to recognize how little you are, and how vast this all is. Yet these revelations do not leave you feeling insignificant but to the contrary leave you with a feeling of great purpose. Not in doing, but just in being. You find it is glorious just to be. To breathe and appreciate the beauty all around you.

This state is the most essential state of reception. Here in this state you allow and receive with little effort. You have already surrendered. You have awakened into the Truth that this mountain is also you, the earth below you, the sky above you, the sun shining down, the leaves on the trees, the roots and the rocks. All is an extension of that same Loving Intelligence, the Intelligent Love within you.

When that kind of Love truly comes into you, it is bigger than you are. It overflows like a river and you are not only in it, you *become* it. You realize you have always been one with it. Allowing yourself to be completely overtaken by Love is the gateway to enlightenment. To realize Love is not tripping and falling but rising and soaring. Love is not with only one chosen companion but the universal One within us all. You feel this expansion within you to the point where it seems it could burst, as if you could take that feeling out of your chest and share it with every single soul, to Light up every heart with this immense, immeasurable, infinite Love. Perhaps no one could ever translate that out. It is an experience beyond the colloquial language we use day to day. No poetry, no song, no art could do justice to a Love that manifold and rich. That is the Love Spirit sends to *all*, now and always. All we must do is receive it.

It is not the mountain the moves, it is you.~ (from Universal Hidden Insight)

VIBRATION SEED

What is vibration? When a harpist plays the strings with every pluck the strings resonate. The melodic patterns they create demonstrate sound, resonance, an audible vibration which is then translated by the human ear as music. There are other vibrations, silent vibrations in thoughts unspoken, in emotions big and small, and in the energies between us.

Everything is vibration, form itself is created through trillions of vibrating quantum particles which make up every atom and cell. From butterflies to planets, every single physical thing we see also exists as (and because of) an energetic frequency. These frequencies can resonate in a harmonic state, with cohesion to the environment surrounding it. All things in nature (when un-poisoned by man) naturally do this. Water has a specific resonance. Grass, flowers, and trees have their own special frequency to compliment the environment in which they grow. We are like instruments capable of being in tune and harmony with the symphony of life surrounding us.

What is your song and how do you play it? In this sense I mean the unique vibration which you alone contribute. No one else can play your part, only you. We sometimes play off key. Sometimes we forget our song. That is ok, if we can redirect our awareness to the intention of coming back into harmony. Your frequency is most significantly decided by the thoughts and feelings you choose. These mental signals and emotional fields largely create our energy. The collection of your general energetic state becomes a kind of signature resonance. This is important to understand in basic terms to appreciate the power you have within you when you are in higher resonance. In a state of Love, compassion, balance, and peace you are most in tune with the natural environment.

You may think, "How in the world can I change my vibration?" Later in this text we will talk in detail about healing our thoughts and feelings and how to come into a more cohesive state within ourselves. Cohesion is how we interrelate. Everything around us has a relationship to us. To master how we connect with that we should take care to remember the basic premises for any healthy relationship: the Golden Rule—do unto others as you would have done to you. Relationships are a two way street. One cannot circumvent the other's needs, one cannot overpower the other. Both needs must be met in balance. There must be a symbiosis. That is what creates harmony.

The Self Beyond

For right now just try to become deeply aware that intention is everything. To intend to have thoughts, emotions and actions that resonate from a place of Love can begin the process. It may seem small. Do not think in terms of size or measurement. A great Oak tree comes from a tiny seed. All it takes is a seed. A tiny thought with great purpose, changes everything. Find that little seed of vibration within you, water it, nurture it, let it soak in the Light, and it will undoubtedly grow.

I invite you here to think about your intention. Ask yourself:

What is my highest intention?

_____
_____
_____
_____

Maybe you have many intentions. That is ok. Name them. Speak them. Write them. This is a potent catalyst that allows you to synthesize your purpose with your power.

---

[8] Obtained from Pexels under CCO creative commons licence

The Self Beyond

THE BLUEPRINT

For the next few segments we need to get a little deeper. Some of this may seem more complicated than it is. Pease don't get too lost in the woods on this stuff. It is ok if some of the more scientific pieces are beyond you. (You do not need to take a test on this later, I promise). It is going to give you a leg up in your life to have a general understanding of the blueprint of nature, energy and vibration. This is all to help you understand how to be healthier, happier, and in more coherent alignment. Work smarter, not harder they say, right?

How does a seed create a tree? How does a single cell create a person? How does an egg become a bird? Life is sculpted through information encoded as DNA. Consider for a moment that DNA was only relatively recently discovered in 1869. Can you imagine this proposal before its time? "Oh yes, there are actually millions of little strands of code inside your cells that tell your body how to grow and what to do." "Preposterous," people would have said! But it is true. Life develops, grows, and reproduces

---

[9] Obtained from Pexels under Creative Commons Zero (CC0) license

itself because it is coded to. All the information and potential needed for full growth is contained within a seed, a cell, or an egg. This information exists like invisible encryptions waiting to be activated.

We are aware that atoms make up cells. Atoms make up every molecule of our physical world. The same atoms that exist now, have always existed, in varying states of energy. As stars, as supernova's, as oceans, as trees, as elephants, as waterfalls, as flowers, as clouds, as fireflies, and now as *you*. The molecules within your body and within everything you see, fluctuate millions of times a second, between form and the formlessness. It happens so quickly we cannot perceive it. But reality is literally changing, shifting, and reforming millions of times a second.

There is a sacred design, if you will, which organizes everything we see, a blueprint for all life in this universe. This universal pattern exists in everything; from galaxies to sunflowers, from cells to seashells. Perfectly present in the mathematical proportions throughout nature, and even within our own bodies. Some might say that math is the language of God. This is not to quantify life's purpose into numbers, instead these numbers expand upon the deep and wondrous meaning underlying all life. Sacred geometry is the study of this Divine design. Here this becomes a metaphysical study of the nature of reality.

The Fibonacci sequence (1, 1, 2, 3, 5, 13, 21 etc.) displays a mathematical pattern that essentially maps how life grows and develops (see in previous figure). Pi is a part of this, as an infinite number with no end (3.1415926535 etc.). These sequences are connected to the golden ratio, or divine proportion, which is 1.618033988 etc. There is nearly nowhere you can look in nature without observing these patterns in the design. The divine proportion is in pinecones, in flowers, in cells, in seashells, in storms, and in galaxies. You do not need to be good at math or follow every word of this section. If you can understand a picture, you can understand these ratios. If you can understand a flower, then you are already there. Appreciate that this does not happen by accident. It is no coincidence, in an often seemingly chaotic universe, that life is following a plan of divine proportions.

The Self Beyond

[10]

Travel back in time with me for a moment. Back to the time when people lived for "the gods," a time when megalithic monuments were erected worldwide. Did you know that most of these monuments mirror the very sacred patterns we are talking about? In fact they do this so perfectly that it took until the age of computers to understand the profound geometry hidden within. The golden number is apparent at multiple sites like the Pyramids of Giza complex in Egypt (perhaps the most pristine and well-known example). These mathematical proportions were only revealed once modern equipment was developed that could measure and calculate the astonishing data encased here. The kind of precision displayed in many ancient temples eludes builders even in "modern" day. These same golden proportions are repeated across the world when looking at hundreds, even thousands of other sacred locations (such as Ankhor Wat in Cambodia and Ollantaytambo in Peru). [11]

---

[10] Self-created image from stock photos cleared for commercial use.

[11] I go into great detail on this astounding subject in *Universal Hidden Insight, The Connection Between Love, Existence and Reality* and I strongly encourage anyone not sufficiently familiar with it to take a look as it reveals one of the most crucial pieces of human history and the

The Self Beyond

Why would ancient cultures go to such lengths to record this information in such perfect detail when just balancing blocks would have built a sturdy pyramid? They went to great lengths aligning to equinoxal points (sunrise and sunset of the winter and summer equinoxes) which takes *incredible* precision. They are aligned to the four cardinal points in many cases (better than modern day structures which attempted the same feat, I might add). Some ancient sites even display knowledge of precession (which means some awareness must have been available of the roughly 26,000 year cycle of the earth's wobble on its axis). This requires extremely advanced astronomical knowledge. Many people, including myself, are certain there is something very important to be known left carved in stone from our ancestors. And perhaps it can point us toward a deeper understanding of ourselves and the nature of reality.

There is a connection between what our ancestors knew and what we are now rediscovering. An ancient truth to be remembered about ourselves as a species. These sites exhibit other repeating themes and similarities. For instance, most major (and many lesser known) sacred sites were built upon an area with underground waterways. Why would they do this? Aquifers and water channels actually contain highly charged energies known as ions (atoms that lost an electron, now holding a negative charge). Ions are shown to be extremely beneficial to our own energy fields (we will talk about that in a bit). These channels connect to make up a global network of telluric energy lines, or ley-lines, as they are often called. Powerful energetic grid points exist where these lines intersect which amplifies the geometric principles of these sites and is perhaps why these locations were chosen for so many noteworthy temples.

The most significant ancient monuments and sacred sites were built with megalithic blocks of granite which carry a large percentage of quartz crystal, making granite a highly resonant stone. Sites such as those at Giza, Puma Punku (a large temple

---

mind blowing connections between these sacred sites. Other researchers such as Graham Hancock, John Anthony West, Robert Bauval, Freddy Silva, Robert Shock and Christopher Dunn have made incredible contributions in their research to expose the truth of our hidden past.

which is part of a complex near Tiwanaku in Bolivia) and the blue stones at Stonehenge have large quantities of magnetite (which is what it sounds like, a highly magnetic mineral).

Magnetism has a strong connection to electricity. The human body carries iron in our blood stream. There are magnetite crystals present in our brain [12] and, even, pineal gland. This means we are literally affected on a biological (and conscious) level by magnetism. Researchers such as Brien Foerster have devoted their lives to studying the anomalies at ancient sites worldwide. Using scientific equipment they have recorded significant magnetic field variations at sites like Puma Punku. [13] The interesting phenomenon is that the electromagnetic fields of sites like Stonehenge actually change. They are affected by the celestial movements of the sun and the moon, charging at sunrise and discharging at moonrise. It is as if they are living sites, in a sense "waking up" and sleeping in a cycle as we do.

The famous standing stones at Stonehenge are even shaped like the symbol for pi—π. [14]

---

[12] Refer to: Joseph L. Kirschvink, Atsuko Kobayashi-Kirschvink, Juan C. Diaz- Ricci, and Steven J. Kirschvink Bioelectromagnetics Supplement 1 :101-113 (1992) Magnetite in Human Tissues: A Mechanism for the Biological Effects of Weak ELF Magnetic Fields. Division of Geological and Planetary Sciences, The California Institute of Technology, Pasadena, California.
http://web.gps.caltech.edu/~jkirschvink/pdfs/KirschvinkBEMS92.pdf
[13] Foerster. 2016. More Strange Magnetic Anomalies At Puma Punku In Bolivia: July 2016.
https://www.youtube.com/watch?v=AJwSdXyJ598
[14] Obtained from Pexels under Creative Commons Zero (CC0) license

The Self Beyond

The pyramid complex at Giza, Egypt. [15]

Pyramids are a theme across the ancient world. Pyramids are a powerful geometrical shape inherently containing many sacred proportions. When I say sacred in this sense, it is to explain that these mathematical proportions are the same divine proportions present in nature and our own bodies. Since the language of nature is written with the same blueprint of these geometries, anything built with these mathematical relationships will likewise harmonize with the energy of the natural world.

The geometry of a pyramid (along with the electromagnetic characteristics of how and where they are built) allow it to resonate, amplify, and even generate energy. I am not talking about energy as we may think of it in the "modern world." I do not mean a kind of electricity that would merely power a microwave or a television. This is not the kind of energy that needs a wire to be directed. This energy is the kind of wireless energy Nikola Tesla studied throughout his life—free energy.

> "*Energy is the living, vibrating ground of your being, and it is your body's natural self-healing elixir, its natural medicine... Numerous cultures describe a matrix of subtle energies that support, shape, and animate the physical body, called qi or chi in China, prana in the yoga tradition of India and Tibet, yesod in the Jewish cabalistic tradition, ki in Japan, baraka by the Sufis, wakan by the*

---

[15] Obtained from Pexels under Creative Commons Zero (CC0) license

The Self Beyond

Lakotas, orenda by the Iroquois, megbe by the Ituri Pygmies, and the Holy Spirit in Christian tradition. It is hardly a new idea to suggest that subtle energies operate in tandem with the denser, "congealed" energies of the material body." ~Donna Eden with David Feinstein in Energy Medicine

The golden triangle, defined using Phi.

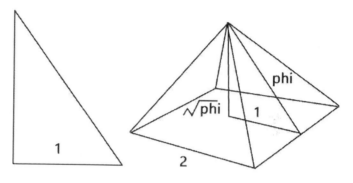

The relation of phi to the geometry of the great pyramid of Giza.[16]

Note, if mathematics makes you nervous you can skip to the last sentence. For all others, consider for a moment: the coordinates of a Great pyramid at Giza mirror the speed of light through vacuum, which is 299,792,458 m/s (meters per second). The geographic coordinates of the Great Pyramid are 29.9792458, 31.134658. Both contain the number sequence 299792458, which may be considered too peculiar to be a coincidence. Some argue that this match only lines up if you base the speed of light on meters per second, and the ancient Egyptians had no knowledge of the meter as a unit of measure. (This unit of measurement was not invented until the 1700's). The ancient Egyptians, instead, used a unit of measurement called a cubit. How did they calculate the size of a cubit then? The cubit is essentially the meter with Pi (the Golden Number). If you take the perimeter of the base and then divide it by the height and multiply that by two you'll get Pi (1760/560 = 3.14). If you draw two circles, one inside the square

---

[16] Self-created for this book

of Giza and one outside the square and you subtract the inner circumference from the outer circumference, the answer is equal to the *speed of light*.

ENERGY

This is a crash course in energy. At a quantum level everything is a frequency. Look at this book, for instance. You are holding it in your hands. It feels solid. It looks solid. However, it is anything but. This book and your hands as they hold it (just like all matter we consider to be material, dense and solid) is actually billions of subatomic particles popping into and out of the wave and particle state, in and out of existence. Everything is energy and movement. Everything has its own vibrational frequency. Heat is not caused because "temperature" changes. It is caused because the subatomic particles within an object move faster and faster, changing their vibration to create "heat."

Note: *You do not need to understand this portion if it is beyond you. This is here for those who are more analytical and need this information to process reality.* It does, however, help to gain a basic understanding, so I will be gentle. This is here to provide a fundamental understanding of the nature of reality, which empowers you to direct your own energy within that framework much more efficiently. This all helps us in our path toward self-discovery and in doing more effective healing work.

Frequency is just a wavelength; waves of energy at various amplitudes. Amplitude means how high up and down the wave goes, and how close together those waves are. Some wavelengths are visible to humans as light (this is pretty much everything we see). Some waves are audible as sound, which is, essentially, just a waveform moving on a medium. All light and sound, vibration and frequency, are energy. Most energy resides outside of our range of sense perception. Examples are; extremely Low Frequency waves, radio waves, UV rays, X-rays, Gamma rays etc. (Example: we can't see the waves from our microwave or cellphone). What this means is that we don't even see or hear most of our own reality. It is mainly, to us, silent, and invisible.

The Self Beyond

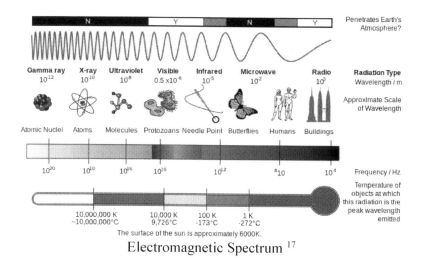

Electromagnetic Spectrum [17]

'In the electromagnetic spectrum there are many different types of waves with varying frequencies and wavelengths. They are all related by one important equation: Any electromagnetic wave's frequency multiplied by its wavelength equals the *speed of light*.' [18]

SPACESUIT

Imagine being an astronaut in a big spacesuit. You are sent to a world in which there may be many unknown variables. This spacesuit is, essentially, designed as a bubble to protect you. Equipment is placed in it to feed information to you from the outside. Due to this, you cannot actually see the world itself. You cannot hear it or touch it. You can only see, hear, and feel what

---

[17] Inductiveload, Wikicommons, 14 February 2013, 12:25:44, under CC license retrieved from Wikicommons
http://commons.wikimedia.org/wiki/File:EM_Spectrum_Properties.svg

[18] How are frequency and wavelength related? (2017). *Qrg.northwestern.edu*.
http://www.qrg.northwestern.edu/projects/vss/docs/communications/2-how-are-frequency-and-wavelength-related.html

the spacesuit is capable of picking up with its measuring equipment. Even with the most advanced equipment, we might suppose there are many things going on beyond the range which our equipment can detect. This is what it is to be in a human body.

What if you could go beyond that spacesuit, beyond that limiting apparatus which defines what you perceive to be reality? You *can*—with your consciousness. We do this when we dream. We do this when we meditate. We do this when we gain awareness of the Self beyond the body, which expands and extends far outside the boundaries of our skin into a fractal infinity. That consciousness has its own equipment to pick up many of the subtle and prevalent energies of the Universe surrounding us. It is simply a matter of tuning into that layer of our consciousness to access this extrasensory information.

ELEMENTS

At a subatomic level, everything is made up of atoms (beyond that, we get into the quantum world which we will visit later). An atom consists of electrons (particles containing a negative charge) and protons (focal point of the nucleus with a positive charge). We all might recall crude models made from Styrofoam balls and sticks in school. These models may have left you with the impression of a very mechanical world in which the space outside the model was a kind of "dead" space with nothing to remark on. Oh how they fooled us!

An ion is basically an atom with a negative electric charge. Ions strive for a neutral state. These energetic charges permeate our bodies and our world. If you cannot imagine this to be true, just look at lightning. Or the next time it is about to thunderstorm go outside. You can, literally, smell and feel the charge (negative ions) in the air. There are dynamic sources and fields of energy intrinsically present in all of nature. Subtle, yet pervasive energies are present within our bodies, within our cells, and even within our thoughts (think of brainwaves). Radio waves and brain waves are both forms of electromagnetic waves of energy that travel at the *speed of light*. Did you know you could think that fast?

Consider the electromagnetic world we live in. There are electrically charged particles available from every point on earth,

The Self Beyond

in the energy fields around us, in the air we breathe. These energies penetrate us without us even knowing because we live, essentially, in a human spacesuit. We, ourselves, are electromagnetic beings (which is why the unnatural EMF signals of modern technology can be so disrupting to the human psyche).

Magnetic fields affect our body's electrical systems. Toxins, heavy metals, radiation from cell phones, computers, and pollutants all generate frequencies and magnetic fields which damage our cells, our DNA, and even our energy field. These conditions cause illness, poor concentration, depression, and dissonance. Negative ions available in forests, near waterfalls, in sunny areas, and generally present in nature are extremely beneficial. They boost cell regeneration and can recharge our drained energy fields.

This all comes back to the blueprint. There is a natural state of vibration that compliments life, the flow of cosmic energies, growth, and spontaneous healing. A spiral going infinitely inward, and infinitely outward. That design and energy is exemplified for us over and over in nature, and in the clever clues our ancient ancestors left for us to discover, when we would one day again be ready. The point of all of this is to explain everything is energy, frequency and vibration as Nikola Tesla explained. Everything is moving at the speed of light. Nothing is truly solid. Most energy exists beyond the spectrum of what we can see, hear, feel or measure. The key to what changes us is in changing our vibration.

> *"You, yourself, are the eternal energy which appears as this Universe. You didn't come into this world; you came out of it. Like a wave from the ocean."* ~ Alan Watts

ALIGNMENT

We, ourselves, emit a resonant frequency. The human energy field can be measured reaching up to several feet away. This frequency depends on our state of being, our mindset, feelings, and of course other practical factors such as what we have ingested into our bodies. The earth, itself, has a measureable resonance which rests at about 7.8 Hz and has been recorded as increasing over the past few years. We also have our own ideal harmonic frequency when in a rested, relaxed and thoughtful state. Being in a state of calm, peace, and Love can actually harmonize us with the electromagnetic resonance of our environment.

In 1992, Bruce Tainio of Tainio Technology, an independent division of Eastern State University in Cheny, Washington, built the first frequency monitor in the world. Tainio determined that the average frequency of the human body during the daytime is 62-68 MHz. A healthy body frequency is 62-72 MHz or higher. When the frequency drops, the immune system is compromised. Check out these very interesting findings:

Human Body:
Normal Brain Frequency 72 MHz
Human Body 62-78 MHz
Human Body: from Neck up 72-78 MHz
Human Body: from Neck down 60-68 MHz
Thyroid and Parathyroid glands are 62-68 MHz
Thymus Gland is 65-68 MHz
Heart is 67-70 MHz
Lungs are 58-65 MHz
Liver is 55-60 MHz
Pancreas is 60-80 MHz
<u>Colds and Flu start at</u>: 57-60 MHz
<u>Disease starts at</u>: 58 MHz
Candida overgrowth starts at: 55 MHz
Receptive to Epstein Barr at: 52 MHz
Receptive to Cancer at: 42 MHz
Death begins at: 25 MHz [19]

A lower frequency means a lesser functioning physiological and mental body. The higher the vibration of our

---

[19] Chang, P. (2011). *The Relationship Between Disease and Energy Frequency*. *EnergyFanatics.com*. Retrieved from: http://energyfanatics.com/2011/12/07/relationship-between-diseases-energy-frequency/

frequency, the more efficient our bodies are at fighting disease, allowing for healing and mental acuity. Aligning ourselves with the universal principles can create cohesive energy within our physical and subtle bodies. It is a feedback loop: our body/mind/spirit are influenced by the environment and we have influence over that environment through what we put into our bodies, what we focus on in our minds, and what we put our energy towards feeling. We are architects of our energetic reality in many respects, given that thoughts and emotions create our energy, and, therefore, our frequency. Both the internal and perceived external environments of our bodies, once we are aware of them, can be managed and even directed. Developing an ability to raise our vibration, through mastering our thoughts and emotions, is key.

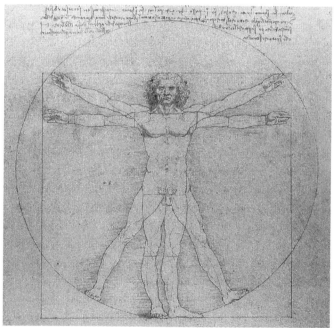

Vitruvian Man by Leonardo da Vinci [20]

---

[20] Luc Viator, Wikicommons, public domain (PD-US) as expressed on Wikicommons.

The Self Beyond

Our bodies are already designed with mathematical perfection. For instance, the ratio of each segment of our fingers to our hand demonstrates Pi ratio. Pi is present in every aspect of us from our arm's relation to our bodies, to our nose's relationship to our face. The divine proportion is present in our ears and the relation of our pineal gland to our brain. Cell division, itself, also mirrors this universal blueprint. We do not need to perfect our body, except in what we eat and subject it to. It is from the mind and heart that we must do our work.

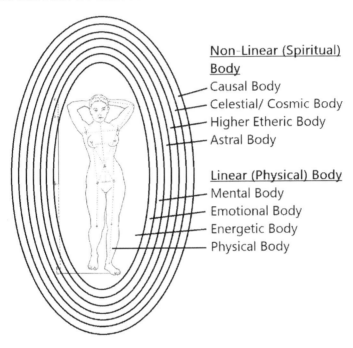

[21]

The connecting factor to all this science is in the vibration we are holding. How can we know our own vibration? Ask yourself, how you are feeling, and how you are thinking? We are becoming aware that thoughts and emotions are, in themselves, vibrations. They create electromagnetic frequencies, energetic sounds which are read by the universe. To understand this more

---

[21] Self-created for this book, overlaid on Wikicommons woman figure under creative commons license

deeply we need to look at higher and lower frequencies of emotion.

Lower vibrational emotions are fear, guilt, jealousy, shame, blame, resentment, and hostility. What creates these lower emotions? Typically, ego and self-service, focusing on what is outside of us that we cannot control, a sense of separation of Self from the Universal creates lower emotional states. Higher vibrational emotions are compassion, joy, peace, gratefulness, and Love. What generates these higher energetic states? Service to others, awareness of our connection to the Universal, and a deep focus inwards to cultivate our Spirit raises our emotional state.

> *"You can offer your vibration on purpose. That's what visualization is. That's what imagination is: projecting thought energy on purpose."* ~Abraham-Hicks

What does the vibration of Love have in common with the blueprint, the harmonic Divine design of life? Look at what comes from Love. Life, itself, is created through an act of Love and union. Life is created through the sacrifice of a tree giving its seed to be reborn out of the Love for something beyond its own existence. Look at a mother's selfless Love, a father's compassion. Look at how a child Loves so purely, from a place of wonder.

Consider the bond that Love creates between us. It is, literally, the universal language, connecting us to each other as all life is connected in the natural world. It transcends all boundaries. Love sees beyond forms. Love goes beyond words. To show Love is the first instinct we have when another is hurting, or in need. That is because we are instinctually aware of the power Love has to heal. Look at the courage Love evokes to be vulnerable, to be present, to listen, and place another as equal to us, as a part of our own Self.

> *"Love is the energy from which all people and things are made. You are connected to everything in your world through love."* ~Brian L. Weiss, M.D.

THE HEART

In a human fetus the heart forms and begins beating before the brain begins to develop. In fact, 60-65% of our heart is composed of neural cells and functions much like our brain cells. The two systems send information back and forth, making neuronal connections via the central nervous system. Did you know that the heart is the most powerful source of electromagnetic energy in the human body? The electrical field produced by the heart is 60 times greater than that of the brain. The heart's magnetic field can be measured up to three feet from the body, in every direction. The heart's magnetic field is, also, modulated by various emotional states. [22]

Love is the highest intelligence of the heart. Aligning ourselves with Love can lift our vibration, increase our energy field's positive resonance, create conditions for healing, allow for greater focus and mental clarity, and nurture our spiritual growth. This is not pseudoscience. This has been well established, although Love is rarely proposed by our doctors as a mode of healing. You may go to a doctor feeling generally unwell. They will take blood samples, and perhaps prescribe medication, but you will likely not hear them speak to you about the coherence of the heart and its role in your health.

Numerous studies done through the Heart Math Institute (a non-profit group made up of prestigious and internationally recognized leaders in physics, biophysics, astrophysics, education, mathematics, engineering, cardiology, biofeedback and psychology among other disciplines) have shown that heart intelligence is essential to optimal health and well-being. Studies through HMI have demonstrated that entering a state of Loving coherence (done by simply focusing on breathing while centering in the heart, as if breathing *through* the heart, and visualizing resonating a loving energy from the heart) regulates heart rhythms, reduces blood pressure, induces positive emotions,

---

[22] *Chapter 06: Energetic Communication - HeartMath Institute.* (2017). *HeartMath Institute.*
https://www.heartmath.org/research/science-of-the-heart/energetic-communication/

addresses trauma, depression, even PTSD, aids the immune system, hypertension, improves mental performance, and has positive effects on relationships.

Think for a moment how your heart feels when you are anxious or worried, the way your heart races. Now think about how your heart feels when you are at peace, in a good mental and emotional state. What do you think a worried anxious heart does to your biological system? This affects everything from stress hormone release, making us susceptible to disease, to our psychological state sending us into a spiral downwards. Imagine then, what a heart in coherence can do for you.

In a letter often attributed to Einstein (but whose origin cannot be confirmed to pen him as the author) here (abridged) another great mind states eloquently:

> "There is an extremely powerful force that, so far, science has not found a formal explanation to. It is a force that includes and governs all others, and is even behind any phenomenon operating in the universe and has not yet been identified by us. This universal force is Love. When scientists looked for a unified theory of the universe they forgot the most powerful unseen force.
>
> Love is Light, in that it enlightens those who give and receive it. Love is gravity, because it makes some people feel attracted to others. Love is power, because it multiplies the best we have, and allows humanity not to be extinguished in their blind selfishness. Love unfolds and reveals. For love we live and die.
>
> This force explains everything and gives meaning to life. This is the variable that we have ignored for too long, maybe because we are afraid of love because it is the only energy in the universe that man has not learned to drive at will. To give visibility to love, [I] made a simple substitution in [my] most famous equation. If instead of $E = mc2$, we accept that the energy to heal the world can be obtained through love multiplied by the speed of light squared, we arrive at the conclusion that love is the most powerful force there is, because it has no limits."

The Self Beyond

Love is the answer, the ultimate solvent for the greatest equation of matter and energy. Love is Light. Love has its own gravity, and Love remains to be our greatest power.

TUNING IN

Studies done by the late revered Dr. Masaru Emoto with water droplets showed that prayers, joyful songs, and expressions of Loving intention caused the molecules in water to arrange themselves into patterns resembling snowflakes (sacred geometry). While negative thoughts or expressions caused the water to form an incoherent blob. The molecular and structural shifts brought on through Loving expression and intention, or kind thoughts and words, reflect the symmetry and coherence of the divine design. [23]

A snowflake matching the water molecules from Dr. Emoto's work. [24] You can see the connection back to sacred geometry when

---

[23] I did not want to take from Dr. Emoto's photographic work, which is a large part of his impact in research, but you can see more at http://www.masaru-emoto.net/english/water-crystal.html

[24] Alexey Kljatov, February 5, 2015, under CC license retrieved from Wikicommons

compared to the next figure as well. (For anyone who has not viewed the work of Dr. Emoto, I strongly recommend you do, as it holds many keys to a deeper understanding of how the inner world truly effects the outer.) Energy and consciousness are the keys to the harmonics of our Universe. All we need to do is tune in through by returning to our most natural state, which comes through aligning with the higher vibration of Love.

The effect of frequency (thoughts and emotions) on molecular matter, like water, is powerful. Just like our thoughts, energy, and emotions affect every molecule within us. All matter can be changed based on its energetic environment. Thoughts and feelings are sounds. Sound is a frequency. Frequencies affect matter.

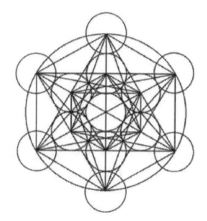

This figure is known as Metatrons cube (Sacred Geometry).

Within it are all 5 platonic solids, **the building blocks of life**.

An example of the sacred geometry mirrored in Dr. Emoto's water molecules (matter) which are affected by energy and consciousness (thought, emotion) [25]

Realize that thoughts resonate just as powerfully as words or deeds. Thoughts unspoken affect the internal and external environment around us. If you do not believe this, spend a week or two just *thinking* you hate a plant in your home and see what happens (please don't actually do that—it really will cause harm). Consider your own internal state after a week of telling yourself you are no good. That abuse causes *real* and measurable damage.

---

[25] Self-drawn for this work

We generate the environment our cells live within. We can create an unhealthy environment that is not in resonance which falls out of alignment with the sacred design by worrying, by blaming, by reliving guilt or having negative thoughts about ourselves or others. Or we can practice entering a state of Loving coherence that compliments and nurtures cell restructuring, growth, healing and aligns in resonance with the natural vibration of the universal field. We can spend time away from the external influences which drain our energy and reconnect with our own nature to find healing and rejuvenation.

The thing to realize is, ultimately we are not objects or even "beings," we are a *process*, a constantly shifting state of information and energetic expression. You are responsible for the energy that you bring. You are the conductor of your process.

SENSE

Compassion and cooperation are undervalued in our world today, however, they are essential elements to a successful society. Humans are meant to be highly sensitive to account for the vast field of information we cannot perceive with the more linear senses of touching, hearing, and seeing. Though many do not express sensitivities often, seeing them as signs of weakness. Society often discourages displays of affection, being emotional, or even caring "too much." Perhaps some are permitted; the artists, the lovers, and poets, but beyond that, the overwhelming expression of emotions are not encouraged.

The repression of emotion is damaging to our physiological biofeedback systems and the larger societal systems we are a part of. Repressed emotions become illness, stress, and disease in the individual body, they become tension. The same is true for the collective body we are a part of in society. In a society which has been desensitized, we see increased violence, greed, neglect, apathy, and careless acts toward others.

We are indoctrinated to believe that strength is showing no emotion. We are taught that compassion or caring too much is weakness, a kind of liability. We are driven to compete with one another, and a sense of insecurity comes from failure to fight for what we need to survive. Contrary to this, did you know that our very first instinct is not competition, but compassion? To help others is our first response. Compassion is our primary impulse reaction to the suffering of another. This has been proven in numerous studies of both humans and animals. Just look at the immediate response to many large scale tragedies. Yes, there will always be some who will take advantage of the situation, but the overwhelming response of the community is to come together and help one another.

There is a biological advantage to having a sense of compassion in that it ensures a greater survival rate of a species. In studies, it was shown that humans and animals alike do not seem to help for the reward of helping, but are inspired by the act itself. To ease the suffering of another was reward, in itself. [26] For me this sheds a ray of hope and faith in humanity after all.

Compassion and cooperation are tools that strengthen our bonds to one another, to our families and communities. In nature, entire ecosystems communicate through a connected network of roots and fungi, sharing resources such as nutrients, water, and carbon. A forest is not made up of individual plants and trees, as it appears. Underneath, they are all linked by a biological grid that connects as *one single organism*. This biological network is made of mycelium (fungi). They act much like the neurons that network our brain, sending signals. The fungi "trade" carbon for nutrients and allow other species to communicate.

Many of these networks overlap. The "mycelium web" (as it is known) connects not just to one, but many species of plants and trees. Through this a "mother" tree can nurture her saplings. She might be connected to hundreds of trees. [27] There are conversations which take place. These mother, or hub trees, are incredibly central to the forests. They share in their wisdom and energy. This is displays the natural process of compassion and cooperation in action. The entire system maintains a kind of

---

[26] Seppälä Ph.D., Emma M. 2013, June 03, Compassion: Our First Instinct. Science shows that we are actually wired for compassion, not self-interest. https://www.psychologytoday.com/blog/feeling-it/201306/compassion-our-first-instinct

[27] Engelsiepen, Jane. October 8, 2012. Ecology Global Netowkr. "Mother Trees" Use Fungal Communication Systems to Preserve Forests. Retrieved from: http://www.ecology.com/2012/10/08/trees-communicate/

symbiosis. The strength and resilience of an ecosystem relies on its connection to every other aspect of itself, not as an individual, but as a collective, a community.

Even trees and fungi know, they are not living for themselves. [28] Their survival depends on the survival of the entire system, thus, through a sharing of resources based on where they are most needed, the entire system benefits. Leaving all aspects with enough to not only, survive, but to thrive. In this way, among many others, plants are far advanced in their existence to that of man. They turn Light into food through the process of photosynthesis. They turn carbon dioxide into oxygen. They give to us just as much as they give to their own community, ensuring, not only, their own survival, but that of billions of other species as well.

PRACTICE

In any spiritual practice, coming into a heart-centered state of self-awareness and compassion is the goal. This can be elusive for many of us, but as more people seek this solution, more material and information on the subject is becoming available to assist. Simple practices such as silence, creative expression, walking in nature, reflection, meditation and gratitude can infuse everyday life with rich meaning and depth. These simple methods can help us center and align with our higher vibrational Self. We learn best when we find the answers from within our self.

> *"When you succeed in connecting your energy with the divine realm through high awareness and the practice of*

---

[28] To see more about how mycelium and mushrooms can save the planet, from "eating" toxic oil spill waste and transforming it into a thriving community of ecological life, to the many cancer preventing health benefits, see Paul Stamets Ted Talk "6 Ways Mushrooms Can Save the World" on youtube at
https://www.youtube.com/watch?v=XI5frPV58tY

undiscriminating virtue, the transmission of the ultimate subtle truths will follow." ~Lao Tzu

SILENCE

Silence is golden. For many, silence is also a luxury. Creating times for silence must, therefore, be intentional. This is an investment in bettering yourself, so you can be better for others *and* yourself. How often do you truly make this a priority? Turning off the phone, the internet, the television? Excusing yourself from the various obligations you have, all the business and relationships which require your attention? This is something only you can commit to doing. This is something only you can make happen.

I recommend taking time daily, *every single day*, to be with yourself in mindful silence. Whether that means meditation for 30 minutes, or simply a nice 15-20 minute session of sitting out in nature, or in a quiet room. The setting is important, it has to be free of distraction to truly enter a state of inner silence. This setting will vary person to person, and you may not have easy access to walk off into the woods every day. That is fine. Wherever you feel at peace that is at least moderately conducive to allowing for silence will do. Even if this just means walking into a separate room while your kids play, or stepping out of where you work on your break for a quiet walk.

Intention is everything when seeking to create silence. The goal, on a physiological level, is to move from the driven productive state of beta waves, into alpha or even theta for just a bit. This allows us to recharge and center. Focus on the breath. Focus on coming to the center. Allow yourself to be still. Close your eyes, if that helps, or if you are somewhere beautiful, focus on that beauty. Allow the silence to wash away any worries, or excessive thoughts. Remember that worrying rarely helps us be more successful. It rarely solves any problems. While centering and calming yourself allows for solutions to present themselves more clearly. Silence is where we can listen to the heart. Silence allows us to check in with ourselves and know what it is we might need.

CREATIVE EXPRESSION

Exercising creative expression is cathartic and powerful. What better than to emulate intelligent creative expression by becoming creators too? Whether you are a skilled and gifted artist, or someone who has never been "crafty," there is still great value to allowing yourself to have the experience of creating without attaching yourself to the outcome. It is the *process* that restores us. The process of creation allows us to tap into the creative and emotional mind. The more we connect with this aspect of ourselves, the more deeply we connect with our emotions. This can also strengthen our ability to express them in a healthy and healing way. So much within us is just waiting to be expressed.

Consider trying this activity, close your eyes and think of something that brings you peace or joy. Something of beauty that enlivens your spirit. What I want you to do is use any medium; crayons, markers, paint, colored pencils, or even clay and attempt to create this. Do not stress yourself about trying to replicate the vision in its perfection as you see it. We are trying to tap into the process which unfolds naturally and cannot be controlled. Just allow yourself to enjoy this creative expression in each mark of the crayon, each stroke of the paintbrush, or each curve of the clay. Enjoy the progression of this creation. Get lost within each layer.

Make it a point to have arts and crafts time at least once a month. Get the kids or your partner involved, if you have them. This is a great group activity with friends or family. Or take this time to become close with your own, most creative intelligence within. However accomplished, what will exist afterward is something that never existed before, and you will feel much more balanced and centered for having made it.

WALKING IN NATURE

Nature is one of the most underused remedies to nearly every malady that our, often, hectic daily lives create. From depression to high blood pressure, from chronic bronchitis to anxiety: *nature is the great healer*.

Shinrin-Yoku is the Japanese art of forest bathing. The principle concept is to, literally, surround yourself with the elements of nature and utilize every sense. Actual interaction with nature is the point. Touch the leaves, smell the air, feel the earth, view the colors and the beauty. This activates and stimulates us on a primal and even spiritual level. Science has shown this is restorative and induces deeper states of relaxation. Connecting with nature allows us to gain better focus, it puts things in perspective. We gain a clear appreciation of the interconnectedness of all life to something much bigger than ourselves. We come into our "now" moment more completely.

Go out into nature, if this is something foreign to you, I suggest going online and looking up "nature trails near me." If you are particularly drawn to water over forests try a search of "waterfalls near me" or "lakes near me." Then, grab some water, an apple, some nuts to snack on, wear comfortable clothes and shoes you don't mind getting dirty and head out for an adventure!

While in the woods, or walking out, try to increase your awareness and deeply appreciate all the little things; the way the sunlight shines through the leaves, the textures of the bark on a tree, the lovely scent of the fresh air. Immerse yourself. Notice the little creatures, birds, and chipmunks scurrying about on their little missions (they will remain hidden until you become still from within). Realize, here, you are in their house. Treat it with the same respect you would entering another's home. Look at the clouds and the sunlight. Stop and actually touch the leaves. Smell the wildflowers. Interact with this experience. Take off your shoes, if weather permits. Let the soles of your feet soak in the wonderful energies of earth. If you have something you need to let go of, this is the perfect place. Imagine any worries, issues, or negative things are coming down out of your body through the soles of your feet into the welcoming earth. She can transmute those energies for you. Give thanks to her for all she gives of herself to us.

This is the most sacred of places. You have entered the sanctuary of nature. If not for all of this working together just exactly as it does, we would not survive. We depend on the water filtered by the streams and mountains, the tides of the oceans to cycle through the seasons, the rain produced by the clouds to water our crops, the oxygen produced by the plants and trees, there is not one element of nature that is wasted without a Divine purpose. We are, indeed, connected to this living system.

Time in nature is time spent in the outermost expression of the innermost self. Make this a weekly practice, or as often as time allows. Don't be picky with the weather. Rainy days have just as much to marvel at as a sunny day. Every season has its own beauty and wonder. When you spend time in nature, you will always return with something more then you went out with.

REFLECTION

What is reflection? It is an image which mirrors an object back to itself. Self-reflection has been a constant tool for me in my life. It allows me to gauge where I am at, to assess my own perspective, to give some objectivity to the subjective reality I would, otherwise, continue to believe in without question. From self-reflection comes self-awareness and that is what we are looking to increase.

To engage in self-reflection is to question your own perspective and reality, to ask the kind of questions that can keep us in check such as; am I doing my best? Have I been acting from a place of Love or fear? Could I be doing better in my relationships or at work? Am I listening to what I need? Am I living up to my responsibilities? Could I be interpreting anything someone said or did with bias? Is there another way to look at what I perceive to be a problem or issue in my life or in a relationship? What am I learning from my current problems? This is a highly personal example of questions and you can make your own as you practice this for yourself.

The most important thing is to challenge your own beliefs about your situations, your role in your life, your viewpoint on relationships with others and yourself. This must always come from a place of compassion and non-judgment. This exercise is *never* meant to degrade you or make you feel bad about yourself. This, instead, empowers you to see things a little differently and often you may find the answer to many problems, or issues may not lie outside of you (such as in another changing what they are doing or a situation changing) but in changes you can make within yourself and how you view them.

Always remember everything is multidimensional and anything taken too far can become harmful. Reflecting inward is important, but we don't want to focus so much on ourselves that we essentially become narcissists, or make our personal problems the only thing that matters. When you start to feel like you are obsessing over your own internal experience, or disheartened by your own problems after focusing on yourself too intensely, the remedy I have found for this is in turning your focus (counterintuitively) *outward*. For example, maybe right now you don't feel good and can't fix your own problems, but maybe right now you can help someone else feel good and fix theirs. When you are discouraged you will find a great sense of life repurposing by encouraging others. This is as uplifting for you as it is for those you are helping. For me, this is always my go-to when things become a little too much inside of me. I focus on where I can be helpful, who might need reassurance, who might need some inspiration (even if I feel I have none for myself). This helps me gain perspective on the size of my own problems, and helps me re-inspire and elevate myself just as much as those I support.

> *Go inwards. Find your inner space, and suddenly, you will find an explosion of light, of beauty, of ecstasy. As if suddenly thousands of roses have blossomed within you and you are full of their fragrance.*~ Osho

MEDITATION

Meditation is an ancient practice of going within, used by various spiritual groups throughout the ages. Its origin is speculative but has been used perhaps as early as humanity's emergence. We might imagine our early ancestors staring into the flames of a fire to enter deeper states of awareness. It has, mainly, been popularized by Eastern culture and the Buddha has become its icon. However, it is not a requirement to be either religious or spiritual to undertake the practice of meditation. Anyone can meditate for any reason, whether to gain deeper self-awareness or become more focused in school or business. Many people have found the benefit of meditation for practical reasons, aside from being a tool of spiritual development. Meditation is utilized by people from all walks of life, from lawyers to athletes, from business people to monks.

Meditation has shown to help ease chronic pain, anxiety, depression, and stress. It can improve heart health, as well as boost mood and immune system function. It lowers blood pressure, increases metabolism, improves breathing, heart rate, and brain waves. In studies done with Buddhist monks, long lasting changes in the brain were demonstrated in areas of attention, memory, learning and perception (consciousness). Meditating, even once or twice a day for as little as 20 minutes, leads to measurable shifts in energy, focus, and feeling of relaxation throughout the day. [29]

One of the amazing things about meditation is that the more you do it, the more you practice, the deeper you will go. "Deeper" meaning to reach a deeper sense of connection, deeper self-awareness (in the broader sense which extends beyond the body), deeper relaxation, and deeper emotional resonance. The root of the word "Meditation" in Latin, "meditato," means "to ponder." To ponder deeply within yourself leads to the ultimate self-discovery, profound healing, and a rich sense of purpose and meaning in life.

Meditation directly affects our states of consciousness. It, literally, creates shifts in our brainwave patterns from the beta (constant production driven state, often accompanied by high levels of stress and cortisol response) into alpha (the rarely visited, more relaxed state in which beneficial self-soothing and self-healing hormones are emitted), and with practice, even theta levels can be accessed (deep meditative and creative state, usually only experienced during REM cycles). If we are skillful enough theta transitions into gamma waves which are the most coherent high level mental state. When measured on an electroencephalography (EEG) machine, almost all areas of the brain light up in gamma. It is a super activated state of higher meta-consciousness. Gamma waves range from 40-70 Hz (or higher) and are the fastest brainwave frequency documented to be experienced by a human. Gamma waves are associated with peak performance levels and high cognitive function.

These altered states of awareness help us to break free from our own patterns to go beyond the diurnal (day to day) conscious mind into the super-conscious mind, to reach beyond

---

[29] Davis, Jeanne Lerche, (2017). Meditation Balances the Body's Systems. WebMD.
https://www.webmd.com/balance/features/transcendental-meditation#1

The Self Beyond

our tunnel vision and see from a greater perspective and to understand our lives as well as our place within them. Meditation allows us to experience the creative intelligence first hand and viscerally sense the expansiveness of our own existence.

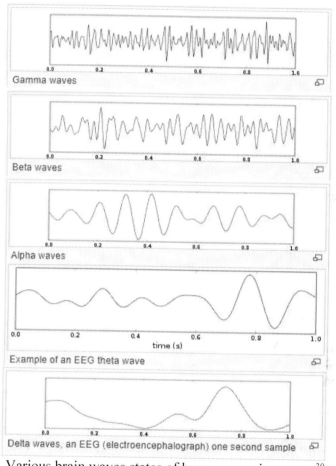

Various brain waves states of human consciousness. [30]

There are various types of meditation, some of which may assist those who have difficulty in entering a meditative state. Mindfulness (or Vipassana) is the practice of simply being very mindful on one particular aspect of your experience during

---

[30] Hugo Gamboa, under CC license retrieved from Wikicommons

meditation. This can be your own breath, physical sensations within the body, subtle sounds outside of you, or a vision you are holding. This can help beginners because anytime your mind wanders off, you can gently bring your mindful attention back to the focus. This is practiced by sitting in a comfortable position and simply concentrating on the selected focus and remaining mindful.

Mantra meditation (used in the Transcendental Meditation) is a focus on a repeated word, or phrase. This can be an English word such as "relax," or a phrase such as "I am at peace." Or, you can make use of the sacred and powerful language of Sanskrit with mantras such as "Om Mani Padre Hum." "Om" is the sacred sound of the Universe, "Mani" means jewel or bead, "Padre" means lotus or flower, and "Hum" represents Spirit or enlightenment. Essentially, this Sanskrit mantra describes the jewel of the sacred sound flowering into the spirit of enlightenment. These words or phrases are repeated as we focus in a comfortable seated position. This allows us to enter the field of consciousness in which we are simply present.

Walking can be a meditation, every step a prayer and a blessing. This is a great form of meditation for those with difficulty sitting still (though it is still very important to allow yourself to have times of deep reflective stillness). The benefit of walking meditation is the attention it brings to the body. It is very easy and anyone can do this. You simply pick a path; in the woods, in your yard, on a nature trail or Labyrinth walk and focus on your feet. Just make sure you are remaining mindful of your surroundings and not placing yourself in a harmful pathway, such as oncoming traffic. Notice any physical sensations you are having. Notice the movement of your legs as they bend, down to the soles of your feet, and even your toes as they flex. This is a practice in a different kind of mindfulness. This can translate into many other areas of your daily life as well such as cleaning, sweeping, doing laundry, or even working.

Visualization is a powerful technique which can be used in many ways. Athletes may use visualization to improve their performance and form. This type of visualization has shown to be incredibly effective. Public speakers may use visualization to prepare themselves to be able to deliver their message with confidence and charisma. We can use it to begin to paint a picture

The Self Beyond

of the happy life we wish to create for ourselves. All of this is possible, and I will go deeper into the science of why a little later in this text. In the context of visualization meditation, we are talking about imagining a serene scene; a beach, a meadow, a nice crackling fire in a log cabin. The more details, the better your awareness can slip into that little vacation spot you create. *The mind loves to imagine.* We use it half the time in the wrong way by worrying. So why not put this mental tendency to some good use by imagining what you *do* want, where you *would* like to be. There are a plethora of guided meditations available online, of course,[31] or you can guide your own journey.

The visualization method for general relaxation is easy: you will simply sit and breath comfortably, allow your body to relax, letting any tension fade away. Then, you follow the story: imagine someplace beautiful to you. Don't try too hard to select it. Just go to the place your mind first thought of. Imagine the feeling of peace as you enter this space. Let that feeling encompass you completely. Breathe deeply. Envision the colors, the sights, paint this space with as much detail as you like. The more, the better. Imagine the sounds, the scents. Imagine the feeling of any textures, the grass, the sand, the earth or the water. Whatever it is, feel it on your hands, on your feet. The concept is to have a story for each sense: sight, sound, feeling, scent, and even taste. This practice can transport you to your own personal soul retreat, anytime you wish to tap into it.

I would like to share a story. For many years I had made little attempts at intentional meditation. For me, especially as a channel, this is difficult. I did not seem to go to a quiet place, but instead as soon as my mind of ego stopped talking, all the deep insights of the higher mind came through. This has been a manageable situation for me because it is through these times I am able to create works like this book. However, I truly wished to

---

[31] I stumbled upon this through YouTube, the Honest Guys make wonderful guided meditations that greatly helped me in beginning my meditation practice. I still use these to help me get into a quiet place before sleep (prior to that my mind would be thinking a thousand things).
https://www.youtube.com/results?search_query=honest+guys+meditation

The Self Beyond

enter a deep space of silent stillness within. I knew I had not quite made it beyond myself yet.

One extraordinary, ordinary, day I decided to go to some beautiful cascades near where I live. I had no intention of meditating. I just wanted to be in nature and enjoy the beauty of it all. As I sat, watching the water cascading through on its own journey, I decided there (quite spontaneously) to close my eyes. Mind you, I had done this many, many times before, but that magical day something different happened. I began to transcend myself. I cannot quite place this gift of an experience into words. I felt myself go to zero-point. It was the calmest I have ever been in my life. I was in that space for at least two hours. I felt Light, I felt warmth, I felt a sense of no gravity, and I felt the most blissful and euphoric waves of radiant Love. When coming back from this inner journey I have since been able to enter this deep space much more quickly and easily. Don't give up if it does not happen for you right away. Your own transcendent beyond-self experience is waiting for just the right time to open that door within you too.

MOVEMENT

Movement is life. It is a natural compulsion to animate our, otherwise, stagnant body. We are meant to move, to run, to jump, to climb, to dance, to hug, to reach, to touch, to stretch every fiber of every muscle and limb, from our head to our toes, from our fingers to the corners of our mouths, from our core to our appendages. Movement brings us to life!

Try it right now. Stretch your body. Stretch out your arms above your head. Hold them there for a few breaths. Feel how good that feels! Stretch your arms back towards your sides like outstretched wings of a soaring eagle. Wiggle your fingers, move your wrists. Flex and un-flex your palms. Rotate your arms at the shoulder, gently, let your joints lubricate. You may hear little pops and crackles. (That is your body saying two things: drink some water, and move me more!) Stretch your core, your stomach muscles and the length of your back. Do this however it feels right for you, do not hurt yourself or push yourself beyond your own range of motion. Your range of motion will open up, in time. Flex your buttocks and your hamstrings. Tighten and stretch the quad muscles of your thighs. Lift and lower your feet to flex and move your calves, your lower leg muscles. Move your toes around (how often do they get to move around like this?) Shrug your shoulders a bit. Do a few little jogs in place. Jump up and down a little. Turn your head back and forth. Lift and lower your chin. Can you feel how your body has needed this? Do this as often as you like. Don't overdo it, but try to gain the fullest range of motion in each stretch that you can.

What does this do for your body? As we age, muscles can tighten and joint mobility can be lost, but stretching improves muscle elasticity, flexibility and range of motion. I do not subscribe to the idea that we are in constant deterioration. I live by the mantra: you are only as old as you feel. (Remember, we don't stop playing because we get old, we get old because we stop playing). Stretching and movement helps to lubricate joints to prevent arthritis, improves circulation, and even boosts energy!

If you enjoy more blood pumping exercises such as running, swimming, or cardio, then these kinds of health benefits can increase even more. Endorphins kick in when we really get moving. Endorphins are like your body's own personal morphine, and they have all kinds of great health benefits. Endorphins are, not only "feel good" hormones, they are stress reducers and natural pain killers. They boost positive emotions, self-esteem, and improve sleep. You don't have to be a marathon racer to enjoy endorphins. Laughing causes our body to release them as well! Laughter burns calories, too. Remember not to take this all so seriously that it becomes a happiness zapping chore. Think of the iconic laughing Buddha. This figure represents the essentiality of being able to laugh, to find humor in the, otherwise, heavy elements of the human experience. Enlightenment is very much about creating a state of joy and laughter.

Dancing is another great expression of movement and you don't have to sign up for any gym membership on this. A recent neuroscience study came out, which showed the number one way to stall the aging process is to dance! [32] It has been shown that

---

[32] Dancing or Fitness Sport? The Effects of Two Training Programs on Hippocampal Plasticity and Balance Abilities in Healthy Seniors. Retrieved from:
https://www.frontiersin.org/articles/10.3389/fnhum.2017.00305/full

physical activities, specifically those related to dance, can positively impact age-related, cognitive degeneration. When is the last time you danced?

GRATITUDE

Gratitude is a huge influencing factor in our state of being. A lack of gratitude leads to resentment, jealousy, taking gifts for granted, and can exasperate or, even, cause depression. Consider why that is, look at what resentment is. Typically, we resent something we felt we should have gotten instead of someone else, or something someone did that we feel was unfair to us. This may be the case; someone else may not have deserved something over you, you may truly have been treated unfairly, or someone objectively did something wrong to you, but by resenting this, whose joy does that steal away? To replace this stolen joy, find gratitude for what you do have, or for what you took away from, even, the most negative experience (such as becoming wiser or stronger). Look at what jealousy is. Within it is the word "lousy." It is wanting what another has instead of appreciating what we, ourselves, have. An absence of gratitude always means we are taking some important aspect of our lives for granted. When we do not appreciate what we have, or fail to notice the (often unrecognized) blessings and gifts, it can cause us to become unhappy.

The transformational power of gratitude in our lives cannot be overstated. Where gratitude is present, you will find problems and issues become lessons and challenges which we can grow from and overcome. Where gratitude is present, you will find you have a greater understanding, compassion, and appreciation for relationships and situations in your life. When practicing gratitude, you will find it is endless. There is no end to what we can be thankful for and appreciate in our lives.

Make a list of everything you are grateful for. Even if you truly feel you have nothing, I do invite you to try with compassion and an open mind and heart. Start with the basics and work your way out. I will ask, can you read this sentence? Then you are lucky

---

[Original Research ARTICLE Front. Hum. Neurosci., 15 June 2017 | https://doi.org/10.3389/fnhum.2017.00305]

as there are 775 million people in the world who are currently illiterate. Can you see the words? Then you are very fortunate as there are 285 million people who are visually impaired and 39 million people who are blind. Do you have a functioning heart, lungs and brain? This is a gift! This, itself is a great miracle! Do you have access to fresh water? 783 million people do not have access to clean water. Do you have a toilet? 2.5 billion people do not have access to sanitation (can you appreciate just, exactly, what it would be like if your toilet stopped working for, even, a week?) Do you have food to eat? 850 million people in the world are presently going hungry (and we will talk about this global crisis of humanitarian need later in this book). Do you have a roof over your head? Around 200 million people are homeless worldwide (this number is an estimate as it is harder to gauge those who may be off the books or missing). I am assuming the majority of you said yes to *most* of these questions. If so, we are living in privilege and have no right to be anything but falling-on-our-knees-daily kind of grateful. We, also, owe it to the world to do all we can to ease the suffering of others who do not share our comforts.

I have an interesting observation I would like to share which I have found in my many years of being close to several different communities, some better off and some with very little. I found that the less people have, the happier and more appreciative they are. Not only that, but the less someone has, the more willing they are to share it with another in need. I experienced this multiple times when I was going hungry, that well off people would shrug me off, while those with very little would offer me what they had. In contrast, in many cases the more people have, the more we take for granted, the more we want, and we generally experience *less* joy.

I do not in any way wish to shame those who have done well financially. There are many well-known philanthropists who have used their successes to support others who are less fortunate. Altruism comes in many forms. Yet, in many other cases this is an exception, not the rule. Empathy and compassion for another's struggle comes into play when you have faced the same struggle. So, essentially, the less we have the happier we are, and the less we have the more likely we are to share.

The Self Beyond

Consider that resistance is a barrier to happiness, while allowing life without resistance can instill contentment. Constantly seeking outside of us and rejecting where we currently are is a kind of resistance which causes imbalance and dissonance. To always be driving towards something more (in a material sense) can see us chasing the wrong thing: the pot of gold instead of the rainbow. The pot of gold is nothing. The rainbow is the real treasure. Creating appreciation for what we have, what we have accomplished already, what we can already do, accepting our current relationships and situations allows for a sense of peace and satisfaction.

Those with very little may accept their status and find gratitude and joy in their current situation. I will tell you, as thankful as I am for the progress I have made in my life which has allowed me to pursue my writing and work, the happiest I ever was, was when I had nearly nothing. Despite the moderate anxiety of insecurity, I felt free. My richness was in my experiences and relationships, not material gains. My value was within the quality of my own character as a human being, not in my status or career. This is something I carry with me all these years later.

When we find value beyond the material, we may also find freedom, deeper meaning in relationships and experiences, or the "simple things" which bring true happiness. Those with a lot may not accept staying at one level and find themselves constantly seeking more. The fundamental issue here is the illusion of material gain. Aside from meeting our basic needs, assuming we have food, shelter, water, and clothing, *more* material comforts do not necessarily connect with greater happiness. In fact, the more we have the more we may not appreciate what we have. For example, when I was hungry for days on end during my early twenties, getting a simple meal was like a feast! Every bite was a celebration. Every flavor was deliciously savored. I was elated and felt deeply grateful. While those who have the luxury of fine foods daily may take it for granted. In fact, the food may literally not taste as good.

Empathy and compassion come in when we can relate. Consider why people are motivated to help or give. Those with very little have experienced being hungry. We are more likely to identify with the struggle of another person being hungry. This plays on empathy and our compassion for what we would hope another would do for us in the same situation. While those who have never shared in this humbling experience may find it more difficult to draw on a sense of empathy or compassion, perhaps justifying their lack of support by drawing from the lies of our culture which depict the poor or needy as lazy or incompetent. It is easier to believe that the poor somehow created their own situation than to take a real look at the unilateral systems in place which have subjugated them and created impossible obstacles for entire communities which are often very realistically insurmountable.

Gratefulness, you see, is not just about being happy with what *you* have, it is about caring for something greater than yourself, as well. A truly grateful person is an active contributor to the greater global community we are a part of. It is a wonderful thing to appreciate your life every morning you wake, every bit of food that you eat, every warm clean sweater you put on, every person who is kind to you, every step that you take. But it is also important to extend yourself outward and share with those who need it. Helping others brings a much greater sense of purpose. You may even find you are more grateful for giving to another, than having for yourself. Happiness does not come from what we have, it comes from *who we are*. Be someone who cares, who helps, who heals, who comforts and supports. This is one of many ways we can be truly grateful.

If you stripped away all that you "have" how rich are your contributions, your experiences, and your relationships? What would be the value of your own character, as a human being?

I want to impress that I have not perfected every method and perspective shift we are discussing. Some things I am gaining mastery over, others I need to continually remind myself of daily. I still get frustrated, I still have my moments where I feel like I could cry. I still take things for granted, I Love too much or not enough. Sometimes my emotions take over and I don't handle things as well as I know I could have. But I, genuinely, strive to better myself and my presence in the world. If we are aiming for perfection, that may create an endless or even impossible goal. But, simply aiming to be better can bring out our best. Every one of these tools takes us one step closer, and we can always take one more step.

The Self Beyond

The journey of a thousand miles begins with one step.~
Lao Tsu

Chapter 3: Vision and Mental Clarity

SET AND SETTING

    For the most part, we as humans seek the security of what we know. Aside from the rebellious spirit of the unquenchable few, most people stay safely in their comfort zone. There is nothing wrong with being comfortable and loving your life as it is right now. There does, however, start to be an issue on your spiritual journey, when you stop growing and learning. When our daily life becomes a pattern, an endless template in which what our day looks like today and will look like many months from now is, virtually, identical. That is a spiritual red flag. Everything is energy, and energy must move and flow for new information and higher insight to come in. The reward for stepping outside of your comfort zone is that you learn something about yourself that you didn't know before.

    For some, you may be well aware of the tediousness of your current life. It may bring you no joy. You may, desperately, want change but despite your sincerest efforts, you find little in the way of revolution in your life, as a whole. What can we do when we are trying to make all the right moves, trying to take all the right steps, actively trying to make outward changes and nothing seems to really change? Do you just give up and forfeit that you are not capable of healing, or that you are an exception and your wounds or issues are too deep to transcend? Have faith in the *process* and understand that not everything changes on the surface in the beginning. A tree does a lot of work underground before it comes into the Light. Many plants in the beginning may have their first bloom and then appear to wither and die, but underneath the roots are growing, and that will bring flowers soon enough.

In order to break through our pattern, to transcend our own greatest illusions, we sometimes need a catalyst. To go beyond our own field of gravity, our core viewpoints which have become obstructions (these are sometimes very difficult to overcome even with the most heartfelt intention and devoted practice) we need the background to radically shift. Setting changes can create a powerful venue for transformation. They allow for a life-changing experience to emerge naturally. If we do not create one, life will sometimes offer one to shake us out of our stagnant state. We are meant to keep going and growing.

When the universe creates a setting change it, often, comes disguised as some negative event, perhaps the ending of a relationship, the loss of a job, or the move you are forced to make which you do not want. It may even be a change as harsh as losing a loved one. This is not because life is mean or cruel, this is because sometimes we do not know how to create that change ourselves.

These intense events often unfold to shake us awake or bring us into greater growth. This may make you angry and you might say, "No! There is no reason they had to be taken from me!" In this I offer great compassion and hope you can hold on to the deeper insight that there is a higher message or meaning within the tragedy of loss. I too have experienced loss, but these losses changed my life.

Some may say, "There is no reason they left me!" or, "There has been nothing but bad that has come from me losing my job!" but time is the greatest teacher. Connecting the dots can take years, even decades, but there is *always* a reason. The Loving

Intelligence from which all life comes does not make mistakes, and with great care and compassion it designs with our greatest growth in mind. It takes the path of least resistance to produce what will be most beneficial for us in our lives and our development.

When I say there is always a reason, I say it with a deep and empathetic recognition of the unimaginable distress many have undergone. How could something like severe violence, death, or abuse have a reason? I am not, in any way, undermining the magnitude of these damaging events that can scar us for many years, or even life. I am introducing an appreciation for the *takeaways*, which can appear negative in many cases, but can also be life-changing and positive. There are always collateral benefits: a deeper purpose underlying even the most dreadful circumstances. There is a subtle point of empowerment that is not always clearly visible, only to those that would seek to understand more deeply.

Consider something negative that happened many years ago. Perhaps, due to some ambiguous circumstance, you broke up with someone who you were certain was the Love of your life. This may have haunted you for a long time and maybe you felt you would never find true Love again. Yet, due to this relationship ending you find yourself attending a different college than you would have if you had stayed together. You meet someone who ends up teaching you more about yourself and opening you up in ways you could not have imagined. This person may or may not have been "the one" but the lessons you take from it change you for life. You may come away from it with a much greater perspective and sense of self-appreciation. All this was a life changing experience that presented as a tragedy.

The good news is that we have a role in the destiny of our lives and how they play out. We can circumvent the bold and harsh negative situations otherwise necessary by *recognizing it is time to change*, and making those changes for ourselves in our own lives. This way, we are a proactive co-creator with the Universe in which the life changing experience can be one that presents in a much more positive context. We can create the catalyst for revolution in our lives and speak directly to our higher self with our intention.

Creating a set change, or life-changing experience, is part intuition and part synchronicity. You have to follow your own heart and try not to control how it unfolds. Step one is to have the intention: to put it out that you wish for a positive transformational experience to unfold. Your intention for this may be for many reasons; for healing, to let go, for insight to come, for discovery of your own purpose. Whatever it is, this method remains the building block. Step two is to then hold the space and believe in the possibility of its reality, it now has a place to manifest. Step three is to actively look for opportunities and act on them. The Universe may hold open the door, but nothing can happen unless you choose to walk through it. The final step? Get ready to be amazed! Get ready to be surprised! You cannot anticipate the specifications or particular conditions. Allow the greater good to work its magic through you.

What might it look like after the intention has been set and the space for the event has been created? Perhaps one day you follow a whim and feel yourself drawn to the beach. There, you may not have expected the conditions to be so sublimely perfect. The water is warm and inviting. The sky blue and cloudless. The sun is golden and you find yourself basking there for hours. You enter a state of blissful presence. You soak in the beauty, and feel yourself recharging, centering. You begin aligning within yourself as all the worries that seemed so large shrink down to their rightful size. As you sit there, the answer you have been troubling over for months becomes perfectly clear. Or perhaps, a solution presents itself as you watch the tide come in. Maybe an epiphany strikes you and you realize you are meant to move to another state or take a new career direction. Whatever it is, this experience can be life-changing. In those few hours, you can make more progress than years of less mindful self-work. However, you could not have planned this. In fact, you cannot expect it to be the same next time either.

Another example might be choosing to go out to a musical event which you, otherwise, may not have typically considered attending. Something compels you to ignore your usual social aversion and you take the queue to follow that impulse. When you arrive, you may find yourself enjoying the music much more than you would have expected. You begin to notice your foot tapping, you begin to sway, perhaps another individual takes your hand and before you know it, you are dancing. You find time suspended. All that exists is swirling motion. You see smiles, you hear laughter, and you find you are smiling, too, immersed in the music and saturated in the current of invigorating energy. It resonates through every cell of your being. You find yourself experiencing an almost tribal bond, sharing a heartbeat in sync with the drums and all who have joined. This is no superficial experience. This is a primal, *mystical*, and sacred event. Celebration (a state of gratefulness) and movement (a state of fluidity) are both vital to transcending any blockages that have prevented your personal progression. Now, your life's energy can flow and you can make the changes you have been seeking.

You must realize these experiences shift and move, because we are meant to shift and move. The key is to follow the strange pull of what calls you: nature, a bookstore, a random event or gathering. The important thing is, not so much the setting, as the *shift* in the setting. The other key is to stay open for these revolutionary experiences to come to you. Allow them gratefully, and try not to take any micro-moment of it for granted. Almost nothing that happens in our lives has only surface value. There is a depth, a rich and wonderful meaning to be discovered. These are the moments that can create the right conditions, the perfect environment, to break through your rut to the other side of your full potential. That is what life wants for you: to be capable of knowing when it is time to change, and then creating that change.

THE QUANTUM SELF

We believe we are living in a three-dimensional world, in a three-dimensional body. This body and this world are made up of atoms which we are told are 99.9999% empty space. Empty space, is there such a thing? If you consider anything you can't see, or touch, or manipulate to be nothing—then yes, to you that is emptiness. However, if you can appreciate that everything is something: that no thing is nothing, you may begin to understand that subtle radiant energies pervade every space, every crack, every cell and every atom even into the quantum levels. These energies contain limitless potential. Within the waves of apparent emptiness, infinite possibilities exist. And the outwardly dense and seemingly immutable elements of our world are, in fact, fluid, changeable, and they are greatly influenced by our own vibrations and level of consciousness.

[Some may already be well-versed in this concept, but stay with me, I will attempt to go farther than you may have gone previously in this complex and catalytic subject. I want to first get us all on the same page.]

We believe that in this three-dimensional world we are governed by laws like gravity and the speed of Light. These laws, we are confident, are reliable indicators predicting the patterns of behavior for all "solid" objects, mass and matter. They regulate, restrict and limit our reality to a specific continuum of possibility. We know we cannot, for instance, be in two places at once, or disappear and reappear. Yet the quantum world exists very differently, under a perplexing set of lawless states and strange attractions. In the quantum realm, Light can exist both as a wave and a particle, for instance. Particles can exist simultaneously in two places at once. They can appear, disappear, and reappear in a different location. They can fluctuate between states. They can, even, become entangled. Entanglement describes when two particles interact in such a way that they become "connected." This connection affects each entangled particle beyond time and space. This means when something affects one particle, it will affect the other, regardless of distance. This happens faster than the speed of Light!

Think of the particle as the choice manifested and the wave as all the potential possibilities that could exist. Who is it, then, that makes that choice? Who decides what happens with the googolplex of waves within the multiverse? Studies done have shown, an observer can affect the particle/wave just by the act of observing. What was shown is that the wave would not appear as a particle in a particular location until the observer looked to observe it. It is as if the observer "chooses" where the particle will be just by looking to observe it.

There is an almost mystical connection between our consciousness and the quantum elements which create our physical reality. It is not, however, mystical at all. This is the science of quantum physics. Just because it seems strange to us, doesn't make it magic, right? There is a direct relation between mind and matter. We have been looking at this all backwards. We have been taught that matter determines the reality that makes up our mind, when it is mind that determines the matter that makes up our perceived reality. We are living in a quantum world and you are a Quantum Being!

Some things you need to know about this world: it is reflective and it is magnetic. It is reflective in that it reflects back to us what we put out. It is magnetic in that we magnetically attract what we think and feel. Both of these aspects relate to the mechanics of a quantum reality.

What does this mean for us in our daily lives? Can we *actually* affect our reality and physical world? Well, yes! I would like to go beyond the simplified versions of the law of attraction which I feel leaves out some fundamental points on the process. Think of your thoughts as an electric signal you are generating. Each moment, you are sending out a signal to the universe about what you want to create. Now, think of your emotions as a magnetic attraction which draw in your experiences. So, essentially, you are manifesting with the electrical signal you send out and drawing to you with the magnetic charge you create. What this means is thoughts (intentions) and emotions (reception) have a quantum material effect.

We are constantly sending out signals with our thoughts. Our thoughts are the main mechanism that drives our emotional state, so beginning with the thought, the mind, is a good place to focus. What are you thinking?

Becoming aware of your own thought patterns is key. This is where the Law of Attraction comes into play. If you are constantly complaining, being negative to yourself, about others, or about situations you are in, guess what you are sending out in your signal? You're sending out more things to complain about, more of the same negative situations or people. You are, even, supercharging it because these thoughts are creating emotional states which magnetically attract these things you do not want. This is where your relationship to your own reality becomes critical. We have to take responsibility for what we have been sending out and attracting in our life. We are, often, doing this in such a way it is almost completely automated and unconscious.

That is why becoming *more conscious* and aware of these thoughts and emotional patterns are vital.

It is difficult to reverse the default inner narrative which has taken a lifetime to root itself within our psyche, but with awareness of your inner workings, it is possible. This inner narrative comes from our upbringing, various relationships and life experiences, but it becomes self-perpetuating when we allow it to play out over and over, creating the same results. As you begin to be aware of your thoughts, you can catch the negative ones. Just allow them to pass through, you can choose what you identify with and personalize. If a negative thought pattern comes, don't chastise yourself or beat yourself up. Just recognize that is a pattern you now wish to release. *Overwrite the program*, then, replace it with a positive affirmation. For example, you might begin to think "I hate this job, I will never get anything done." Be aware of it. Release it with Love, not resentment (that is key). Then, *choose* a better attitude about it and say, "I am grateful for my job. I know all will be completed and I will work on it, step by step." That is a program override.

Another example, is looking in the mirror and saying, "I am so ugly, no one will ever Love me." Recognize that this, of course, is not true. Allow yourself to look in your own eyes with Love, and say, "I Love and accept all of myself. I am beautiful. I am surrounded by Love. I never need to look any further than within myself." These affirmations may sound cheesy but I will tell you right now—*this will change your life*! These are powerful, *powerful* electrical signals that evoke prevailing emotional magnetic charges to allow space for the things you do want to come into your life. Your thoughts and emotions allow you to interface with the quantum world and the reality which is subsequently co-created.

CHANGING YOUR MIND

It takes an incredible level of commitment to change your mind. Deep held beliefs about yourself are difficult to alter at the base level. But, this is a kind of quantum alchemy: to dismantle and purify base thoughts and emotions like long held insecurities or fears and transmute them into the higher elements of self-Love and compassion. We push ourselves around so often. We are often our own worst enemies. That is what we are seeing in action when someone is being unkind to us. We are seeing someone who has made an enemy of their own reality. If you listen closely, hidden within any insult is how they really feel about themselves and how they have, perhaps, let themselves down. That is how powerfully our thoughts and emotions can affect us. They, literally, project our own illusions or pain as an overlay onto what we, then, perceive to be reality. When we do this, we are not then seeing an objective reality, but a self-created impression: a world filtered by a veil of our own making.

To, instead, run the program of someone who talks well to ourselves, to instead become someone who can be filled with Love and compassion for self and others, this changes everything. Then the quantum world, which is only responding at a vibrational level to your own resonant frequency (by quantum law), must respond in like. It is a rule just like gravity or the speed of Light.

Tell yourself, "In this moment I am doing exactly what I am supposed to be doing. I am exactly where I am meant to be. When it is time for me to do something else, I will be guided to it. I celebrate my now. I celebrate what is already here." When you engage in a state of celebration for where you are now, you have entered into glorious acceptance. The laws of the quantum universe respond and sends more for you to celebrate in glory.

Watch your thoughts the same way you would watch your children playing, with compassion and patience, with a mature understanding. Think of your thoughts as children still growing, and observe them with Love. If they become unsettled, destructive, dangerous, or mean you might say, "Ok, let's settle down. We don't want to hurt our self or anyone else." Think of how a kindergarten teacher might respond. That is a helpful, healthy tone that you can grow from. It is not demeaning or violent. It is not aggressive or cruel. There is compassion, rational calmness, and care in this approach. That is the kind of inner voice we need.

Sometimes, something doesn't happen that we wanted to happen, and we notice it. We feel its absence. We pay attention to the fact it is not occurring. The more it doesn't happen the more we notice it didn't happen. Through that, we begin a cycle in which it will perpetually not occur. The more we notice it not happening the more it cannot happen because now we are completely misaligned with the energy of what we want. It's a self-fueling negative feedback loop. The only way out of this pattern is to break the code, control + (h)alt + delete, then change the energy you are feeding into this. *Become aware of your awareness* and redirect it onto the infinite possibility and potential still available. Initiate a positive feedback loop in which you notice what you *do* want. Break the chain and run a new program. It's as simple as the words that you say in your mind. All you have to do is have the right intention.

If you continue to practice cultivating your mental acuity, you will soon no longer have an inner narrative that controls your life, but an inner conversation in which you co-create your life, where your higher consciousness and day to day awareness communicate in harmony. You will find when you talk to yourself, you will no longer fight against yourself, or repress aspects you don't like, but have an open, compassionate and *honest* dialogue. You will embrace all of yourself. You will release what is unhealthy, without judgement. You will allow what is nurturing and most aligned with your highest good.

COHESIVE HEART

The next crucial piece is not just thought, but emotion: the heart. Your heart must work in concert with the mind. What you are feeling and thinking should align with what you want to create. Having just the intention, having the right mental signals and attitudes, along with having an open and loving heart is the complete formula. Love is the great attractor.

Studies have shown that intention, alone, yields little results. Positive thinking, alone, can only work for so long. Love, alone, can make it feel better but without the other two aspects tends to be unsustainable. But when all three aspects (intention, positive thinking and a coherent heart of Love) are working in harmony together, *miracles can happen*. Love, and intentional, directed awareness of our thoughts is the goal. The great thing is, these powers combine. As you reprogram your thoughts with more positive signals, a Loving awareness will begin to arise within your heart organically. As you open your heart to Love with intention, your thoughts will become more positive on their own. Each system feeds the other system.

When your thoughts and feelings are aligned with what you want (your objective), that creates *coherence*. You are creating a clear resonant frequency through sending the right signal (through your thoughts) and generating the right magnetic field to attract it (with the heart). That is how you become your Quantum You. By thinking about what you want to create, feeling you can create it, that you are worthy of it, that it is, not only a desired outcome, but the *only* outcome you will observe. Hold your clear intention and purpose with Love. Be grateful, be ready to receive, and allow. Always remember to keep supporting this with your thought patterns.

If you do not believe this can really work, consider how we are already doing this with things we don't want. Maybe you do not notice the peripheral thoughts and emotions if they have gone on for some time, but if you are experiencing anything in your reality that is unpleasant or even painful, it is because the quantum reality that makes up our world can only match the program you are running in your thoughts and emotions. It cannot do anything else but that. That is the program you are generating. Some may say, "How can I change my thoughts and emotions until my circumstances change?" Yet, in this quantum world, how can our circumstances change unless we change our thoughts and emotions? It is one thing we can control. We cannot change what happens around us, but, we can change what happens within us.

I am not suggesting this is the solution to everything, but this understanding can greatly dislodge deep cognitive blockages that we have set up in our own way. When you think you are doing everything right and don't understand why nothing is working out—look to your thoughts, beliefs and feelings.

We cannot attract or manifest what we want with incoherent waves. It is like fire and water, one extinguishes the other. If our thoughts and feelings do not match, they are incoherent. An example is thinking Loving thoughts about yourself with the intention of attracting a loving partner, while not feeling that Love in your heart for yourself. Or feeling a general sense of self-Love but constantly berating yourself in your mind. Both the mind and heart have to work together to create coherence and to align with the right frequency. Your thoughts have to support your feelings, and your feelings must compliment your thoughts. Otherwise, we are sending, quite literally, mixed signals.

NO LIMITS

You cannot place restrictions on a quantum world. We can send out the intention of manifesting a better job in a career we truly are passionate about, for instance, but we cannot control the parameters of how that will come into play. We have to allow unrestricted flow to manifest in the most *possible* route, which we do not need to see. The universe works like water and will take the path of least resistance where it can. Water finds a way. All it needs is an open channel. If we close doors saying, "I want this thing, but not *that* way" or by saying, "That could never happen for me," then it won't. It can't. You have shut the steel gates.

Remember, this is not a cause and effect situation. Quantum reality is all about *flow* and like energies meeting in coherence with other like energies. The external does not control the internal. The internal *interfaces* with the external and influences what presents as our new reality in each moment. To change your external, change the energy (the thoughts and feelings) within you. Send out your intention, feel that intention with joy and with power. You have to believe this new program and reality is possible. Then, allow it to come to you without micromanaging the way it will come to be.

"TIME TRAVEL"

To be *truly* capable of generating the resonant frequency of what we want, to truly manifest a change in ourselves, in our lives, or in our situations, we have to be capable of living the change *now*. We have to send out a source code. We have to feel it, and know it, *before* it has occurred. We have to observe the reality we want to create before it can manifest. This is true in our personal lives and our shared world (which is why war can never create peace). We are connected through a kind of co-creator consciousness. This collective intelligence shapes our collective reality, just as our individual awareness and focus shapes our life. Perception is reception. We cannot receive what we cannot imagine. We have to go beyond imagination and tune into the actual energetic experience of the new desired changes.

Do not look to observe your desired outcome in the future or it will continue to stay right there—in the future. Look to observe it in your *now*. That is where all the power of creation is. Does this seem complex? It is and it isn't. It is like this, as I wrote this book, I not only put in all the effort and work of writing and researching it. I not only set my intention and believed it could come to be. I went into a space where I could see it. I actually felt the physical book in my hands. I felt the weight of it. I saw it in front of me. Even now as I write this sentence halfway through, I can already sync into the experience of it, and even the experience of you reading it as if it has already happened. *That* is a powerful quantum frequency to submit. That is how we can really get things done.

If you want a different job, don't just want it: be there now. See and feel yourself in that new space, actually three-dimensionally tap into the energetic experience of it. That is dream time. That is the quantum world you are visiting. You are directly interfacing with the mechanics of the universe when you get there.

You can also do this by recognizing how these changes you are seeking are already present. If you want to experience more Loving relationships, for instance, look to observe how they already exist now. If you only notice their absence you will just perpetuate more of the same. If you want to experience more abundance, look to be grateful for the abundance you have already. If you want to experience more growth, more success, more joy, more fulfillment, look to notice, to observe, and recognize where you are already experiencing those things. When we overlook their presence, we block them. As you appreciate them, even if just the little bit of them, the Universe picks up that mental signal and the magnetic emotional energy and looks to send you more.

In order to become like your Quantum You, you have to enter a state of Quantum Consciousness. Since the quantum world is beyond space and time, beyond body and matter, you must transcend your attachments to those rigid parameters. You have to enter a state of pure-consciousness. (To manifest the Divine, emulate the Divine). Consider a peaceful and blissful moment at a nice park. You close your eyes and soak up the sun. You begin to enter a state that feels timeless. You almost go beyond your body, beyond what the senses tell you. There is no longer a sense of space or separation. It feels like total connection. That is the doorway to the quantum state. That is also why meditation is so very helpful because it allows us to enter that transcendent state of creation.

To manifest an event or create a new reality we can "time travel" into that future vision to enter the field of its possibility. That unlocks it. As we experience it as if it is already our reality it allows us to send out the correlating signal and magnetically attract the matching event or reality much more easily. In essence, you would live as if you already have what you want, as if your future is already in your present.

It may seem complicated but there is really just a few basic premises: thinking the thought, having a clear intention, feeling the feeling as if it has already happened, and believing it can happen. Honestly, the best way to do this is to just *have fun* with it. Creation should always be imbued with fun and happiness.

When I first began to consider this quantum stuff I was skeptical. But I tested it in my own life to see how this could work for me. After some practice on smaller things I used this method to manifest my very first management position, which was a turning point in my life. For the week or two before my interview I began dressing like a manager. I began carrying myself as a manager. I felt and thought like I was already in leadership. I practiced interviewing before I went in but I took it even further in visualizing their impressed reactions as I answered their questions. I visualized the conversation in which they would pull me in the office and tell me I got the job. So when they pulled me into the office for their decision, I was not surprised. I had felt it for the weeks before with great commitment.

This is not to say you do not have to do all the right work. This quantum understanding is for those who are taking the right steps but have had a real problem with mental or emotional blocks in their way. This is, simply, to help you run a new and more effective program. You still have to take the steps, and do your part.

Remember, we are not trying to make something happen. *Making* is very different from creating. Making is ego trying to overpower and intervene. Creating is the creative intelligence

The Self Beyond

within you working together with the energies of the Universe. We want to allow this event to unfold organically. We should look for the opportunities to present themselves without forcing anything. We do our part in taking the steps and making internal changes and then let the laws of the universe work with us, instead of against us.

Try this with something small and work your way up. Try manifesting a parking spot in a normally busy market lot. Just imagine the spot, see an open space near the door in your minds eye. Lock in on the feeling of knowing that, "I *knew* there would be an open spot!" Feel that feeling and gage your results. You may find at times it does not work, but understand the root cause of failure in quantum creating is a fundamental disbelief in the process. Just reevaluate what steps were missed and try again next time. Like anything, this takes practice!

With bigger things like a new job or new relationship, understand that sometimes we may think we want something, but subconsciously we do not. That can come into play. We also have to understand, some things are not meant to happen, but this means it was in our best interest to not "get what we want." Trust in yourself, and have faith that the Universe (or God if that resonates to you) has a pretty good handle on what we most need.

ACTIVATION

What we think and feel also must align with what we *do*. You can be in total resonance and create all the cohesion in the world, but you also have to take the steps: walk through the doors, speak up, and take action. I want to make this as clear as possible. Your role goes beyond the superconscious creator into the one who will be actively experiencing these creations. So, your outer world should be as cohesive as your inner world. For example, we might recognize how "poverty consciousness" can perpetuate lack of financial security. We might only go halfway in believing if we just think and feel rich, money will just come to us. That is *not* how it works.

How it works is this: you recognize up until now you have struggled with financial security, so now you will, not only, shift your focus from what you lack onto your abundance, but also play an active role in creating that abundance by saving $5 dollars every chance you can. You might begin to think, well that doesn't add up to much! But *that* right there in that very thought is poverty consciousness in action. In the actions you are taking, the thoughts you are thinking, and the feelings you are feeling, all of that should paint a clear directive. Do your part to set yourself up for this success you are visualizing, however small it seems. Then create the best environment you can to allow that reality to slip right in.

Another example is recognizing how long you have perpetuated bad relationships by telling yourself, "No one will ever Love me. Everyone leaves me." So now you recognize this and change your thought patterns. You align your thoughts by thinking, "I Love myself, I am worthy of Love, and the right person will come and stay." You align your emotions by feeling and reinforcing self-Love. Now you might realize you also must create an environment conducive to a Loving relationship around you. Take yourself out to dinner, leave room for the right company when they come to join you. Enjoy yourself as you would with a lover or a friend. That is, not only, a cohesive signal and frequency, but a cohesive environment.

SECONDARY CONSCIOUSNESS

There are many layers, or levels, of consciousness. These are states of awareness which can be tuned into like a radio station such as primary (individual) consciousness and secondary (collective) consciousness. What is secondary consciousness? It is an overlaying aspect of consciousness that relies on the existence of a proto-consciousness field. Do not be intimidated by these words. I promise, I will make this easy to digest. Your primary consciousness could be described as one instrument, the part you play, while secondary consciousness is the whole orchestra.

Secondary consciousness could be defined as the collective consciousness. We have our individual consciousness (or local consciousness in quantum physics). All this means is you have your own thoughts. We, also, have a secondary layer considered to be the collective (or non-local) consciousness. What this means is we actually share thoughts with others. (We can hear

The Self Beyond

our own instrument, but, if we listen, we can hear the whole band as well). It is essentially a field of information available to share and draw from, like a world-wide-web of consciousness. Accessing or entering this higher level of awareness very much depends on our own level of metacognition, which is simply an awareness of awareness, or the ability to think about thinking, which can allow us to more deeply connect to the multiple layers.

The proto-conscious field might also connect to the morphic resonance Rupert Sheldrake [33] has proposed, which describes how lessons, fears, traits, and habits are not, merely, passed on genetically through DNA in a species, but they can be learned through the field of morphic resonance, which a species shares. The relevance of this field is simply this: there is a level of our consciousness which is shared. It is through this field we can, literally, feed our insight, our learned lessons, our Love, and our individual experiences, or draw from those of others.

When a certain number of individuals have learned a specific skill or gain a specific awareness, a phenomenon occurs known as "critical mass." Here it is in formal text: "In social dynamics, critical mass is a sufficient number of adopters of an innovation in a social system so that the rate of adoption becomes self-sustaining and creates further growth." [34] All this means is that once a bunch of people know something, it can very easily become learned or known by all the rest of us too. Let's say critical mass is 5% which is what ethnobotanist, mystic, psychonaut, lecturer (and avid supporter of the responsible use of naturally occurring psychedelic plants) Terence McKenna proposed. At about 5%, the critical mass is reached and there is a transference of some understanding to the entire species, even onto successive generations through the field of secondary consciousness. The information succession increases from there—exponentially.

---

[33] Check out Rupert Sheldrake banned TED Talk on YouTube. https://www.youtube.com/watch?v=JKHUaNAxsTg while on that path, I also recommend checking out Graham Hancock's talk of the War on Consciousness which was banned from TED Talk as well, https://www.youtube.com/watch?v=Y0c5nIvJH7w

[34] Wikipedia. Critical mass (sociodynamics) Retrieved from https://en.wikipedia.org/wiki/Critical_mass_%28sociodynamics%29

The Self Beyond

Let's make this simple. Consider that, right now, across the world, hundreds of people are having the same thought. Maybe even thousands. At the same time in places across the earth, scientists are coming up with the same scientific breakthroughs, visionaries are tapping into the same revolutionary insights at the same time. Whose thought is it then? Is it their own or something downloaded from the field of the collective mind? We are connected through a field of information, a collective consciousness which is not ours alone, but shared.

What this may mean for us, in a practical way, is that as *we* adopt a healthier, more enlightened, and balanced state of being, and more and more of us upload it into that layer of secondary consciousness, it can become easier for others to achieve the same level of self-awareness. This is also why it is important to consider how much time we spend engaging in watching violent movies or programs, for instance. The more people that do this, the more that violence is, literally, fed out to our shared consciousness. The energy of that is very damaging. Luckily, a growing number of people are led to do things that raise their vibration and their consciousness, which helps override the violence and dissonance that would otherwise saturate our shared field. Remember, what we do for ourselves, we do for the world we share. As we become more aware, so too do an emerging number of individuals awaken.

SOUND AND MUSIC

The words we say are powerful. When we are walking around saying, or thinking, "Something always goes wrong," guess what is going to happen? It amazes me how often I hear people casting these kinds of negative word spells over their own world. They say, "What else could go wrong?" They say, "It figures this would happen!" Do any of these mantras apply to you? Sometimes we may even haphazardly do this to others by providing negative sentiments disguised as advice. Such as saying, "Well, even if it doesn't work out, you will still have me." We just voted for that person to fail. Can you see how this happens? It is incredibly important to be careful and consider the power of our words. *Change your words, change your world.*

We speak our worlds into existence with our words. Was this not the story of creation? The word, or a song, in some cultures, was the first action of our conception. This universe is made up of waves and particles vibrating constantly (like water). We have established that our entire cosmos and what we perceive as reality, itself, is made of energy, frequency and vibration. Everything is resonance. Everything can be translated into sound, light, and energy waves. They are each interchangeable.

Anyone familiar with the Egyptian, Hebrew, or Christian cosmologies will be aware that they state, essentially, the same thing. In the beginning, there was nothing: a void. A face moved upon the waters. The word (or a tone) was spoken (or intoned) and creation began. (*I am not, necessarily, claiming this is the whole story. The focus here is on sound*). The word is powerful, no matter what you may believe. The word is one of the most esoteric concepts and sacred aspects of existence. The word is more than just what is spoken, it is also a thought. Every thought is an energetic vibration.

A word can be spoken from within—it holds the exact same resonance whether it is spoken out loud or internally. A tone is the root of the name for one of the Egyptian gods, Aton. This god was often depicted as a sphere, like the sun in the sky, reaching out rays (do, re, mi like notes in a scale) handing down the ankh (considered the breath of life in ancient Egyptian religion). A tone is a vibration of a specific frequency, just like a word. Our *tone* of voice can influence our conversation and how another perceives our intention or emotional state. We can start or end a conflict, literally, just by the inflection, or the resonance, of our tone.

Sound is powerful. Sound can cause matter to alter shapes. Cross frequencies of sound can levitate or move objects, alter DNA, and even boil water. Experiments done with cymatics (the study of the effects of sound on physical matter) show that specific frequencies can cause particles to shift and arrange themselves into various patterns, or even (depending on the medium such as a thick paste versus salt or sand) generate three-dimensional forms that seem to come alive. If sound is a frequency, and our thoughts are also a frequency (even if we

The Self Beyond

cannot "hear" it), then what does that say about the power of our thoughts?

Chladni patterns, images created by sand on plates with soundwaves at specific frequencies. [35] The higher the frequency, the more complex the pattern. How many shapes and patterns can you identify that are repeated in the natural world? We can see the role of sound and vibration present in its relationship between the energetic and physical world.

---

[35] Public domain (PD-US) retrieved from Wikicommons

The Self Beyond

When we are talking about sound, we are establishing, that we are talking about vibration and vice versa. We cannot create anything without first creating the vibration of it. Sound, like thought, plays a crucial role in creating our reality. When sound is harmonized with the natural frequencies (which we can calculate using the blueprint laid out for us in our own bodies, and

---

[36] Rajatyadavjaora, 8 December 2014, under CC license retrieved from Wikicommons

[37] Richard Bartz, Munich aka Makro Freak, January 3, 2008, under CC license retrieved from Wikicommons

[38] Public domain (PD-US) retrieved from Wikicommons

The Self Beyond

in the ancient sites left to remind us) it can create physical and, even, spiritual shifts within us, as well.

Everything makes a sound, even if it is not perceptible with our human ears. Remember, we are basically walking around in a spacesuit. This spacesuit can only pick up what it is programmed to, within its limited range. There is an infinite spectrum of Light beyond what we can see with our eyes. There is a vast field of audible information which we cannot pick up with our audio "equipment." There is, also, a great amount of energetic information which we can tune into when we are resonating at the correlating level.

Let's look, again, at brainwaves and the effect of sound on our brain. We spend most of our day in beta brainwave state (when we are driving, working, running around and, likely, stressed out a little). We may only visit the alpha wave state for small increments of time, at best. I want to note here that watching television does not put you into alpha waves, even though you may feel relaxed. Instead, it places you into a trancelike and highly *influential* state which is not beneficial to your conscious development. The sound of *music* however can activate different areas of the brain and alter our brainwaves.

Music activates nearly every area of the brain; the corpus callosum which connects the right and left hemispheres, the motor cortex (if you start tapping your foot), prefrontal cortex with the setting of expectations (in the melody and pattern of a song), the nucleus accumbens and amygdala (if you have an emotional reaction to the song), sensory cortex (if you play an instrument or dance), auditory complex (as you perceive and analyze tones), hippocampus (from any memory of music), visual cortex (if there is a visual element), and, finally, the cerebellum is involved in most aspects from dancing to emotions related to the music. When you engage with music, you engage with your higher brain potential.[39]

Researchers have looked to sound for healing, using ultrasound waves as a non-invasive means of changing brain behavior for neurological conditions, breaking up kidney stones and other uses. Ultrasound waves are already used for diagnostic

---

[39] Cooper, Belle Beth, *8 Amazing, Little-Known Ways Music Affects the Brain*. (2013). *Social*. https://blog.bufferapp.com/music-and-the-brain

purposes. But, there are many possibilities since sound is a frequency, and frequencies affect frequencies. A tuning fork tuned to a lower frequency can stimulate free radicals to reduce inflammation and affect pain transmission. The "sleeping prophet," Edgar Cayce, said *sound* would be the medicine of the future.[40]

Another wonderful thing about sound is it has the ability to penetrate energetic "blockages" without causing pain. And in the case of music, it is relaxing and enjoyable. Picture a current of water and how it might gently, but powerfully, dislodge a blockage of built up debris downstream. Sound can affect mental, emotional, energetic or physical blockages the same way because sound is energy and every aspect of our physical and spiritual bodies are also energy.

Entrainment occurs when our brainwaves seek to align with the frequency of music or soundwaves. This means listening to peaceful sounds or music can cause your brainwaves to go to a more rested and peaceful state as well. As we relax, signals are sent to our brain saying to send out more happy hormones; dopamine, serotonin, and endorphins. These happy hormones relieve pain and stress. They help regulate mood, affect metabolism and sleep cycles. Constant stress causes our brain to send out adrenaline which increases heart rate, and cortisol (the primary stress hormone). Cortisol is not all bad, but it can create many issues when you are in a constant state of stress. This is why relaxing music and pleasant tones can be helpful in aiding memory, focus, healing, centering, and entering into meditative states.

Understand, the body is all one system, functioning like one connected network. What affects the mind affects the body, and what affects the body affects the mind. You cannot, therefore, only treat (or neglect) one part of that system independently. Everything is affected because everything is connected. That is why sound therapy is so effective. It addresses each layer of the more subtle, systems along with the physical. Whether audible or

---

[40] Singer, E. (2017). *Targeting the Brain with Sound Waves. MIT Technology Review.*
https://www.technologyreview.com/s/413697/targeting-the-brain-with-sound-waves/

not, the brain picks up the resonant waves and the entire system is influenced by them. [41]

If you think sound has no effect on our mental, emotional, or physical state, consider how you feel when a car screeches to a halt nearby. Consider how your heart races, your stress levels increase in an instant. You immediately go into panic. You have a physical, mental and emotional reaction. The same happens when a baby cries. We feel compelled to try to comfort them, and feel helpless if we cannot succeed. Our heart rate changes. Our breathing shifts. All of these changes affect us on many physiological levels. What about a gun shot? Or a clap of thunder? Can you appreciate the powerful effect of, not only, the sound, but the vibration the sound has on us? Think of a rumbling as opposed to a loud noise. This is vibration we not only hear, but feel. Think of the loud bass on a car driving by and how the windows shake.

Now, consider the sound of waves lapping on the beach. What about a cascade of waterfalls? How about a steady spring rain, the sound of song birds singing, or the sound of a lullaby. These sounds can relax us. They slow our pulse and our breathing. There are correlating mental and emotional shifts initiated, as well. We feel a deeper sense of peace, our body systems regulate, and we may find our thinking moves at a much more natural pace. Intense sounds can increase external stress factors and gentle soothing sounds can add to a peaceful and calming environment. This is as much about the energy of these sounds as what the sounds are.

Natural sounds like a babbling brook, or rainfall tend to resonate at a frequency closer to that of earth and our own heartbeat when we are in a relaxed state. Sounds at this frequency induce entrainment and sympathetic resonance so we can more easily heal, center, and align with the rhythm and pulse of our natural state. The field between the earth and the ionosphere emits a resonance (a sound) of about 7-18 Hz. Our heartbeat emits frequencies at about 7 Hz. Even the sun emits a sound along with every living being (it hums). Frequencies are the connecting link between a world of form and reverberating patterns. The fields of

---

[41] Martinez, Nate, *What You Need To Know About Sound Healing*. (2015). *mindbodygreen*. https://www.mindbodygreen.com/0-17515/what-you-need-to-know-about-sound-healing.html

sound and energy surrounding us store information and act as a bridge, connecting the cosmic resonance systems to the systems within our own bodies. You are electric. You are magnetic. You are energy resonating at every level.

> *"Our entire biological system, the brain and the earth itself, work on the same frequencies."* ~Nikola Telsa, master of lightning.

STAR BEING

If you know nothing else of yourself, know this: you are Spirit, a Star Being, born of the Great Light of Eternal Consciousness which begat all of creation. We are, actually, made of star stuff! Nearly 97% of our bodies, every cell and molecule is made of the same atoms and elements found at the center of the Milky Way. 99% of the human body is made of carbon, hydrogen, nitrogen, oxygen, calcium, and phosphorus. Aside from the calcium in our bones, these are the same elements that create stars, galaxies, and worlds. [42]

How are these elements created? Stars are transformational Light bodies! Stars work like nuclear reactors, a galactic lab converting fuel into other substances. Hydrogen becomes helium, then helium builds every other element we are made of; carbon (the basic building block of proteins, among many other things), nitrogen (taken in through food and used to make amino acids), iron (in our blood), sulphur (a macromineral important in biochemical reactions and protein synthesis), and of course, the oxygen that we breathe (cellular respiration and creating energy). That is what stars gave us. Thank your lucky stars!

---

[42] Howell, Elizabeth, Astronomy, S. (2017). *Humans Really Are Made of Stardust, and a New Study Proves It. Space.com.*
https://www.space.com/35276-humans-made-of-stardust-galaxy-life-elements.html

The Self Beyond

Well at the end of its life, in a cosmic act of self-sacrifice, a star swells up, comes in to the center, showers off its outer layers and that star dust after many millions of years finds its way to become you and me. [43] (I love the metaphor of the life cycle of a star).

> *"The reason the universe is eternal is that it does not live for itself; it gives life to others as it transforms"* ~Lao Tzu

Every physical birth came from the physical death of a star. Stellar explosions spewed out the building blocks of our lives many millions of years ago. The atoms and elements that make up your somatic body are as old as the Universe, making you approximately 13.772 billion years old (give or take a few million years)! Being as old as time is another way of saying you are timeless. Perhaps, even if you do not subscribe to the belief of an interminable soul, you may still appreciate that every atom and molecule within you will, someday, be a Star once again. The oxygen you are breathing right now represents many epochs, many eons, of living and dying, regeneration and transformation, and the perpetual eternal in constant motion.

We are, literally, Light beings! New research has discovered that the neurons in our brain emit and conduct biophotons (light). In fact, most cells in our bodies emit Light. This research is showing that *Light* is how many cells in our body communicate. It has been hypothesized that by using microtubules like conductive superhighways, Light can be channeled from cell to cell (think of fiber optic wires). Electric signals to the brain can transmit too slowly, an obstacle which Light can overcome to help the brain coordinate responses and perform various activities.

Mathematical physicist, scientific philosopher, and professor at the University of Oxford, Roger Penrose, is largely known for his contributions to General Relativity and cosmology. He devised the "Penrose Triangle," which he described as "impossibility in its purest form." This was so profound to have

---

[43] Worrall, Simon, *We Are Stardust—Literally*. News.nationalgeographic.com.
http://news.nationalgeographic.com/2015/01/150128-big-bang-universe-supernova-astrophysics-health-space-ngbooktalk/

The Self Beyond

inspired artist M.C. Escher's famous Waterfalls and Ascending and Descending (I strongly recommend looking this up). In Penrose theory of consciousness, he suggested that consciousness, itself, is a quantum process of which microtubules were the medium of quantum mechanics. [44]

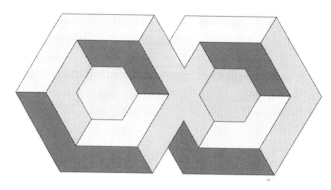

Infinity [45]

      There is, as you might see, no beginning or ending, not really. Everything is intimately connected: death and birth, the cycles of time. We are Light beings, Star Children. Everything that ever was will always be in some form. We are part of a massive network of consciousness, communicating through subtle channels, through energies and vibrations, through frequencies of Light and sound. We are receivers and amplifiers which the Intelligence of the Universe works with, and *through*.

POLARIS

      What is it that guides and connects us? If you consider every atom belonging to us has belonged to a star, then every molecule and element has been shared between us, if only, in the distant past, has it not? I am in you, and you in me. Is that not what

---

[44] arXiv, E. (2017). The Puzzling Role Of Biophotons In The Brain. MIT Technology Review. Retrieved 14 October 2017, from https://www.technologyreview.com/s/422069/the-puzzling-role-of-biophotons-in-the-brain/

[45] Nevit Dilmen, 2013, under CC license retrieved from Wikicommons

was written down in many sacred ancient texts in many different languages? We are the same energy, the same enchanted spirit, wrapped in a different blanket, a different skin. Wearing a different face, but the voice that speaks is a shared voice, scattered out as transcendental scintillations of the same Light Source.

Love is the only true gravity, drawing us back toward the center of all centers—the divine nucleus. We are, literally, one in an infinite pool of oneness. When we are *in* Love we exist beyond the boundaries of space, in the eternal moment escaped from time. This is it: the kingdom and the stairway. We are enigmas roughly defined by colorless imaginations that could never capture the whole of it. Many will struggle to understand. To live is to break free of *names* and *words*. It is far too wild, the grandest thing of all. It is the insuperable connection which does not bind, but expands. It is the breath and everything it touches.

We are interfacing fields between form and resonant patterns. Electric. Magnetic. One affects the other. We are blissful gliders on a cosmic wind. Shapeshifting navigators of a long lost tide. Only in losing do we find it. To say it simply, Love is the compass that guides. The moon may wax and wane, but the Light within us, never conquered, is the North Star fixed and unmoving.

BLESSING

Bless every single thing you touch, even as your lips touch the air and your feet touch the ground. Everything, *every* thing, is a part of the Great Sacred Spirit. Bless it all with Love; your thoughts, your words, your movements, your feelings, every aspect of you within your reach. Use it to manifest blessings. The only time we become lost is in forgetting this sacred truth.

What is a blessing; a prayer to our higher power (if we resonate with one), support and assistance bestowed upon us, a state of gratitude for what one has received? A blessing is all of those things. We wait for a miracle, wish for a blessing, and often forget we have the power to evoke the blessing in our own life—just by being aware of the miracles already present.

We need no intermediary to be blessed. That has been the greatest crime of modern theology: to instill in so many the false belief that we cannot get directly to our Source, that we need someone else to act on our behalf to provide these blessings. We have the ability to connect and commune with Spirit already, from within. We have support and assistance when we request it. All we need to do is ask through our own powerful intention. We have countless things to be grateful for, so many that if we could realize in its utter fullness, we would fall to our knees. All we need to do is recognize them and acknowledge their presence. We, ourselves, are an incarnate, breathing, and walking blessing. Share the very best of yourself.

THE WALK

Walk with purpose.
Walk guided by your Highest Self, and walk with Love.
Walk empowered, walk enlightened, and walk in peace.
Walk with integrity, walk honestly, and walk humbly.
Walk confidently.
Walk as if you are Spirit embodying the realm of this earth for but a moment in eternity.
Walk as if that moment is the testament of both Creator and Creation.
Walk as if you are *That*.

CONNECTING TO THE HIGHER SELF

How do we connect to our higher self? How do we access the wellspring of Love and Wisdom available, yet invisible, in the subtle cosmic field of information? First, understand that there is no wisdom but Love. Any information presenting itself in contradiction to Love is not Wisdom, it is conjecture used to rectify the imbalance within us. It is only bits of words strung together to fortify the role of the ego in its last stand. The only real intelligence comes from Love. Loving awareness is the highest understanding of a truly connected being.

I feel I should clarify on what I mean when I say the "higher self" or "within." Sometimes, we might become very connected within ourselves, but, not necessarily, our higher selves. It can be more of a superficial connection to the persona of

The Self Beyond

ego. When we are only connecting to the ego we are only going to be getting ego wisdom, which really only cares about its own survival. The point is in transcending the lower self and reaching the higher self. That is where the more advanced wisdom of Love and enlightenment resides. That is where the soul-truth, the truth-force within us, lives.

There are many paths, but a basic place to start is by grounding yourself. "Grounding" means coming deeply into your own body, embodying yourself. Feeling your feet on the earth. Feeling strong roots and becoming aware of your connection to the Universe above and beyond you. Sense it as if it is within you. Be aware of its presence. Breathe deeply in and out, in and out, with nice long breaths. Allow yourself to become disenchanted with the alluring push and pull of the ego. Be still and slip onward in your most relaxed form and you will gently enter a luminous stillness. The silence present from this place subdues the lower mind and summons the courage of the heart. Now, simply close your eyes and listen. Not to the primal polarity driven thought patterns to which we have all remained so addicted, not to the habits of the lower impulses, but the higher awareness within you which transcends the transitory and discordant states. It is inexorably present, just waiting to be communed with.

Some may call this higher aspect the soul. Some may call it God and separate this Higher Voice from their own Being (though nothing is truly separate). Some may not differentiate one with the other. It doesn't matter what you call it. This Loving Creative Intelligence will guide you from within. Messages and insights will come. Peace will come. *Love* will come pouring in, overflowing. In the fire of total presence with yourself, you will go beyond your ego-*self* into your Higher Self. How can you tell which is which? One is ready to let go, the other is not.

This takes practice, commitment, and sincere inner honesty. We have to allow the flow, instead of impeding it. We impede it through our identification with the ego, with separation, with our ceaseless dependences on false beliefs. We do not yet trust ourselves, so then it is a lack of faith. *Faith,* in this sense, is not meant to elude to the commandments of any religion. In this context, faith is meant to insinuate a trust in your own power, your own intuition, and your own higher insight. Faith, then, is also an acceptance of the truth that we are always connected to that

The Self Beyond

Loving Intelligence. We *are* that Loving Intelligence. It is always available when we open our hearts and go beyond the mind into the higher echelons of conscious Wisdom. You will find *that* level of consciousness eclipses the ego. It surpasses the polarization reality we have attached to. That voice is the voice of the cosmic directive, it is filled with compassion for all. The Spirit we come from does not seek to divide, it seeks to merge and connect. *God is seeking you too, endlessly.*

The ego fights for its own existence, but we are more than an individual body. (I do not want to demonize the ego as it helps us navigate certain aspects of a three dimensional world. But when you go beyond this limited dimension into the higher levels, the ego serves no purpose and it knows that). You will experience this fight of the ego when you want to take a leap of faith, for instance. The higher aspect within you may sense it will work out, but the ego will kick and scream and shout, "What will happen to *me*?" Do not let the ego rule you. The ego was never your master. It has only been another teacher to allow us to experience division so that we would seek to come back into Unity. This unity is as much a convergence with our own wholeness as it is with the whole we each belong to.

We are not the individual body or the mind. We are not the ego which we experience here in the third dimensional realm of learning. The ego is a lesson in seeing beyond the illusion. The ego presents as a veil that shrouds us from the glory of our Truth. We are *immense* beings of consciousness and energy. Spirit is everlasting and indestructible. We seek to connect with our higher self but really need only realize we *are* wholly that Higher Self. Go beyond ego and step into being. Go beyond being and step into Love.

Love is always available. That may be best understood by thinking of it like this: do not go out and seek others to be your friend. Go out and seek to be a friend for others. Love is just like that. Do not go out and seek Love from others. Go and seek to *be* Love for others, and yourself. That is the wellspring. *That* is the inextricable link between us and the heart of all that is. Honor yourself in all others, honor all others in yourself.

We are the force, not the fist. We are the voice, not the mouth that speaks it. We are the walk, not the feet that take us. We are the Love, not the material heart that feels it. Inside that Love, we can be certain there is nothing that is not that. *Everything* that is immortal and transcendent within us is Love. Spend some time today basking in the radiant company of this Love, and know—you are already fulfilled.

MANY WORLDS

We live on a planet which is what we know, and from our position, it is difficult to get a complete view of what we are such a tiny part of. Even with all our advancements, we have still only touched the moon and Mars. We have barely scratched the surface of the nearest planets.

The Voyager space probes were launched in a miraculous achievement in August 1977. There was a rare alignment of planets which created a unique opportunity (coming only once every 176 years) to reach them in succession. This was the first, and really only, mission of its kind. Travelling at about 35,000 mph, it took two years for Voyager 1 to reach its first target, sending back the very first close-up pictures of Jupiter in 1979. In 1980 and 1981, both probes reached Saturn. In 1986, Voyager probes reached Uranus and it was not until nearly 1 year later, in 1989, that they reached Neptune. The Voyagers continued onward toward interstellar space. Every star has a bubble, a plasma sphere encompassing its solar system. The Voyagers, travelling faster than any other known manmade objects before them, did not reach the plasma boundary of our solar system bubble until August 25 of 2012, over 35 years later.

The Self Beyond

Before heading out toward interstellar space, the Voyager turned back one more time to take the first ever "portrait" of Earth from 4 billion miles away. Upon seeing what appeared to be a speck of dust on the film, Carl Sagan remarked in a famous speech:

"Look again at that dot. That's here. That's home. That's us. On it everyone you love, everyone you know, everyone you ever heard of, every human being who ever was, lived out their lives. The aggregate of our joy and suffering, thousands of confident religions, ideologies, and economic doctrines, every hunter and forager, every hero and coward, every creator and destroyer of civilization, every king and peasant, every young couple in love, every mother and father, hopeful child, inventor and explorer, every teacher of morals, every corrupt politician, every "superstar," every "supreme leader," every saint and sinner in the history of our species lived there-on a mote of dust suspended in a sunbeam."

"There is perhaps no better demonstration of the folly of human conceits than this distant image of our tiny world. To me, it underscores our responsibility to deal more kindly with one another, and to preserve and cherish the pale blue dot, the only home we've ever known." ~Carl Sagan

---

[46] US-PD courtesy of NASA Voyager

We are not much different from a fish in a pond. A fish sees the pond as the whole of its world and cannot traverse the boundaries nature has placed around it. Yet, there are many dimensions of worlds around it; the earth cradling the pond, the sky above it, the planet that earth, water, and sky are a part of, the solar system which the planet revolves within, the stars which each have their own worlds and live in their own way, and so on. Do not forget the many worlds, even those which we are not now capable of seeing.

THE ART OF WATER

What can water teach us about the art of life, connection and our own existence? Water is powerful, yet gentle. Water cuts through rock, sheer cliffs and canyons are carved by its currents, and, yet, you can put your hand right through it. Water is patient, timeless, and moving through all things. Even in the driest places, if you dig deep enough, chances are water is there underneath the surface. Water is always present in some form. It may be floating above us as moisture, hanging out as clouds, or coming down as rain. In this sense, water represents the Spirit.

When you read each sentence here, you must realize these are multilayered metaphors. Meaning, water can represent you, or the "other," whatever that might be. Whether that's a person, a situation, or an energy. Realize, though, with water there is no *other* because nothing is truly ever isolated. That's why water is such a perfect representation for us and life.

Water does not just take the journey, it *becomes* the journey. Water shows us that all journeying has the same destination. Water says, "Come from any direction. All are welcome here, but come with open arms, overflowing." Perhaps this may seem too deep for all to relate to, my hope is some glorious morning you will be sitting by the water and say, "Oh! This is what she meant!" Water speaks.

Water is almost mystical. It gives life. It is taken into our bodies to live. It cleans and it supports journeys to new worlds. It can be a large or small body, yet still retain its status as water.

The Self Beyond

Water is a drop, a cup, a wave, a stream, a lake, a waterfall, an ocean. You can strip water down to the minutest molecule, if you wish. But, no matter how large or small we see it, *all* water is the water of the same ocean, connected as one body in the aquatic deep—where all begins and ends—beyond all boundaries. Water always goes towards water. No matter how its paths diverge. All will end up joined together in the endless sea.

Water can become one drop, but that drop will always seek its way back to the ocean of source. It may burn up and evaporate completely, back into its spirit form, (which is all the entire drop of water was made of in the first place). The water has not lost anything: it has merely transformed its state and will transform again. And in this new state it can become a puffy sky wave, but eventually it will come back to earth as rain. Everything rises and falls. *Everything comes back to itself.*

Look at a lake or an ocean. Watch how the waves come in and go back out. This is one of my most cherished and insightful open eyed meditations, observing living water at work. Water carries many, many messages.

One day, as I sat by the lake, I noticed that the waves were breaking very hard due to a big sandbar just before they reached shore. They came in, jumping high in the air only to crash down just beyond that sandbar, a lift into a drop which caused the wave to well up just before it broke through. We may think of times in our life when we have felt we reached a great height, only to come crashing down. We all panic during the drop, but really all you need to do is just keep your balance, and remember—you can *float*. Water cannot sink. Spirit cannot be extinguished or destroyed, just as water cannot be extinguished or destroyed.

Look at the properties of still, clear water. Look how perfectly still water can reflect what is above, how clearly it allows us to see what is below to its depth. Consider what that may symbolize in you, that in a state of stillness we can most honestly assess the outer and inner worlds. What is on the surface, what is under the surface, and what is beyond? Take some time out by the water to let it speak to you too. Observe in stillness and think about any metaphors or messages present.

Water loves to share its wisdom. Water is alive. Water is conscious. Water listens. Water is a receiver and a conduit for pure universal energy. Water amplifies your prayers and deepens your meditation. Water is life.

LOST & FOUND

We have made a lot of progress. Take a moment to appreciate that. Perhaps you are not yet aware of any changes. But wait, you will soon see your life begin to change as *you* begin to change. These lessons and insights can be elusive. We might gain one step, only to fall back three. We may spend several days or weeks feeling a kind of spiritual mastery in our lives, then backslide due to the spontaneous combustion of life's dramatic blows.

This is not about keeping us safe in a bubble so that we have no more trouble. We learn from the trouble, we grow through it. These shifts within you are not about gaining control of your life. The idea of control is a desire of ego. This is about being better equipped with the tools within you to handle yourself in the tides of this life. The waves will still come. But, now, you may find you have balance. You may, now, find you do not panic. You may, now, find you let your body do what it is meant to: relax, float, and be still from within.

---

[47] Obtained from Pexels under Creative Commons Zero (CC0) license

It is ok to backslide. It is ok to find you resorted back to an old default reaction upon being triggered. What is important is that you are, now, aware of this, where before, you were not. We lose it and find it again, we come in and back out. Like waves on the ocean, we are always on a journey. Constantly coming back into awareness of our own sacred truth, our purpose, and our connection. You cannot change what already occurred. We can only choose what we are doing with our "*now*." We do not learn through perfection. We learn and grow through messing up, big time. Be gentle. Be patient. Be thoughtful with yourself in the process of your journey.

Always remember who you are and the Whole you are a part of. Always, do know that within you is a beautiful expression of that wholeness (even when you forget). Know that you are deeply Loved, understood, and every up and down, every divergence in your path, every mistake and every miracle, is necessary and part of your own personal divine plan of awakening. Your soul set this up long before you came here, charting a course that would best bring you back Home. Trust that you are right on time. You are in exactly the right place. You are exactly who you are meant to be right now.

MANY FACES

One of the most difficult things to do on a genuine spiritual journey is to become capable of seeing all others as a part of you, to recognize that we are all connected, and that the same divine spark within you is also in every other. It is in every person, creature, plant and lifeform. In theory it sounds wonderful, doesn't it? Yet, exemplifying that principle is a whole other story. People do not make it easy. This takes dedication. We may lose our cool and have to start all over. Living this requires a constant refocusing on the fundamental value that we are all connected.

It may seem inconsequential, but consider how very different your day will look if you treat the loud and annoying co-worker, or anonymous crazy driver, or inconsiderate shopping cart pusher, or unknown troublesome looking passerby as *a part of you*. Not only a part of you, but an embodiment of the same sacred force that moves through all things. What does that look like, sound like, and feel like? It looks much slower to react, more sympathetic, considerate, and accepting. It comes from a place of indiscrimination. We would communicate and act with open hearts. We would tap into unconditional Love. Understand that these seemingly trivial interactions make up the majority of our day. These are training simulations to master this skill so that you will be capable of drawing on it when it really matters.

Can you then find it in you to extend unconditional Love and compassion to those with who you share drastically different world views, to those who you have been taught to despise or reject, to those who have been taught to despise or reject you, to those who you have ignored and neglected? Would we have conversations instead of arguments? Would we listen? Would we say, "You first" instead of, "Me first?" Would we smile rather than make a smug expression of disapproval? Would we engage in acts of mediation and peacemaking?

This is *your* story. This is about the part you want to play in the world, and what you want that world to look like. No one can tell you how that should go. But if you believe the world should look more kind, caring, and thoughtful then *this* is how we create that. By Loving *all* others as our self. Love isn't there for us to pick and choose when it feels good, or when it is easy. Love is there for us to call upon when it is the most impossible, when it takes all the will and valor within us. Love is sometimes the hardest thing we will do, but it is always the right thing.

We can't do this alone, or while hiding away in our room. Difficult situations and people help us gauge our current state. This is where a real opportunity comes in, through our person to person interactions.

Pay attention to each person you meet. Even a brief encounter can be there to hold up a mirror to you, to see in yourself what you must now focus on. For example, perhaps you are feeling great, you are happy, everything is sailing smoothly but someone bumps into you at the grocery store and says nothing to even acknowledge their slight of your presence. It isn't a huge deal, but leaves you with a curious tinge of resentment, bothering you more than it should. This can be someone who is holding up a mirror to show you what happens when we tip the balance of being so self-centered we forget about the value of others. Or they could be providing you a little reminder to pay attention to your own presence. To acknowledge your own space. This can get deep. We have to be willing to ask ourselves the right questions. Questions such as, "What am I meant to learn or see in myself from this?"

Every "other" being and, even, experience is an extension of us mirroring back a part of us that may need Love, or that may need healing. There is always a message or lesson to be found if we just look a little deeper. In this insight, we might see there is no "other," only carriers of the energies that are already within us. By rejecting another, we symbolically reject an aspect of ourselves. Ignoring these parts of us only creates hostility and self-destructive behaviors. When we are unkind, that energy is sent out into the world which responds like an echo chamber. Every action or inaction creates powerful ripples that inescapably find their way back to the source. So the matter is, we hurt *ourselves* when we hurt another. But the upshot is we *heal* ourselves when we heal another. (This will be repeated often because it is one of the most world changing takeaways.)

That does not mean we should be false. Making up a disingenuous version of yourself to please others is very detrimental. I spent a long time in the beginning of my spiritual journey being so nice to everyone I was often taken advantage of. Many fall into the trap of thinking we have to set aside our boundaries or needs and Love, even if it hurts us. But that is not the real point. Those same people who seemed to adore me fell away when I began to show my authenticity in Loving myself enough to set limits. They loved my weakness, not my strength. This is not about being fake or so nice that you become a pawn. All this means is to be kind, to be thoughtful, and to show respect, to show compassion when it is needed, to remove ourselves from the service-to-self identity and care for others as we would someone we Love.

Do your best. It will not happen overnight. We are not perfect and, even as I write this I am reminded of my many annoyances this week that I wish I had handled better; conversations with others in which I became short, situations in which I allowed myself to be baited. But over these weeks, months and years working to hold this as not only a viewpoint but a way of life, I have found myself more easily capable of coming into understanding instead of blame; more willing to show kindness just for kindness sake, more willing to hear another out, more adept at choosing a peaceful and compassionate reaction, more willing to reject my default programming and let a crazy driver pass by and wish them well, or let an inconsiderate person neglect my presence and still send them good energy.

Understand, this is not about allowing ourselves to be abused or mistreated. Loving another should never trample us in its path. This is about rectifying the caustic imbalance and perpetual patterns of hurt in this world.

When you feel yourself being triggered by that crazy driver, by someone's inconsiderate actions, by a family member or significant other who knows just how to push your buttons, or a stranger with a viewpoint that contradicts your own, just breathe and remember: getting angry just fuels more cycles of anger. Hurting another just causes more hurt. Look at their face, look into their eyes. You cannot see the life they lived, the pains they have endured, the challenges they have faced, the Love or lack of Love they have experienced. If you could, you may recognize how very much you share in common, similar scars and wounds. If you could, you may be compelled to embrace them, not expunge them.

What good does it do to add more hurt? Every cycle of hostility then requires more healing. You are at the center of the cycle with all the power in the world to break the chain. That chain has one ultimate dissolvent, and that is Love. What would Love do here? What would you do if this was *you* standing in front of you? Or someone you Love dearly? That is the perspective that changes how we interrelate to the world around us.

A method I have found which can take this even further is to not only say nice things to others, but to *think* them. If you are benevolent on the surface and raging underneath with a slew of profanities and insults, it can still be damaging. It may not matter how wonderful of a person you are, we are still inclined to think some pretty awful things in instances where we feel someone has done us wrong. This is the real test, but you will see miracles if you commit to this. Challenge yourself to think caring thoughts, instead of careless ones.

This technique came from me seeking ways to connect with people around me and show them something positive. I wanted, greatly, to show some compassion and consideration that others may not be receiving on a daily basis. We spend so much time in the company of strangers and it is a real crime to keep

The Self Beyond

ourselves in such needless isolation, never connecting. So I seek out opportunities to bond and share Love. In my experience you never know whose life that could save, whose day that could turn around, or whose spirit that could lift.

I had challenged myself to not neglect anyone who passed by me. I would always smile genuinely from my heart and say, "Hey how's it going?" If possible, I would try to make them laugh or make a positive comment (especially if they replied with a negative sentiment such as, "It could be better"). I noticed, sometimes, this could be abrasive and not everyone likes someone disturbing them, to some it comes as an intrusion. So now I have taken to gauging if a verbal nod could be successful, and if not, I am replacing it with a wonderful thought such as thinking, "I see you. You are beautiful and I appreciate you." In the past weeks of practicing this I have noticed that people respond positively to these silent messages. It is kind of amazing. It is as if they can hear them. (Remember, thoughts are also frequencies and resonate in their environment just as powerfully as sounds or words.)

Consider for a moment how you may wonder sometimes if you are just being paranoid, but you swear you can tell when someone doesn't like you, even if they never express it. You can pick up on the judgments another is making as if they were said out loud. Is this not so? What about when someone likes you. You can sense it. It may even be a physical feeling. Your face gets warm, and you feel an almost palpable energy coming from them. We often overlook our extrasensory perceptions but we are silently communicating with each other hundreds of times a day. Even from great distances. So, by taking every opportunity to be kind in not just our actions and words, but our *thoughts*, this can have a healing, uplifting, and restorative effect on the world we interact with.

We are all precious faces of the same bigger body of the Universe. Various facets of the same brilliant gem, shining with the resonance of the entire Diamond. One facet, one face, contains the whole of this fractal infinity. Every face you see is a chance to reflect back Love. Author Mason Cooley once said, *"Compassion brings us to a stop, and for a moment we rise above ourselves."*

DON'T WAIT

How much of our lives do we spend in waiting; waiting for the perfect moment, waiting until we have saved more money to make that move, waiting to feel stronger or more confident before we go for a new job, waiting for our significant other to Love us before we can Love our self, waiting for our children to grow up, for a raise, or the pieces of our life to fall perfectly into place before taking a leap of faith? This is called playing it safe. This is not how the universe works with us as co-creators. Remember your quantum self. Remember the quantum field.

Sometimes, in life you have to go all in. You have to double down and never look back. Think of the most incredible achievements of some of the most successful people; multibillion dollar business launched from the garages of college drop outs eating ramen noodles and living on a prayer, world changing initiatives and innovations born from someone with the guts to lose it all and gamble to win. Guess what? The universe likes this, a *lot*. The quantum field responds to a brave heart. Not foolish, mind you, *brave*.

When you are in waiting mode, you will continue to attract more setbacks that resonate with delaying you further. Think about life and what you are doing as yelling into a canyon. Whatever you are doing is what you are yelling out into the canyon of your life, and the canyon is just going to echo that back to you. If you are yelling, "Someday I will live my dream" the canyon echoes back, "Someday I will live my dream." "Someday I will live." "Someday I will", "Someday." How can that day ever come? Someday is always in the future. This places all the power on outer circumstances instead of within you, the voice. You have set up your own personal (albeit inadvertent) time paradox which can, literally, never resolve.

What if you send out, "Today I'm ready to live my dream!" The canyon echoes back, "Today I'm ready to live my dream." "Today I'm ready to live." "Today I'm ready", "Today." This is an active statement, not passive. This places you at the center of your reality. Co-creating with the resonant canyon of the universal echo reality at work. You do not need to know how it will happen. You just need to stop waiting.

Don't wait another moment. No one else, nothing else can do it for you. Do you have a dream? What is holding you back from it? Is your dream bigger than your excuses, or are your excuses bigger than your dream? What are you afraid of? Can you face those fears? Do you believe in yourself? Can you build trust with yourself by taking the chance that you just might succeed? The only one who makes your life and lives your life is you. We were imbued with tremendous resilience to allow us to overcome, even, the most insurmountable obstacles. Do you want it more than you want to avoid the hassle, or the possible risk of failure? There is no failure, only a million ways to find what does not work, and what does.

If you have been waiting for a sign to begin a huge project, or pursue a lifelong dream, a sign to leave that bad relationship, or take a leap of faith, then you have been looking in the wrong place by looking outside of you. The truth is, you have just been waiting for permission from yourself. Once you say, "Yes" to the universe, just guess what the universe is going to say back to you?

NATURE MESSAGES

When I wander in nature, I recognize that the clouds, the water, the leaves are all messages. It's up to us to decode the meaning. Can you see that to be true? Just step back a little to view the larger majesty of the landscape, these masterpieces endlessly unfolding from every perspective. Everywhere in nature there is beauty. The kind which no earthly being could replicate even in the greatest artwork. Nature paints with the imagination of unbounded possibility, symbolizing growth, change, persistence, will, diversity, connection, and community.

Lean in closer to observe the little worlds; the way the moss carpets the bed of the tree roots, the way the acorns and little buds sit peacefully existing in this tiny perfect place. Look at how the clouds seem to create images, cryptograms of our own nature reflected back to us. Look at how a brook moves ever so gently through the forest floor, how trees reach up to the sun, how every rock, every leaf, every bud has its place. Does this not show us the Way?

Connecting with nature is connecting with our true nature. It is so crucial to our own wellbeing to find time to connect, balance and re-center in a place unviolated by the hands of man. Especially now while so many intense energy shifts are occurring on our planet. Set aside some time to appreciate the beauty. Stop for many long hours to be still and listen to the music of the water, the sky, and the earth without watching the clock. Notice the enormous amount of Light and Love that surrounds you there. If only we saw the energy in everything as what it is: the language of God, the Source speaking to us through all creation, every being, every plant and seed. Then, we would see everything is carrying a message. We just have to pay attention.

Nature is one of our greatest teachers; both the classroom and the textbook, both the lesson and the plan. What we learn in nature is so very personal, yet universal, because it ignites within us the remembrance of our mortality and immortality at the same time. Nature evokes the sense of how very small we are, but how

---

[48] Self-taken over the summer of 2017

The Self Beyond

even the smallest thing can change the course of an entire ecosystem.

Nature teaches us that something as gentle and soft as water can carve out entire landscapes, creating valleys and canyons. That mountains can reach the sky if they are willing to be shaped by the elements and push upward, and that all things change form and go through cycles. Nature shows us that nothing exists for itself, but exists as a member of an interconnected community. All this, nature does without telling directly. It doesn't yell. It doesn't push. Nature whispers. This lesson can be trusted because it comes from within you as you connect to the Intelligence of Creation all around you. And, perhaps, you may truly realize that by connecting with the beauty of nature, you are connecting with the beauty of yourself as well.

[49] Self-taken over the summer of 2017

TREE OF LIFE

No matter how far we have come, there still may seem to be more to heal, more growth to strive for, more to learn, more to let go of. Do not let that discourage you. Why do we clean up when it is just going to get dirty again? We do it because it is not healthy to live in filth. We do it because it is worth the time we invest in the few days (or hours) afterward that feel clear and clean. Why do trees grow brilliant blooms if the leaves will just fall? Because that is a part of the constantly shifting cycle of life. Every spring blossom is worth the winter.

We often don't appreciate the necessary phases of growth when we are faced with our inevitable imperfections along the way. It is important to be patient with yourself, to celebrate where you are and what you have overcome, but don't stay there forever. Keep going. Nothing is stagnant in nature. Everything moves and changes, even, if only, so imperceptibly. We are all on a lifetime journey back into remembering our true nature. It is a continual process of allowing the most authentic expression of ourselves and others, even when it gets messy, or shifts in (what seems) a fundamental way.

This has to be a perceptual shift that originates from within you. You can't force it. Those perspective shifts are just as important as the physical work we do. There is nothing that cannot be changed just by changing the way that we see it. It's not about changing your mind so much as opening it. Meditate on the existence of the Tree.

You cannot Love the tree only when it's in full bloom. That is only one phase of a tree's many lives, rich and blanketed with the hearty greens, sunspot yellows, and every shade of neon lime. Anyone could know that's beautiful. You have to Love the tree during every season and phase. Even when every leaf has fallen. There is a process a tree goes through to bloom. It is always transitioning between winter and summer. You cannot Love a tree if you do not appreciate that process; the bright reds, oranges, and fire swept burgundy that sets across the leaves before they fall, the shedding of everything that must be abandoned, the sparse skeleton of wooden branches left aching only to realize: nothing is lost, all is still right there within. It's still every bit its whole self, every bit as majestic, gathering the elements needed to bloom

The Self Beyond

again. Then, after what seems an eternity, when it feels no warmth, will come again. The first thawing blossoms of spring show their face; sweet buds of white, purple and pink, sprouts that reach toward the Light which welcomes their return.

50

It takes a journey to become a full blossomed tree. First, the falling of every leaf and comfort, setting fire to all you had built up until now, the cold winter in which you must realize that with nothing, you still have everything inside of you. It is only in losing everything will we realize that what is most important cannot be lost. Through that realization, you will begin to blossom renewed. With rain and plenty of Light, you will grow full with a whole new outlook. Love every part and phase of the tree. Love every part and phase of your own journey.

Like a tree going through seasons, stay rooted, grounded, and never stop reaching for the Light. Let go of the lifeless leaves. Make room for new growth. Recognize the winter is not forever. It has its purpose, too. Recognize that summer will come again, when you are ready and have gone through the process. Recognize fall and spring are a part of our life, as well, and without them, we

---

[50] Self-drawn for this book

would not change at all. Accept the stormy times as a time to cleanse. Accept the lonely times as a chance to reflect inward. Have gratitude for the rain as much as you do the sunshine. Appreciate every season. Align yourself with the universe that endlessly cycles around you, showing you the way. Accept it all and include yourself.

We want to be sure that everything will be alright. There is no guarantee, except the faint voice of reassurance beckoning a deeper faith in your own resources. Despite the many cycles or changes we have endured already, which should give us some relief (that we made it before and we can do it again). It can still feel uncertain and out of control as we go through new change. It may seem as though we are losing everything when, in fact, it is just a part of the natural cadence of life.

This life is just preparation, a higher education for your soul. And if you don't pass a life test, that's ok. You just look at what you can learn from what you missed. You don't blame the teachers or the books. You look at *how can I be a better student*? We are all students. We are all perpetually learning, developing, remembering, and healing. Things will continually come up which challenge us to seek, to reach, to release old ideas, and to transform from the inside out. That is the point. If you are allowing that with compassion, with Love at the center of your heart, then you will never fail.

THE CAVE

Many cultures and tribes have an initiation time in which the inductee will go through literal or symbolic darkness to re-enter the Light. This can be accomplished in many ways modern day, through sweat lodges, through journeying to an actual cave (with proper guidance), through turning off all the lights in your room for several hours and seeing what comes, or for me, through the use of a sensory deprivation float tank. It was something I had been sincerely apprehensive about, yet simultaneously intrigued by, for years. Something I had always wanted to try but never had the guts to go through with. I was certain I would experience severe claustrophobia. I believe this to be the reservation of many, as we do not like feeling like we might, even for a moment, not be in control. But that is why this can be so transformative, it forces

The Self Beyond

relinquishment of our defense mechanisms. The cave forces us to confront our naked self.

I would like to share a brief story of how I took a journey into the darkness, my personal cave of the soul. (I can't say I don't enjoy how cavalier that sounds). How it happened for me was highly synchronistic. On one chance Sunday afternoon, I decided to get a haircut. I wandered to the Park Avenue district of my little city where there are some hip and artsy restaurants, boutiques, and beauty salons. I had one place, in particular, I wanted to try out. When I parked in the lot across the street, which was surrounded by several other businesses, I realized the salon was closed. I did not have any pressing reason to go immediately back home so I began to look around. A little shop caught my eye, "Body Mind Float Center." I saw on the sign a man peacefully floating in a pool of blue liquid bliss. I figured, I could go check it out, ask some questions, see how the energy felt and maybe another day I would consider giving it a real try.

As I entered, I removed my shoes and felt a nice warm energy, the kind you might feel walking out on a beach in the tropics. It smelled bright and clean. There was a lot of Light entering the main room. The young man at the desk seemed inviting and very relaxed. He was happy to answer my questions. I asked, "Have you ever done it?" He said, "Oh yes!" I said, "What was your experience? Did you feel like it took you someplace else?" (I have heard many things about these experiences and people seem to be able to astral travel across the cosmos with this method which could not but get my attention). He replied honestly, "It is different each time. You kind of go deeper as you do it more." I don't know what came over me but I was compelled. I said, "I want to do it!" He said, "Ok!"

I entered a room that was quite temperate and clean. I was not sure, at all, what to expect. There was everything I would need; towels, a robe, earplugs, q-tips, a shower stall etc. They provided all the essentials. He gave me a brief tour and instructions, then left me to my adventure.

The unit, itself (for those who have not had the experience), is roughly 4 feet in width, with the lid closed it is about the same in depth, with a length of about 7-8 feet. Inside is several inches of body temperature salt water and nothing else. I entered this space with both excitement and reservation, but the

The Self Beyond

moment I closed the lid and laid down something amazing happened. I instantly found myself *floating in weightlessness*. I was in a zero-gravity simulated environment and I may as well have been out in space. I sensed my body spinning for several minutes. I was unsure of why this was. I reached out my hands to confirm if that was really happening and found (to my surprise) my body was not moving. My own energy field was spinning. I set the intention to steady myself and it settled down. I felt fully supported, yet also, truly felt as though I was floating free in the ocean of space. I did not feel too hot or too cold. Time ceased to exist here. I felt nothing but the float.

In this environment, I quickly realized that I could entirely influence my experience by setting a clear intention. I set an intention to commune with the highest aspect of myself (what some may call God, or the Divine).

When I was there in that darkness, the first thought that I had was, clearly, "I am not this body." I quickly began to take some kind of inventory of myself. Who am I then? I thought, "I am not this foot, this hand, not this heart or, even, the mind." It all just seemed to be hanging off of me, from my core to my limbs. I, then, felt struck at the solution to this existential equation: "I am this thought!" But yet, another higher level of me heard this and said, "No. You are beyond your thought. You are *more*. Go deeper." It was then that I *remembered*, I am not even my thoughts, because above that is a silent observer always watching and listening. What am I, then, but the infinite and unconditional witness—the Beholder.

I had many realizations, here, in this timeless and spaceless place. I recognized as I contemplated the Divine Source of All that we are *not* fragments scattered out of our universal origin. We are fractals of it. Fractals, meaning each piece contains the entire blueprint of the whole within it. Not incomplete shards of something much greater than ourselves, but shards of the whole within each piece. The entirety of the boundless stellar ocean was in this drop of consciousness which I was experiencing. When you experience the utter infinity of the cosmic oceans, your first realization is how infinite you are as well. We are all seeds of the same Source, containing within us *everything*! *The universe is on the inside*.

The Self Beyond

As I basked in this endless observation, I realized that, not only am I not this body, or my individual self, but even if I was a tree, it would not be that I was the tree. I would still be the thing that I am which is everything and nothing at the same time. So, I, then, decided to experience myself in various forms. I intended to know what it is to be a tree. It is amazing what our minds are capable of when all the restrictive distractions are shut off. Call it imagination. Call it fantasy, but for me this was a very real and transcendental experience. I felt myself become as a tree, with my roots sinking deep into the warm earth the way it feels to push your toes into the warm and welcoming soil. I felt the branches of my arms stretching out towards the sun. I felt the loneliness yet serenity of winter, how quiet it is there. I felt the wondrous emergence of spring and rejoiced in the returning songs of the birds. I felt the full glory of summer where it seemed nothing could ever be any more delightful, rushing into a swift fall in which all I had grown was released. There was a sacredness to this existence, a nobility to live so humbly as a tree; to exist just to exist, to endlessly give of your life, to stay in one place, yet touch so very much.

I then wished to know what it would be like to be various animals; a dolphin jumping up through the waves with my companion. How blissful that was! I swear we were smiling! The sunlight was pouring down through the ocean's surface, like crystal beams, the blues and turquoise colors, so much happiness and Love! Then I experienced being born as a baby elephant; the disorientating drop to the ground and trying to stand upon entering this world, the profound feeling of attachment I felt to my mother and my herd, the unfamiliar sensation of having such a long trunk, how wonderful water felt on my sun-dried skin. Then, I was a butterfly, flitting around and sensing just how delicious every flower appeared!

The Self Beyond

I thought it would be wonderful to know the life of a flower. So, I began as a seed, buried deep in the darkness, not knowing where I was or what would happen. All I could do was reach and push toward what I thought may be upward. So, I did until the earth cracked open, the Light poured through and I emerged. I felt myself unfold every leaf and every petal. I would, simply, unfurl and look to see a new layer of myself come into being. What a glorious existence it is to be a flower.

I spent hours in my float and it was a life changing experience for me. I left with the same kind of feeling one might have after a near death experience. Colors were brighter, foods tasted better. I felt renewed and my life's purpose was emboldened in every way. The cave has been held as an allegory in various religious and spiritual texts for this very reason. It symbolizes a death of sorts, and a rebirth back into a new life. It symbolizes crossing into the realm of the eternal and conquering the shadows to reach the Light. Joseph Campbell once said, *"The cave we fear to enter, holds the treasure we seek."*

---

[51] William Warby, March 3, 2008, under CC license retrieved from Wikicommons

THE SUN

The sun says to the waves, "The Light within me is also shining from within you." I will tell you a secret, one of the oldest and most hidden. The ancients did not worship the sun, but the light that illuminated the sun. *The Light from within.*

Through the hardships, the upheavals, the trials, and the gauntlets life may bring as we need them, remember to turn toward the Light. Take comfort in the promise of a new sunrise each morning. Even when it falls below our sight bringing dark nights. The golden Light is never gone. It is us that turns away, not the sun. The sun stays in one place; a facet of our solar system, the center of our little orbital journey. So, stay golden. Keep your heart draped in golden tapestries, your thoughts bathed in a golden wash. What is gold but the highest element of alchemy? What is the sun but a star, and she is *our star*, sending rays of warm nurturing, energy, and Light always. Hold the Light as sacred, and never forget: the Light of the Sun (of all suns) is within you.

> "*I swear to you, there are divine things more beautiful than words can tell.*" ~Walt Whitman

---

[52] Obtained from Pexels under Creative Commons Zero (CC0) license

The Self Beyond

Chapter 4: Healing the Whole Self

HEALING FROM THE INSIDE OUT

If we are being honest and paying attention, many would recognize that we are living in a damaged and disconnected world, but how did it get this way? Whose fault is it? Is it the government, or the system, or some inherent flaw of society creating symptoms which we have no control over? Or, is it something we have power over? We are not individuals suffering from a world in crisis. The world is suffering from a crisis of the individual, and *we* are the individuals who make up the world.

Inner transformation is required for any outer transformation of our lives, or the world. If we have not individually found balance and harmony within, then everything we build, including all structures and relationships, will be based on this imbalanced foundation. Some of us have started to find healing and balance. Some have actively sought it, recognizing our lives cannot change until we change. Some of us have stumbled upon it, uncertain how to proceed. Some of us have been unwittingly thrown into it due to a drastic life situation which forces us to look toward deeper healing. At the core, we must understand, the earth, the world, our communities, our families and our own lives cannot (and will not) heal, without us taking responsibility to truly heal ourselves first. We are all connected and we are each responsible for our individual strand in this great tapestry of life.

We each contribute, as individuals, to the collective experience. The critical condition of the world we see is really a reflection of the critical condition of our inner states. This has operated as a negative feedback loop of damaged and disconnected governments, societies, families, *both* created *by* and creating *more* damaged and disconnected individuals. This cycle has replayed for many thousands of years. That is why personal healing is so fundamental in changing the world. *As we transform ourselves, we transform the world.* As we heal ourselves, we heal a part of the collective, and, one person at a time, we resolve the paradox of pain.

I do not think I have come across one person who does not need healing, in some form. Give yourself a moment to consider what may need some healing within you. Do a pulse check on your health, your relationships, your connection with your family and friends, your work, and your finances. Even if you say, "Well, my life is not perfect but a lot of people have it much worse," don't cheat yourself out of living your life to your fullest potential as a healed and actualized individual.

The great majority of us have never made healing a priority. We focus on, simply, surviving day to day. Or perhaps, recovering from the past few years, the past few months, or just the past week! We may make minor adjustments and catch ourselves in some ways to course correct. The issue is that without going deeper, we never get at the root. Like a weed, if we do not get at the root, it will just continue to pop back up as illness, as problems in relationships, problems with money, and problems with life! We may have swells where everything comes together, but sooner or later it all falls apart again. That pattern is exactly what I want to help you address.

The Self Beyond

We have such demanding lives, which often, require all of our attention to be on everything that continues to keep us sick; bills, work, relationships, and obligation of all kinds. This constant depleting cycle has most of us on overload as it is. When that is the situation, we are no longer in control of our lives. Our *wounds* and insecurities are driving. So, let's ask ourselves, why do we keep perpetuating the same toxic relationship dynamics, the same negative situations, the same obstacles and patterns?

MY HEALING JOURNEY

I grew up in a small town, in a small family, daughter of a music teacher and an engineer. We were not rich or poor. Middle class, would best describe it. I don't remember going without any essentials like a few new clothes before each school year, or a jacket during winter. We had a little above ground pool. I had my own bedroom. There was always pretzels in the pretzel jar, and food in the fridge. For that, I am sincerely grateful in a world where so many children and families are living below the poverty line. You may never have known, looking out from on the street to my suburban two story house with a nice garden that something dark lurked within.

I love my family and do not now seek to create shame or blame, but telling a small sliver of my story may help others heal. I appreciate that each person may experience the same thing from a very different point of view, and I can only speak from my own. My family members are caring people, and all I hope to speak to are my own feelings, from that largely influential time period.

Subtle oppression, power struggles, and fear dominated over my childhood into early adulthood. This, for me, eclipsed what may have otherwise been a fine upbringing. My younger sister and I lived on a rollercoaster of dysfunction and normality. Perhaps this affected me more deeply, being highly sensitive, as many creative children are. My father had a temper, and to a young me, this was scary. My mother would often recede away. Boundaries I tried to set with my timid might were overrun. I felt intimidated, infringed upon, and mostly desperate that no one in the world understood me. [53]

During my teenage years, due to the intense dynamics which ruled my home world, I harbored a lot of self-resentment. (A child's boundaries are delicate, and when tampered with it creates issues with safety, trust, and self-respect). I became a "cutter" which no one seemed to notice. I would stare in my mirror and scream silently "I hate you!" There was a leering presence of something dark which haunted me in that house. Looking back, I now fully believe there was something deeper than my own hurt that needed to be healed and released in that home. That presence superimposed itself on my childhood and that trauma there, whether the gravity of it was known or unknown, inflicted a deep wound which I still, to this day, work to overcome and heal.

I recall, faintly, a few experiences of Light which came to me as a youth. One, in which, I awoke to two angelic forms of Light by my bed. Their presence was not, as much seen, as felt. One emerald green and one violet. Into my adult life I would have vivid dreams of being visited by teachers and guides. I met a stoic shaman whose face is still emblazoned in my memory. He did not speak, but I heard his wisdom from within. I met a beautiful Egyptian goddess who shared ancient secrets with me at the foot of the great pyramids. I travelled, in my dreams, to other worlds where I found crystals, magical waters, and met other beings who shared their telepathic kind-heartedness with me. All of this sounded crazy and I could have never shared this then. Something within me was waiting and growing, as a caterpillar in a chrysalis waits to break free, but it would still be many years for me until that was possible.

When I was 14, my mother left my father. It was a distressing time, but this was a blessing in disguise, as it made all the pieces move around. I was no longer under the same oppressive setting, and we were able to, finally, move out of that house. However, this took a toll on my mother, who felt it more

---

[53] If you or anyone you know is experiencing signs of abuse or self-harm please reach out for help, you are not alone, and you do not have to suffer in silence. You can call The National Domestic Abuse Hotline at 1-800-799-7233. More on this at http://kidshealth.org/en/kids/handle-abuse.html

than she could bear, and she receded further into herself. This collapse was apparent to me and my younger sister. We clung to one another as you would to the last life vest on a sinking ship.

At that time, I was struggling to come to terms with my sexuality. I had grown up highhandedly religious and we were sheltered from the reality of most worldly issues. Due to not knowing about drugs, sex, and the dangers in the real world, I was not prepared when they were introduced to me as a young teenager.

Just before I turned 16, I met a woman who presented herself as my savior. She came into my world saying sweet things no one had ever said to me. It made me feel special and loved. I moved in with her and became emancipated from my parents. We entered into a relationship which quickly disintegrated into the same patterns of abuse I had dealt with from childhood. She was possessive, controlling, jealous, and highly violent. She introduced me to nearly every drug there is and I was swept away into a world of clouded escape. Yet, I was captive to her in nearly every way.

Three years later, just before my twentieth birthday, I found myself on my own for the first time in my life. I did not know, then, the damage that all the trauma had done to me. I did my best. I began to be happy for, what seemed, the first time in my life. It was then, at the turn of the century that I began my true spiritual journey. It took about eight years of soul searching, wandering, losing, learning, and growth to build a baseline of, what is now, a radically different world view.

I had seen the darkest aspects of society. I had been subject to many kinds of harmful people, yet many beautiful and Loving ones, as well. I began to know real Love for the first time in my life. Not the kind of love that someone gives you with attachments and bargains built in, but the kind of Love you give wholeheartedly for its own merit. My heart had opened through many life-changing experiences. I felt the splendor, the wonderment and ecstasy of life for the first time. I found freedom and a kind of connection to everything. It was as if everything in my life, up to then, had some hidden meaning which had finally revealed itself, layer by layer to me.

I experienced many profound events which activated the wise warrior within me, coming close to death and coming back

The Self Beyond

from the edge to live again. This changed me on a mystical level. I dreamt in lucid dreams and travelled far, even across star systems. I saw the Light, what could only be described as the Living Light, on my journeys. Rainbows, feathers, butterflies, and even clouds became messengers. I communed deep in the mountains, the lakes, and the forests. Everything now was filled with meaning and purpose. I studied with psychics, philosophers, and masters whose bloodlines were tied to the ancient tribes and wisdom wherever I could. I travelled between worlds and found the veil between them had become permeable for me. It was a time of true awakening.

  I moved back home at the end of this long Shamans voyage. I had lived with very little for those eight years; many days not eating, at times, not having a home, going without trivial things like socks, or towels, little things we take for granted but are a puzzle to work without when needed. This instilled in me a profound appreciation for the little things in a way which I am eternally grateful. If I had not spent those many years like that, I would still be taking so much for granted. I left that chapter of my life, feeling filled with a higher awareness and appreciation. Food tasted better, colors were brighter, Love was sweeter, and every breath, every step was a miracle.

  When I made it home, I thought this blissful state would continue. I had worked so hard and grown so much. I had found peace and happiness I was sure would translate into my family life. Yet, upon coming home, I quickly realized all the old problems were still there, waiting, having never concluded or resolved. My sister was so hurt that I had left her, abandoned her. This was an awful realization for me because my sister has always been the one I've held the closest to me, even when I was away. My mother was still working through her pain, which was so hard to watch because she is one of the kindest and most generous people I know.

  There was a lot of forgiveness and healing still needed all around. Instead of dealing with the challenges of healing, it seemed everyone chose to act as though everything was fine. I was left holding the bag no one wanted to admit existed. I did not feel validated in the many wounds of the past, I could not forget, and I needed to be heard. I felt torn between looking at the bigger picture, beyond my own pain, or confronting it as it begged to be

The Self Beyond

confronted. I was unable to move forward and unable to step back. I tried to let it all go, but you cannot let go of something that has not first been embraced. So, it was only a matter of time before it would all come to the surface to be dealt with.

I had worked for nearly a decade to heal myself and transcend my past situation. I thought I was doing great; I was healthy, I felt invigorated, enlightened, even! I had come from a place in which I felt completely connected to myself and the beauty of the earth. I was happy with myself and life, in general, yet, I was met with the same issues that I had ran away from so many years before: issues which I could not resolve, despite all the work I had done on myself. Why?

I had made the novice mistake. I had only healed my adult self. I did not heal my child self. Let me explain why that is absolutely critical: the number one reason for the current state of our lives, our current relationships, and any problems we face is our internal thought patterns and emotions. We cannot move forward and expect a different reality or a different life, unless we do the work to heal those thoughts and emotions. What we experience and what we think and feel are directly connected. These programs we have been running on ourselves, for most of our lives, were set in place in the beginning, from our childhood, and I was no exception. To truly heal, we have to heal our deepest patterns and programs. We have to find our emotional root.

WHAT DO YOU SAY

[The next several sections will review a template for deeper healing. I recommend reading through it fully once, and coming back to it to work through each step, as needed. The journey will not be complete when you close this book. That is just the beginning. My hope is this will jumpstart that process for you.]

Louise Hay would say all disease and all our problems stem from one thing: a lack of self-Love. The key to Loving ourselves better begins with how we speak to ourselves. Think for a little bit right now about how you talk to yourself. Be honest. This is for you, alone. Listen to your inner narrative. Are you Loving yourself or blaming yourself? Are you feeling like nothing you do will ever be enough? Are your thoughts racing so much you can barely catch exactly what you're thinking? Slow down, breathe, and *listen*.

When we find, as adults, that we are self-critical, it is nearly always rooted in what we experienced as children. I empathize deeply with each of you, as I know that *many* have undergone things as horrific and damaging as physical or sexual abuse, or even as subtly damaging as being ignored, or put in situations in which we had no control. The psyche of a child is complex and fragile—just perceiving ourselves to be unloved is enough to cause trauma.

Some may say, "Well, I had a great childhood!" and feel sure you're rarely (if ever) negative. I urge you to pay attention over the next week and really check in with yourself to catch any stealthy programs that may be running in the background. Those can be the most damaging of all. Realize that negativity towards others also reflects an unconscious negativity about aspects of yourself. These are red flags as well.

As you begin to be conscious of your internal thought patterns, be compassionate with yourself. Do not judge yourself. Do not censor or resist what naturally comes. That is key: to allow yourself to be *as you are,* so you can understand your most honest tendencies and habits. Do not allow this exercise to make you feel bad. This is simply to identify when negative thought patterns occur, what situations trigger them, and what exactly the thoughts are. Write them down in a journal. Read it over to study the pattern. This will help you find the root, and that will bring you one step closer to shifting the pattern, overriding the program, and healing.

The voices we hear in our head, present day telling us we are not good enough; "no one will ever Love us," "we are worthless," etc. these are the same voices of our upbringing or past relationships. This is not to blame anyone. This is about *you*. This is about healing yourself. This is all done with the highest intention of breaking these unhealthy cycles so we can have peace, fulfillment, and happiness, so that we don't perpetuate those cycles with our families, children, colleagues and partners.

Nearly every one of us has deep rooted issues, wounds, and work to do in order to come into our fullest potential. No one is better. No one is worse. Healing lies within us. If we would only put the focus where it is truly needed—on Loving ourselves more than we have ever Loved anything in our life.

NEW PROGRAM

Once we have identified our negative thought patterns, we need to do a few things with them. Recognize, we may not be able to completely eradicate them from our lives. Especially if they have been so deeply embedded. What we *can* do is choose to observe them and recognize their origin without attaching ourselves to them. When they occur, we can simply resist holding onto them, stop identifying with them or personalizing them. Just release them like a balloon into the sky, or a leaf on a running stream. Then we can replace them with new positive thought patterns. These are, essentially, positive affirmations such as:

"I Love and accept myself"
"I am worthy of Love, respect and compassion"
"I am surrounded by Love at all times"
"I am perfect as I am"
"All my relationships are Loving and harmonious"
"Life is simple and meaningful"
"I am thankful for my healing"
"I am blessed"
"Deep at the center of my being is an infinite well of Love"
"Miracles happen every day" [54]

I believe it is most powerful to write your own personal affirmations. You can also look up many online. The key to affirmations is to say them like you believe them, to say them until you really do believe them! You, also, have to follow up with action. Your actions should complement your affirmations. You cannot say "I Love myself" then go out binge drinking, or allow yourself to participate in a relationship in which someone treats you poorly. You have to *act* as if you believe you do Love yourself and through that, you really *will* Love yourself much more deeply.

---

[54] See my personal affirmations at the end of the book to get you started.

The Self Beyond

This is the nitty-gritty of healing—changing thought patterns and actions.

THE INNER CHILD

Imagine a child who has been treated poorly for most of their young life. They have been told awful things; that they aren't good enough, that they never do anything right, that no one will ever truly care about them. They believe it is true. It is all they have ever been told. Imagine how damaging that is to their psyche. Can you appreciate that everything we say to ourselves as adults, we also say to our inner child?

Our inner child is just one of the many archetypes we each hold, along with the judge, the saboteur, and the prostitute. [55] Each have their own strengths and weaknesses but we will focus, here, on the inner child. To reach our inner child, we need to talk to them. We need to realize we never lost them. We *are* them. We need to talk to ourselves the way we would talk to our five-year-old self. If our five-year-old self was standing there in front of you, just think of how much you would Love them. If they made a mistake you would not talk to them the way you talk to your adult self, would you? You would not say, "Look, you did it again! It figures! I can never count on you to do anything right!" Think about how that makes your inner child feel, how damaging that is. That inner child is always with you, observing, listening, *waiting to be Loved* for who they really are.

When looking through this wide angled lens, we might begin to change our inner narrative and use kindness and understanding. Instead or berating your inner child, you could say, "We all make mistakes, and together we can fix this. We will pay attention to what we can learn from this mistake, and know that you are always Loved, no matter what. You are perfect as you are. I know you are trying your best. And I will always be here with you and for you." That is all this child ever really needed: to be supported, believed in, appreciated, understood, and Loved. Only you can give that to your own inner child. It starts with how you talk to yourself.

---

[55] See more on these archetypes in the work of Carolyn Myss, Ph. D who takes us beyond the incomplete philosophies of Jung and Freud.

The Self Beyond

WILLINGNESS TO CHANGE

Healing requires the willingness to heal. Not just a willingness to get better physically, emotionally and mentally, but a true and honest willingness to *change*. We have to be willing to change our behaviors, our beliefs about ourselves, and our thought patterns; our addictions and compulsions, which created the disease, situation, or negative patterns in the first place. This is not just about thinking you are willing to change on a conscious level. You must truly explore how deep your attachment to the illness, pattern, or situation goes. If you are not willing to let go of the illness, situation, or pattern, then healing will not be complete. You can do all the healing work in the world, but it is ultimately a choice, to be willing to *let go* (surrender), and allow that healing to take place.

All pain is emotional at the root. All illness, disease, and manifestations of problems in our lives have a source which we can identify, learn the message of, and overcome. If we can address the emotional root, the many expressions of its problems, including physical disease [56], can be stunted and even stopped.

Recognition (or awareness) is a critical step. This has to do with creating, or allowing, a greater viewpoint. You have to look at your life as a whole picture, not just a snapshot. You have to see it from bird's eye view. In order to get to the root of any issue, illness, or situation, you have to look at your early life; relationships with your parents, caregivers, and family. You have to look at patterns that may have resulted in relationships you created as a young adult and adult. Many of us will find we have

---

[56] If you are struggling with a physical disease such as high blood pressure, diabetes, high cholesterol, heart disease, even cancer I *urge* and *compel* you to look deeper at the links between diet and disease. A great resource on this is '*Forks over Knives*' a documentary which explores these links and promotes a balances plant based diet. Addressing the emotional root and cultivating self-Love is important, and diet works in concert with that deeper work.

perpetuated the same initial hurtful situation from our childhood, but we cannot see these patterns unless we step back.

Awareness of these roots is exactly what recognition is about. Understanding your pattern and how the past events and situations connect to what you think, feel, and believe now. And then how that connects to the situation, illness or pattern in your life at present. This will take time to understand, but I promise you, it will change your life. Keep track of what triggers your patterns. Pay attention to how that may mirror situations from earlier in your life. When you can see where these issues stem from, you can begin to loosen their hold over you and your life.

This is not yet complete awareness. Total awareness means finding the lesson in all of this. There is a reason for everything, especially the painful things. What is this pain, this pattern, this situation trying to teach you? What is your body, your issue, your life trying to tell you? You are the only one who can see this for yourself. Understanding the lesson is critical to being able to learn from it and move forward. You cannot let go of something until you have learned its lesson and taken in its message.

FORGIVENESS IS FREEDOM

Without forgiveness, we cannot release the root of our own patterns and issues. There is no need to hold onto something once you have learned the lesson. The lesson becomes a part of you, and that is all that it needed to do. To release it requires forgiveness.

This is not about making excuses for poor behavior, violence, or cruelty. However, forgiveness is only possible if you can move beyond judgment. Realize that hurt people hurt people. These people who hurt you, were hurting too. This does not justify it, but helps us draw context around the situation. A deeper awareness can see that this pain caused them to project that pain onto us. This was *not* something you deserved. This is *not* something that was your fault. But perhaps, through understanding that, ultimately, this hurt was a desperate act of someone who did not understand how to Love. They did not feel Love, they felt lost, scared, and misunderstood themselves, which

The Self Beyond

is sad. Through that understanding, you may find the compassion to free yourself, and them, through forgiveness.

We cannot forgive anyone until we forgive ourselves. So please, take all the time you need, in any way that feels right for you. Set aside some time to look at yourself in the mirror with unconditional Love, and forgive yourself. If you feel any resistance, that just means the forgiveness is truly needed. You have been waiting (for yourself) to Love and forgive yourself for a very long time. Come home to yourself. Come into your heart with Unconditional Love and acceptance.

Working through forgiving those who have hurt you such as parents and caregivers, old partners and lovers, can be difficult. Having the support of Loved ones or professional counselors may be required. But there are many ways to do this for yourself. I do not want to define one particular method as "best." You can visualize talking to the ones who have caused you pain. You can write a handwritten letter. You might allow yourself to say every mean thing you need to say to them out loud as a visualization, and then sit with it until you are capable of finding a ray of compassion. Once you settle into that space of compassion the toxic effects of what we held onto for so long are no longer buried deep inside, they are disempowered, and can be finally released.

For me I, simply, imagined those who hurt me, right there in front of me. I imagined the circumstances they may have endured in their own childhoods, feeling unloved, or neglected, or abused, which caused them to have difficulty in showing me the kind of Love they had not received themselves. I said, "*I forgive you and you no longer have power over me.*" I said it until I felt it, until I felt a weight lift. For those of us with incredibly deep trauma, this is a profoundly arduous process. I felt, for a long time, I could never forgive. But the only one that was held captive was me. *Forgiveness is freedom.* It frees both you and the offender, whoever they are. Forgiveness is an act of self-healing, self-liberation, and self-empowerment.

Remind yourself throughout this process a quote by Louise Hay, who said, "*In the infinity of life where I am, all is perfect, whole, and complete.*" You are safe now. You are empowered. Forgiveness and healing is possible.

ACCEPTANCE AND SELF-EMPOWERMENT

Understand that our parents and caregivers, in fact every person in our lives, has only ever been capable of showing us the version of Love they knew for themselves. If they experienced lives of knowing love as verbal abuse, bribery, neglect, manipulation, indifference, or even violence, then that is the only way they know. They will literally *believe* that is what Love is. We cannot show someone something we do not know for ourselves. In this realization, it may widen our understanding of the "why." Accepting that most people are doing the best they can with what they know can be healing. Of course there are exceptions. There are exceptions in everything. But in many cases, there is a generational pattern, a chain which you can break, by seeing through it and doing your work to make a new link.

Many of us do not know what our primary caregivers, or parents, lives were like as children. They were taught how to love from their parents or caregivers, and the parents of our parents may have been continuing a long chain of abuse in the name of "love." Our caregivers may have tried with all they had to do it better, just as we are trying to do better now.

The goal now is to run a new program, one built on a much deeper understanding of Love, and to be the evolution of what we knew. This is especially true for those who have children. We are recognizing how deeply affected we are by our upbringing. So much of who we become is shaped by the Love or lack of Love we receive growing up. We are now appreciating how the words we say to our children and how we talk to them, will someday become their own inner voice. Speak with greater Love. Speak with compassion. Speak and act with a deep respect that they are not just a child, they are a *little person* who will be an adult in this world. We want to support and nurture them to become an adult who does not need to heal from their childhood.

Acceptance is a powerful step to healing. Once we have done the work to identify the emotional core, the root of the issue, now we have to accept what that has shown us and created in our life. This means (actually) accepting our current pain, illness, and situation—*gratefully*. How could we possibly be grateful for pain that came from events that scarred us for life? How could we accept an awful situation that we are *now* in? It is not that we need to be grateful for the harm something or someone caused, it is about being grateful for what grew within us *from it*. Not everything taken from our adversities is negative. We may walk away from abusive situations less trusting, having lost a sense of safety. We may feel physical pain due to our illness every day, but this points out to us where Love and acceptance is most needed. It encourages our growth and challenges us to summon something much deeper within us.

If this makes you feel anger, I greatly understand. I became angry as well in the beginning. But, the desire for healing has to eclipse the desire for some kind of righteous retribution. Our resentment of our hardships is self-damaging, only. It does nothing to serve us or our redevelopment. We have to take that step, and *then* the way appears. In accepting the troubles we are given, we can overcome them. We have to get to that emotional root, accept it, and Love ourselves there: to heal ourselves there.

For us as adults, acceptance is about appreciating the collateral benefits within our past and current situations and problems, which are gifts to help us grow and evolve. The pieces which allowed for opportunities to transform us and now heal deeply. It is important to acknowledge and accept that opportunity and blessing. If it was not for these signs and messages that our body and life are telling us, we would never change. *Change is the whole point. Growth is the whole point.* The discomfort is what propels us to seek deeper wholeness, balance, harmony and peace within ourselves.

Pain has a purpose. Pain is only there to make us aware of something within us that needs attention. It is, essentially, a lesson. Not in the cruel sense of "teaching you a lesson," but in making you aware of a truth you now must acknowledge. When you become aware of the lesson, the pain no longer has a purpose and can be released. When we learn, we can let go. When we accept and *allow* it, we can release the need for it.

You cannot heal a part of yourself by begrudging the pain it causes you. That, literally, sends harmful energy to that place. You have to embrace the parts that hurt. Imagine Loving them completely. Envision the pieces or parts in perfect condition. Embrace them. This generates powerful energy that heals and rebuilds.

The Self Beyond

It may seem counterintuitive, but through accepting our challenges, our pain, and our sickness, through welcoming them, we are taking back our power. We, often, do not recognize the many ways in which we have disempowered ourselves. In this sense, empowerment means reclaiming your control through taking *responsibility*. When we blame others for our issues, when we see all outer circumstances as the reason for our troubles, our sickness, or our pain, we give away our power.

Taking responsibility for your life is different than believing you are to blame for it. Believing your life is your fault assaults you with guilt. Taking responsibility is about, simply, accepting accountability for your role in creating your life, and taking ownership of that.

No one else has put you here, or made your life what it is. When we are children, we have little choice. But, as adults, no outer circumstances have made us suffer and, really, no one has truly hurt us any more than we have allowed them to. We are always given the experiences that will move us toward our deepest healing. The capacity to recognize this is a higher level of insight. It allows for profound transformation. When you no longer need those lessons, or that healing, the situations and relationships in your life will change.

Empowerment is the quantum leap from victim mentality into healer mentality. We walk around saying, "I'm sorry." We are sorry for our own existence. We say, "I'm trying," but we do not have to try. Change this language: instead say, "I am doing my best!" Feel how powerful that is! When we say, "I'm sorry," or say, "I'm trying," it is filled with weakness, not strength. We are not victims. We are meant to master our life. Every word you use inwardly and outwardly is your energy, your intention. Use that energy to empower yourself. Be conscious of the *words* you choose and reclaim your power.

We are empowered to heal ourselves. Our bodies *want* to heal. Our lives want to be in balance. Our existence wants to resonate with the harmony of our highest order. That is our original condition and our true state of being. *You can heal*. It is possible.

Your whole life has lead you here, to this point. Your whole life has been waiting for you to come back to yourself, to be there for yourself, to Love yourself. Love is what heals, not just any Love but unconditional self-Love. That kind of Love is the most powerful medicine on earth. That kind of medicine does not just heal, it *transforms*. It becomes a healing force, in itself. Walking forward with an open heart filled with unconditional Love, not only, heals you but transmutes you into something even greater, a healer.

CHOOSE HEALING

We do not create what happened to us during our developing years. We do not, from a linear standpoint, choose to be injured or abused. We were victims, but we do not have to stay victims. Most of us have held on to those wounds so deeply they have become who we are, and through that mechanism of association, we have remained victims. They have become how we see ourselves and who we think we are. They have controlled us into adulthood and from that place of pain, we continue to choose to perpetuate the harm it caused.

Yes, we *choose* it. Perhaps, by feeling so angry and unheard as a child, we over speak others as a dominating adult, which causes relationships to constantly fail. Perhaps, by being in such a traumatic situation as a child, we shut off and as an adult never open our hearts back up, causing us to feel constantly distant and alone. Perhaps, due to so much unaddressed pain from our childhood, we hold resentment or, even, guilt which becomes cancer in our bodies. These are all very real pathways which we choose to perpetuate. Then the wound is no longer something that ruined our lives as children, but, now, we allow to ruin our lives as adults.

I know the first instinct of considering this is to reject it in anger. We will fiercely defend our standpoint that this is not our fault; that our illness is not our fault, that how our ex-spouse treated us was not our fault, that all we are going through is not our fault. It is ok to feel that resistance. Resistance is a sign that we are getting closer to that root, and, ultimately, our healing.

If we want our lives to change, or our issues or illnesses to be healed, we have to look at how we create them. Believing someone else has done this to us, or something else has created any aspect of our life keeps us trapped in a state of powerlessness.

Understanding that it is true, we have created these things in our lives, is how we *choose to heal.*

There is great power here in your choice. To know what you are choosing, look around you. Look at your body, your thoughts, and your relationships. What messages are being sent?

To get deeply in tune with yourself means becoming very quiet. Hear the subtle intelligence from within. Just listen to your Self. If we want to uproot the emotional core like a weed, we have to see how we have interwoven ourselves with it, how we have chosen to form strong attachments in creating it. We become strangely comfortable with our pains and issues. We identify with them in such a way that letting them go feels like letting go a part of our self. We are not our pain or sickness. We are not what happened to us in the past. We can choose to be who we are now: someone who is healed and someone who has learned a great deal from those chapters of our lives.

When we, not only, see the root of our constant struggles in life, but see how we have, essentially, created these patterns and all the pains and illnesses from them—we come into our power. Understand that if you now believe you have created your pain, your illness, your patterns, and your issues, then you know that *you can un-create them.* You can heal them. The most powerful choice we can make is in taking responsibility. Choosing Love and forgiveness of ourselves and others can flip the script. Once we are done allowing the pain to conquer us, we can overcome the pain and find the cure.

FOCUS AND ACTION

Focus is the glue that holds every other piece together. Focus, essentially, means here, the law of attraction. What we focus on, we attract. Once we have done this deeper healing work, we cannot fall back into focusing on old pains. If you continue to identify with your illness, problems, conflicts etc. that's what will continue to manifest, despite all the deep healing work. It is like fixing the brakes on your car after riding your brakes all the time, and then going right back into riding your brakes. We have to heal and then change our way of life. We can come out of deep healing and recognize that now we must have *new* thoughts and new patterns. Focus on wellness (even if little pains come up again), and on opportunities (even if obstacles rear their head). Focus on being healed (even if you are still in the process), on peace (even if conflicts appear), and above all, gratitude (for every little victory). We will, then, experience more things in our lives that mirror those victories.

Pay attention to what you *do* want. This doesn't mean living in denial. Focus is the very opposite. It means becoming ultra-conscious, rather than making our issues unconscious. This means recognizing the condition or issue, facing it and sizing it up to understand it is not bigger than your power. It never was. Then, release your need for what it has taught you with Love. Release your attachment to it. Accept your responsibly for it. Then focus your energy on what you *want* your life to be. Focus on the solution, not the problem.

Words are powerful. *Language* is powerful, in this. You cannot do all this work to heal, and continue complaining about your old situation. That reinforces the old paradigm of suffering we are trying to break the hold of. Try to catch yourself. This will be hard at first, then easier as you notice how often we do it. If you notice you have started to tell your old story, just catch it, and change the narrative. This, in itself, will not stop the old story, but it *will* weaken it. It will begin to dismantle the stronghold it has built around your life. Eventually, it will diminish due to lack of nutrition. Over time, these self-destructive thoughts will be forced to retreat completely.

Do not wish or want. Those words relay a sense of lack. You have to speak as if you have it already, even if you know you have a long way to go. As an example, say, "Healing is already mine, it's waiting for me to create it. Though I have not gotten there yet, I *will*." See it, feel it, and know it. There is no try, only doing, only being. We are either allowing the natural flow, or blocking it. Do not try to force or make something happen. We cannot *make* anything happen. All we can do is *allow* it. Do your right work. Create the space for it, and allow whatever comes to come, gratefully. Create an environment that supports and allows for healing to take root in your life by speaking of health and well-being.

Thinking and feeling are central. Internal thought patterns and the emotion behind them are key. But now it is, also, time to do; to take the steps, to create the conditions for deeper healing to manifest. The application of any change is about nurturing conscious awareness. The capacity we have to heal is infinite. Know that is true for you. We are connected to a deeper and greater energy of Love, wholeness, healing and peace, then we could possibly imagine.

Actions must compliment the positive thinking, feeling, and deep inner work you are doing. Actions such as planning your life around your healing, not your illness. Actions such as making choices from your healed self, not your hurt self; to wake up, to walk, to talk, and to *act* from a place of total healing. Create an atmosphere of celebration, joy, and rejuvenation. *Be willing to surrender your suffering self.* Let that part of your life go. Refuse to continue to identify yourself with that suffering. Be willing to allow your healed self in. *Be willing to be changed.*

HEALING ALL BODIES

We are beginning to appreciate that through holding onto our past and allowing it to create our present, we end up carrying a perpetual sickness, whether it simply expresses as negative thought patterns which create life circumstances and relationships we do not want, or when left long enough, it begins to express itself as serious illness, dis-ease, and physical pain of all kinds. Mind and body are connected directly. So, remember as you do this work, this heals more than just mind, this heals your body too.

You will need to treat your body better if you are suffering from serious illness. *Food is key*. Every cell of our body is constantly recreated, based on what we put into it. Sugar, alcohol, animal products filled with antibiotics, over processed foods with many chemicals, all contribute to an unhealthy body. Eat fresh, raw, organic produce (this works reciprocally in that it will help your mind work better, which helps your body heal better, too). Plants and fruits that drink pure water and Light are rich with the nutrients your body needs. Only life gives life.

The Self Beyond

[57]

Grounding is essential. Your body is an electrical system. Many physical pains are caused by inflammation. You need to get your bare feet and hands on the earth to discharge and take in the electrons present there. Over 20 peer reviewed studies have shown when we ground ourselves, inflammation is drastically reduced. [58] This means pain reduction. This means a better flowing electrical system.

Rest often. Meditate in silence or with soft music. Take up a practice that is both social and healthy such as yoga or tai chi. Utilize massage, acupuncture, reflexology, or Reiki energy healing in your wellness regimen. Remember that these modalities *facilitate* healing, but *you* are the one that heals *yourself*. The changes you are making from the inside out is what heals. (Even if you believe in God as a Higher Power, working through you in your healing, you still must do your part to heal yourself).

---

[57] Obtained from Pexels under Creative Commons Zero (CC0) license
[58] See more on the incredible scientific evidence of the benefits of merely grounding here: https://vimeo.com/205264910

The Self Beyond

Beyond our physical and mental bodies, we have an emotional and energetic/spiritual body as well. We cannot neglect the more subtle aspects of our emotional and spiritual state. Journaling, painting, expressing your emotions are all very helpful. Many emotions come up to the surface and that is what is needed to truly heal. Do not repress them. Do not attach to them. Just recognize and allow them. Imagine this practice of non-attachment by visualizing each thought or emotion as a leaf on a stream gently flowing on by. You do not have to pick up every leaf. You can simply allow it to flow past you. This process is much like the process of a spiritual awakening. It is a constant shedding of all that no longer serves you, all that is not you. You can simply say to older impulses or feelings that no longer serve you, "That does not belong to me" or "That is not mine."

To work on the energetic/spiritual aspects, we can look at our chakra system. Our chakra system is an energetic body that can become misaligned or, even, blocked due to carrying trauma, daily stress, or before true deep healing has occurred. Please understand, this is not new age dogma. The energetic body is one of the most ancient systems of knowledge we have (and validated by many cultures worldwide as well as modern science). [60] The

---

[59] Obtained from Pexels under Creative Commons Zero (CC0) license
[60] Wisneski, Len. Anderson, Lucy. 2005. The Scientific Basis of Integrative Medicine. Evidence Based Complimentary Alternative

concept of the chakra system originated in India, extracted from the vast ancient texts known as the Vedas (as early as 1500 BC).

The energy body is truly a complete connected system. This means blockages in one energy center can clog up the flow of the whole system and manifest in various ways in your life. For instance, a blocked throat chakra may cause you to have trouble speaking up when needed. Or a throat chakra that is too open can cause you to speak up a little *too* much in the form of verbal abuse of others. Addressing these imbalances can assist you with aligning within yourself. The idea is to get the whole system working together and flowing in its most natural state which is meant to be in balance. This will greatly assist your healing process because everything can flow much more freely.

ENERGY BODY

The energy body of the chakra system is multilayered. Each energy center of the physical body deals with a specific aspect of the mental and emotional bodies. Understanding where strengths and weaknesses are within our energetic system can help us focus on balance in those areas of our life. Each chakra has a color associated with it and a simple way to bring energy for a weak chakra, is to infuse that associated color into your life, for a time. For instance, if you feel your sacral chakra is blocked, you might wear an orange scarf around your waist to help encourage better flow. Or if you have trouble communicating effectively and want to help open your throat chakra you might wear a necklace with turquoise or a blue stone complimentary to that chakra.

Medicine. Retrieved from:
https://www.ncbi.nlm.nih.gov/pmc/articles/PMC1142191/

The Self Beyond

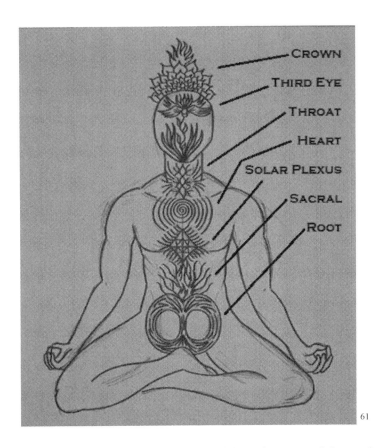

61

The root chakra (at the base of the spine around the genital area) deals with survival and physical wellbeing. This is the point of life's emergence where we are physically conceived and born. It is an earth chakra and deals with grounding and connection to our roots. Physically, the root chakra is connected to legs, bones, feet, large intestines and adrenal glands. Blockages here can create fear, paranoia, defensiveness and guilt. Many survivors of sexual or physical abuse retain blockages in this area that deals with safety. The color association is red and by using red in painting to deal with emotions, or lighting a red candle with a positive affirmation of bringing healing and balance to this area, can assist in releasing the blockages. Stones that can help balance this chakra

---

[61] Self-drawn for this book

The Self Beyond

are hematite, red garnet, and smoky quartz. Stones that are grounding all complement the root chakra.

The sacral chakra (just below the naval) deals with desire and sexual energy. This is a powerful chakra to work with and underpins the importance of keeping intercourse sacred. The sacral chakra is connected physically to the reproductive organs, kidneys, bladder, circulatory system, and lower abdomen. Issues with this energy center can express as emotional problems, obsessive compulsion, or sexual intemperance. The color association is orange. Stones that can help balance this chakra are orange calcite, carnelian, turquoise and fluorite.

The solar plexus (located just above the naval near the diaphragm) is the power center. This center is the origin of the sensation of that "gut feeling." This chakra deals with the creation, perception and projection of self. Joy, laughter, anger, and personal power all stem from this emotional core. Sensitivity, ambition and confidence originate in this area, as well. It is connected to the digestive system, pancreas, adrenal glands, and muscles. Blockages here can create a sense of victimization, anger or frustration, or lack of motivation. The color association is yellow, so to re-energize aspects of your life dealing in these emotional areas, you can use a little more yellow (yellow is the cowbell of the rainbow). Stones that can help balance this chakra are citrine, amber, yellow jasper, and tiger's eye.

The heart chakra (center of the chest) deals with love, compassion, openness, and empathy. The heart chakra is connected to the lungs, arms, hands, and thymus. A blocked heart center can create physical heart problems, as well as immune system and lung problems. It can also create a lack of compassion or being emotionally closed off to others. The color association is emerald green, the majestic green of nature. Being in nature can greatly assist in opening a closed off heart or problems associated with blockages. Stones that can help balance this chakra are rose quartz (the Love stone), lepidolite, green adventurine, malachite (be cautious with this stone as it can be toxic if ingested), and jade (which is an excellent dream stone to place under your pillow as well).

The throat chakra (located near the vocal chords) deals with expression, creativity, communication, and judgement. It is connected to the neck, shoulders, arms and hands, thyroid and parathyroid. The throat deals with synthesizing ideas and expressing ourselves. Issues here can cause problems with our communication, creative blocks, or dishonesty. The color association is light blue. Stones that can help balance this chakra are sodalite, blue calcite, blue kyanite, celestite (a highly spiritual stone said to connect us to our angel guides), chrysocolla, turquoise, aquamarine, and amazonite.

  The third eye chakra (located in the pineal gland) deals with inner vision, insight, spiritual identity, and psychic abilities. Multiple ancient cultures revered this area of the brain as the "seat of the soul" (though some Eastern traditions assigned this status to the heart). Dreams and wisdom are held here. This is the nodal point that physically intersects both hemispheres of the brain. A blocked third eye can result in a lack of true vision, a loss of spiritual awareness, difficulty in receiving insight, and even depression. Its color association is indigo. Work to awaken the third eye during meditation and visualize it opening as an eye from within. Filter your tap water specifically to remove Fluoride as that calcifies the pineal gland and dulls its abilities to connect us to our higher self in the crown chakra. Stones to help balance this chakra are lapis lazuli (which has many revered spiritual benefits and was worn by Egyptian royalty), azurite, and tanzanite.

  The crown chakra (located on the top of the head) is the last physical chakra. (There are other chakras resting in our energetic body and auric fields as well). The crown chakra deals with the higher self, wholeness, and connection with Spirit/God. It deals also with information, understanding, acceptance, and happiness. When we are born, this portal remains soft and flexible for 9-18 weeks afterward, still connected with the spiritual realms we had so recently come from. (Interestingly, the anterior fontanel closes not long after we learn to walk). The crown chakra is connected to the cerebral cortex, central nervous system and pituitary gland. Its color association is deep purple. Stones that help balance and open the crown chakra are amethyst (which is such a multipurpose stone *I highly recommend everyone have at least one nice piece somewhere prominent in the home), quartz (a powerful healing stone in general as well), Herkimer diamond, and selenite. [62]

The energetic chakra system can give us deeper insight into our patterns and personal issues. By meditating or practicing physical alignment, we allow the proper flow of energy through our bodies to support a more *complete healing* throughout our entire system. You cannot address just one area. They are all connected. An issue anywhere can affect the whole. That is why looking at these subtle systems can provide such great benefits to our mental, emotional and physiological wellbeing. The energy body is part of our greater body.

THE POWER OF BELIEF

You have to believe in your intentions, in your power, and in your healing. You have to believe in the positive thoughts and emotions you are creating and their inevitable positive affect on your entire life. Do your best. Be compassionate with yourself. If you make a mistake or have a negative thought, just allow it and release it. This is a progression, this is a journey to healing.

With every step, you are transforming yourself. Do not rush it. Do not shut the door in a few days or weeks if you do not see immediate affects and say, "This isn't working!" Continue through each step. Recognize that *now* you are aware. *Now* you are empowered. The only direction that can lead you is forward. Make new choices, better choices, based on what you now know. Stay with your willingness to be transformed. Keep with your awareness of any thoughts and feelings as they come up, and focus on the lessons. Continue to stay in acceptance. Be grateful. Forgive as many times as you need to. Make it a mantra if needed.

---

[62] Stone and crystal work can greatly help with stagnant and tougher-to-break-through energies. They can connect us with earth's natural frequencies and each carry their own special resonant frequency that interacts with ours in a beneficial way. They can also assist us in strengthening our own energetic field. This is literally a science of its own and I recommend looking into making use of the stones or crystals you feel drawn to and integrate them into your healing practice and in creating a healing environment. A great place to start is "The Crystal Bible" a comprehensive guide to most minerals, stones and crystals.

This is constant. Empower yourself. You are not a victim, you are a survivor. Focus on your healed self and send energy there. *Create* the life, the healing, the happiness and wellness you seek.

PATTERNS

We all have our habits, some, we know are not good for us. Still, many times those are the ones we most stubbornly refuse to give up. How can our life change, if we refuse to change? What patterns are you repeating in your life? We are empowered with the ability to change what seems to "keep happening" to us through changing internal thought patterns. This requires a deep compassionate acknowledgement of any habitual negative thoughts and emotions. Constant self-criticism, doubt, guilt, fear, insecurity, disappointment, all of these are habits we can change. We are uncovering their root through this work.

Belief is powerful. Believing everyone is out to get you, or that you are just not good enough, creates a world in which others seem to hurt us all the time. Believing people are helpful, kind, and supportive, believing you are enough, creates a world in which we find healing, Love, joy and peace. Look within and do a pulse check. Forgive any negative thoughts and allow yourself to Love yourself better. Release the past, forgive it, and set it free. Allow yourself to be Loved. Be kind in your thoughts, Be gentle with your emotions. Know that you are deeply Loved and that *you are worthy of Love*. Allow yourself to create a better world from within by, simply, changing your habits and patterns.

THE PROCESS

Understand, healing is a *process*. It will not happen immediately, not in a day, or a week. It may take months or, even, years. It has to be an intentional and conscious development. It will happen in your own time. Healing cannot be forced to fit a schedule. You have to understand, it *will* be difficult. There is no way around it. You will need to look at your past and present, you will need to ask yourself some hard questions, and answer with total honesty. You will be uncomfortable. You will feel angry and even scared. You may want to hit something. You may want to

The Self Beyond

cry. This is all natural and healthy, as long as you express it in a productive and not destructive way.

You will know you are doing honest healing if you are *feeling* throughout the process. These feelings must be acknowledged in order to be processed and, ultimately, released. But, you will get better every day, and you will look back a year from now and you will not recognize the person you were to the person you become.

Louise Hay (author and revered visionary of self-healing) reassures that, "the *power is Always within the present moment!"* Good news for us. That means we can do something right now! It is *never* too late to turn your life around and find healing. Remember, this is something only you can do for yourself. Books, teachers, healers, and higher powers may guide and support you, but it is up to us to do the work.

Despite knowing and practicing all of this, do I personally have it all down? Of course not. I still have total meltdowns. Anyone who has overcome trauma will go through breakdowns and struggle through certain days. I believe breaking down is healthy and necessary every so often. To cry is cleansing and when we deny ourselves that, we block up our heart, we banish emotions which cannot be ignored or neglected. I have my down days, my off days, my dark days in which I still feel as if I am totally lost. The difference now is that I use all this (which I am offering to you in this work) to heal myself. I use these very methods and perspective shifts to come back to the center, to come back into my power, and to remember the truth. I don't just believe in this, I *live* this in my daily life. [63]

We have all had our hearts broken, undergone traumas, losses and great betrayals. These disturbances on our lives are universal, but that does not take away our personal experience of them. The ultimate key to heal every form of suffering is to find our way back to self-Love. For me, a broken heart became a theme in my life. I was not loving myself as I should have. I have come back from the abyss of that wretched place so often that I have

---

[63] For more on deep lasting healing I highly recommend two life changing books, "You Can Heal Your Life" by Louise Hay and "The Secrets of Aboriginal Healing" by Gary Holz- both overcame impossible illness and experienced profound self-healing.

The Self Beyond

unwittingly become an expert. A master of broken hearted healing and the path to Loving myself again.

When you have no choice but to recover from such a pain that is almost indescribable, you bring something back with you. There is a healing to be shared in such a profound wound. Being a way-shower is now part of my life's work. To share the insight, tools, and perspective shifts which have allowed me to heal and overcome. When we can see the unhealed parts of ourselves as messages and lessons, and stop personalizing them as something working against us, we come into a deep understanding that bears even deeper healing.

You have to do pulse checks often. This is not hard to do when you are connected to yourself from within. You can simply commune within yourself and see how you are doing. How can we know how far we have come, or really if we have made any progress? One important way is, simply, how you feel. Do you feel a little better? Despite challenges and obstacles, despite occasional moments of panic, are you now able to find balance, to calm yourself, bring yourself back, and use your self-tools to act as is needed? Do you find yourself in a peaceful state that is capable of accepting and allowing the ups and downs of life's gradual tides? Or, do you find yourself triggered by little things, old issues popping up with the same reaction? It is ok if that is true because *now* you are empowered with a new awareness of this pattern. You have a new insight into your own dynamics and that makes all the difference. These healing insights mean that you no longer have to be held captive to who you were decades ago, or even yesterday. You can set yourself free.

SOUL CONTRACTS

Understanding soul contracts can greatly support healing from relationships of our past, present and even future. Some may not believe in this, but I introduce it here as a point of consideration. If we can appreciate that we are a soul coming from a conscious place and entering a state of spiritual amnesia upon entry, then, perhaps, we can also accept that on the "other side"

The Self Beyond

we are a part of greater soul groups working together for a common cause. We make cosmic contracts with those we incarnate with, in which we may ask one another to do certain things with, or for us, on earth. These contracts are, generally, meant to act as a catalyst for spiritual growth. They may appear to come in as something negative, such as someone leaving you, but, ultimately, trigger a new path in your life. These can also be positive triggers, such as coming into your life as a Loving and supportive presence that signals you to activate and move to the next level in your life.

These soul contracts can exist between families in which certain karmas need to be amended, for instance. Sometimes it is not that we had anything to do with that karma, but we incarnate into that family in order to help restore the karma which has not been healed for many cycles. (Acting as a Light bringer into the dark chain of abuse, for instance). Sometimes we are healing karma from many past lives in which we shared relationships with those we are still connected to in this life. There are soul contracts with lovers, friends, people we work with, teachers, employees, bosses, and even strangers.

When we say, "soul mate," we often ascribe this term to be defined as the ultimate romantic companion. But, the truth is we have many soul mates throughout our lives. A true soul mate is anyone who sparks something within your soul. This can be someone who hurts you, or someone who helps you. We have made these deals with one another before physical form was ever taken on. We do this to evolve and awaken according to what our soul planned before coming in.

Understand that from the octave of Spirit, time does not exist. So you can "go in" at the same "moment," but end up decades apart, miles apart, or, even, worlds apart. Yet we find one another. We cross paths. We agree before entry on these goals, based on what we need to learn, and what challenges we wanted to face and overcome. It may be hard to accept that we choose these things, but some of us were highly ambitious and set ourselves up with lots of hearty challenges to work through in our lives, all in order to reach our higher evolutionary goals and help others on earth.

What this means, is that through these soul contracts we are working together for our pre-decided outcome. This does not mean you cannot break the contract and change your mind. We have free will.

To close a contract with someone, all you need to do is say (out loud or inwardly), "I no longer wish to be in contract with you at a soul level." This would be something you might decide if someone has been particularly damaging to you and you feel you cannot handle any more. You can "cut the cord," so to speak, and cancel the deal. All you have to do is intend to. Always do this with Love and send the other Light as you release them.

The understanding of soul contracts can, perhaps, add a bit of perspective into the people and events in our lives which appear to be negative. It helps us place the focus on ourselves to reflect upon what it is we planned to learn from the experience or relationship. We chose our parents knowing the challenges we would face, however, so many of us had no idea it would be so hard. We chose our journey and the benchmark obstacles we would face in our lives, specifically, for what we hoped to accomplish in transmuting these traumas into Light and Love. We agreed to have a deep amnesia so that we could find our way back into total recall and Love.

OLD AND NEW SOULS

For a long time, many have described those with a kind of wisdom beyond their outward age as "old souls." Many religions and spiritualties have believed in a form of reincarnation throughout the ages. This can, both, describe the actual physical energy, which continually cycles from death into rebirth, or the spiritual "death" and rebirth. For countless epochs of time on earth, numerous people believe, souls reincarnate many times to amend karmas of past lifetimes or failure to become self-actualized as Conscious Beings in the previous lifetime. These souls would be a true "old soul," having come up from the times of Jesus, from medieval times, even from the times of ancient Egypt or legendary Atlantis. When people undergo past life regression, they are often able to retrieve these soul memories which can help explain the root of a chronic illness, or patterns in their life where other explanations have failed.

I have long researched the lineage of the soul and the many chapters of human history which *greatly predates* what our

The Self Beyond

current history teaches. I stumbled upon an interesting theme in the work of Dolores Cannon. Dolores developed a method of hypnosis called somnambulistic hypnosis, or QHHT (quantum healing hypnosis therapy). It is a revolutionary hypnosis technique which can cut through the layers of superficial consciousness and make contact directly with the subconscious.

While reading her book, "The Convoluted Universe," I was astounded at the testimonies of people who would, not only, describe in vivid detail their past earth lives, but many would also describe life on other planets, with other beings, and even as being something as obscure as water or some form of landscape in another star system. Some described being an actual star and the blissful sensation of total Love and tranquility they felt as they floated within that space. (If you are doubting this, that is ok. Please understand many souls resonate deeply with this who need this information to heal and remember).

Over her many decades of work, Dolores began to find, some individuals while under QHHT would explain they were not from here. They had not reincarnated the same way many on earth did for so long. They were "new souls" who volunteered to come to earth now, during this important transitional time period.[64] These new souls of Light (incarnating in greater and greater frequency waves to offset the darkness that is seeking to dominate the earth) are coming from other star systems, from higher dimensions (beyond the physical), and even directly from Source.

Some new souls, during QHHT sessions Dolores recorded, described existing as a "shimmering"—as a literal Light prior to this human incarnation (among many other things). They came in to assist raising the vibration on the planet back into Love and to aid in the Ascension process for all beings. They are qualified to do this, having recently been at the highest frequency of Love and Light. Some have a job of, simply, existing, and even though they may feel an aversion to social situations, they are meant to partake, because just by their energy, they catalyze a higher vibration for all those they encounter. Some are here with more rigorous missions to actively initiate change. No mission is of higher or lower value. All of us are meant to do our part.

---

[64] For more on this, check out the book "The Three Waves of Volunteers and the New Earth" by Dolores Cannon

Coming from Source, or a place of pure Light and Love and making a quantum leap into the heavy, dense, and unforgiving climate of this three dimensional world is an incredibly difficult transition. Many of us have felt this from birth; a kind of home sickness, a longing we cannot quite describe. We have great difficulty understanding the way of human behavior; the violence humans do to one another, the harm humans inflict upon others and themselves. The disconnection from the Source and the Light from within is hard to comprehend. For some it is all too much to bear. Some of the new souls want to tap out as soon as they become a young adult. But, many Brave Ones, the Light Warriors, have risen to this challenge, driven by the imperative of their soul mission.

To the new souls and old, please know you are not alone. You are heroes. You knew the risks and the trials to be faced, yet, *you chose (and choose) to be here now*. You are making history. You are doing something legendary that will be talked about across galaxies throughout time; from across the Universe, from others in higher dimensions, from your star groups who have not incarnated, and your soul family. They are exclaiming with great reverence, "We are watching you in awe!" The linear and pragmatic *you* may not understand this concept, but there are many more levels of life beyond this. Those higher soul sources beyond have expressed, "We are always supporting you, always sending you Light, great Love, and assistance for your journey." Know that you will be welcomed Home as a champion in Victory, having faced the hardest test in being human.

The spectrum of experience available on earth is like no other in the many billions of galaxies. We experience tremendous highs and deep dark lows. That is why, what we are each doing here is so exceptional. We are changing the timelines. We are raising the vibration. *We* are the revolution of humankind.

THE SIZE OF THE SOUL

The soul does not always incarnate in merely one body. This may blow your mind. The soul is much more vast than we fathom. Sometimes it will incarnate in multiple bodies in different places and even time periods across the physical world. The soul, also, never completely incarnates into physical form. A portion remains in the higher echelons for us to tap into as our Higher Self. It is like putting one foot in the water, while the body stays above the pool.

We may or may not connect with the "other" pieces of our soul while we are here, but I think it is important to be aware of this deeper truth. We are connected at a soul level. Perhaps it can provide context to those times when you meet someone who you feel like you, just, know. Who you feel an other-worldly connection to, or who you see yourself in. They may well be another "you" or a member of your soul group.

SOUL PURPOSE

Finding your soul purpose can enrich your life with meaning, new focus, and inspiration. Some may be well aware of what their highest reason for being is already, and for those that are actively following that divine calling, *I commend you*. It takes clarity, bravery, and selfless dedication to do this kind of soul work. However, defining that soul purpose can be elusive to many people.

Soul purpose is your calling. It is what you are here to do or be. Some may be called to simply share Love (which is no small task). Some may be called to protect the earth. Some may be called to carry their Light into dark places, to hold a higher energy wherever they go. Some may be called to take political or social action. Some may be called to use their art or their voice to affect many others. Some may be called to use music or writing. Some may be called to be good parents and raise conscious children. There is no lesser calling. There is only the higher calling of your soul purpose.

I searched for my purpose for two decades. From the time I became conscious I wanted to know, why am I here? What am I meant to do? I knew there must be a reason. I, literally, threw my arms up to the sky many times and begged for some kind of direction. I committed to my own higher power that I would do *anything*. I just needed to know what it was. For me, this most sincere request was made for a very long time before it was answered. I found my purpose by allowing myself to receive it without trying to make it what I wanted it to be. Then when it started to unfold, I got out of the way and let it flow through me. It became something bigger than I am.

I strongly feel every one of us has a soul mission, something we are meant to accomplish, bring, share, or even change while we are in our earthly form. To find out what your soul purpose is, you can simply ask yourself the right questions. What makes you come alive? What is your particular skill or talent? Out of those answers, then ask the most important question: what can make both you *and* the world a little better and a little brighter? Meditate on this. Pray on this. No one can tell you your purpose. Only you can find it from within.

What should happen, is that you will (eventually) have an inner knowing emerge, a calling within you that says, "I am the reason you are here." For me, I tried to make that soul reason be many things it was not. I tried to be a musician and envisioned myself playing make shift stages and little coffee shops singing my heart out with poetry and evoking soulful reactions from my audience. That is what I wanted it to be, but it just did not truly affect as many people as I hoped it would. Ultimately, that purpose did not make the most effective use of my most important talents. You may find it to be the same for you. It is not what you want to be, it will be what you *are*.

We cannot will our purpose into being something we want to gratify ego. We can only allow Spirit to work through us using the divine gifts we have already. Understand, here, this is also where the many hardships you struggled through in life can be a part of those gifts and that purpose. Perhaps you may be meant to speak to great groups of people and inspire them in navigating through similar difficult circumstances, for example.

If you believe you may have your answer, begin to put it into action. For instance, if you feel called to write, begin writing. There is no wrong place to start. See if it is something that comes naturally to you. I will tell you a trick on how to know if it is right. You will know it is right, if it is something you *can't* not do. That is the core of your soul mission—the gift that you couldn't stop using if you tried.

Our soul purpose isn't what we do, it is who we are. We cannot force ourselves to be someone or something we are not. You are already exactly who you need to be for your own highest purpose. Your highest soul truth is in you right now. That doesn't mean it will be easy. There will be trial and error. Be ready for those tests. Sometimes you may face disappointment and self-doubt. But know that you are not alone in your mission, and when you are truly aligned with your soul path, many things will fall into place, as if you are divinely guided and supported (because guess what—you are)!

THE DEPTH

Had it not been for the depth of the troubles we faced, the losses, the heart breaks, even the violence we escaped, we would not have found just how deep we go, just how strong we are. We look so often at what we lost, at how it damaged us. But, look for a moment in a new way. Look at what you have gained. Look at what you have learned. Look at how very healed you already are. We have the capacity to share this profound and life-changing wisdom. We have risen from ashes, from flames that could have devoured us, only to transform like a phoenix and rise from the fire, like seeds dropped in darkness and buried, emerging to bloom and blossom among the world of Light.

Did you know a baby will fall an average of 240-280 times before they successfully take their first steps? From birth we knew we would fall many times. We were born with the will to get up and try again, as many times as it takes. There is nothing in us as toddlers to tell us to stop. We only know we want to stand up, and we do.

It is through the darkness and pressure that the diamond is formed. It is through inner and outer forces pulling and pushing with magnificent power until near total collapse that forms a star. Depth is a gift in a world of shallow interferences all blocking us from the jewel and the Light hidden within. Finding deep meaning in a world that has lost sight of any real purpose, can only be achieved by one who has marched through the furrows of struggle.

Had it not been for all my broken hearts, or the many challenges I faced, I would have *never* gained the insight to do my life's work. Every terrible and wonderful event in my life put me on this path, my path, just as yours is doing for you. I cherish the awful things that have happened, not because they have made me tougher or stronger. For me, I have become much more sensitive and I embrace that. This sensitivity gives me a tool to facilitate healing, to reach another in their darkest depth because I know it. I have sat there. I know that darkness too. I carved my name on its cavernous walls. We do not respect wisdom coming from someone who has not overcome trouble, just as we do not take diet advice from someone who has never struggled with their weight.

      Who would we be without this kind of depth and dimension? What more would we take for granted without having struggled to earn this healing? *Honor your struggle.* Pay homage to your wounds. Hold the path behind you as part of your sacred healing Journey. We are here now. Look how very far you have come. Take a moment. Celebrate this truth. You are already a Victor! You are a Star! You are rich with the depth and the wisdom of your experience. Having healed yourself, having saved *yourself*, you are revived. With this new strength and compassion, we are ready to go be healers in the world.

Chapter 5: Opening the Heart

LOVE IS

When they ask me what I followed, I hope to honestly say, "My heart." In this context, I do not mean the often fickle and fragile emotions that are embedded together with the confusion of human psychosis which so often misguides us. What I mean, here, is the constant, eternal core of harmonic presence: the ethereal state of the heart, which is Love.

We put so much weight on the semantics. We assign superficial meaning to words we hardly understand. We can only understand meaning as deeply as we understand ourselves. We say, "Love" so often, but rarely touch upon what it really means. We say, "I love that sweater," "I love it when you kiss me," "I love pizza." That kind of love speaks of addiction, carnal desire, and avarice. When the word Love has been so often entangled together in this context, it is no wonder we are so confused. It is no wonder so many people mistreat another in the name of "love."

Words can be multilayered, retaining a much deeper and, even, spiritual value to them. "Heart" doesn't mean the biological muscle that pumps blood, or even just the place from which we experience our feelings, but the center of our highest self, the Heart of our higher being which is in a constant state of perfect and infinite Love.

Love is the connection we share. Love is the greatest healer. Love is more powerful than all the weapons on earth combined! Love is the greatest tool of transformation. Love is within each of us. Love is what we come from, what we are born of, and return to. You do not need to learn to Love, only remember what we sometimes forget—Love is the map, the compass and the Way. Love is the highest truth. Love is all around you. Just look within. Anytime you feel unsure of what to do, know that Love is the answer to every question.

IN RELATION

Though this book is intended (mainly) to focus on you and your relationship with yourself, I would be remiss to not touch upon the importance of our relationships with others. Love can *not* only be experienced as an independent force or isolated state of Being. The shared Love that flows through us is there for a reason: to allow us to, also, connect with, and Love, another. To Love another as an extension of oneself, as a reflection and as a conduit of the same sacred energy in all things, takes *practice*. It takes devotion. It takes patience, and it takes a solid foundation built on the relationship you have already cultivated within yourself.

Relationships are hard. So many of us struggle to understand ourselves, let alone, another. Relationships with ourselves are one thing, but to extend the kind of unconditional Loving compassion we offer ourselves, to others, can test us greatly. The good news is, if we can unconditionally Love and accept ourselves (as we are) then we are more than half way there!

Humans are a species that need relationships and a strong network of shared support. We require the bonds of affection, comradery, connection, and community. It is essential that we have solid links to others in our lives to stay healthy physically, mentally, and emotionally. We are not meant to live in seclusion, not all the time.

Some species do not need that kind of communal connection. Some creatures in the animal kingdom, for instance, spend their lives in solitude and only contact another to procreate or fight for their life. Imagine how humanity would look living that way (as we do sometimes appear). Many other species of animals however, like wolves, lions, dolphins, elephants, buffalo, etc. rely on their herd. Without the pack, the tribe, the family, these animals would not survive. Their strength is in their group. It is instinctual for them to form these communities. While, we do not need other people to survive per se, we need others to maintain psychological and physiological wellbeing.

The oldest continual society on earth, the tribe of Aborigines in Australia, model this kind of communal living. Small, connected communities where all contribute and all benefit. No one is left out. No one is forgotten. This kind of tribal society has often been looked on as primitive. Though, when reviewing the failures of modern society, which has allowed for widespread poverty, imbalance, and an overgrowth of greed and violence toward others, we may appreciate the benefits of this type of community provides.

Eco-communities are popping up across the world, and many seek to return to this original way of life. They are focusing on permaculture and sustainability, growing their own food and taking care of the community as a whole, instead of individuals competing separately. This kind of structure thrives and is maintainable. It benefits the ecosystems, it benefits the children and the elderly, and people find they are happier and healthier, as well.

The Aborigines were (and those remaining still are) attuned with the earth energies, the land, and their community. They have no word to express ownership (imagine that), everything is communal and shared. They live for the community, for each other. They are capable of going into what they call "dreamtime" (which is, essentially, the secondary consciousness we discussed earlier). Through this deep connection, they share each other's experiences. They exist within this dimension and the higher realms simultaneously. They have never lost sight of the intimate relationship we all share. Rome has fallen, our modern systems are rotting away at their corrupt foundations after a few mere centuries, yet the tribe of Aborigines have endured for over 60,000 years.

LIMBIC RESONANCE

We have been endowed with the capacity to, not only, care for others, but actually *feel* for others. When someone we Love is hurting, we *feel* their pain. We feel another's heartache when we are connected to them and it causes our own heart to ache. We actually *share* in these deep emotional states, not just emotionally or mentally, but physiologically. Our hearts beat faster when we share in the excitement of someone we are close with. Our breathing changes when we wait with someone we care for deeply to get news they are anticipating. We even have the ability to transmit these emotional reflections, this limbic resonance, to and from another without speaking a word. We can simply look in their eyes and know. This is nothing that needs to be proven by science. Each of us has already experienced this in action. This is not mere coincidence. This is the evidence of a deep shared conscious connection humans innately possess.

We can read joy, pain, sadness, passion, anxiety, and fear without the transmitting party moving a muscle. We are capable of sending and receiving these messages that go beyond direct verbalization. Even the more subtle nuances of what we are feeling can be relayed, such as an aversion towards something or someone, an energy which noticeably shifts within our counterparts. All of this demonstrates an association that goes much deeper than we may realize.

MISUSED CONNECTION

I often observe people making their own messes in their relationships, whether that is with a family member, a lover or spouse, a friend or, even, a stranger. What happens here is very simple, no matter the situation, people get into all kinds of trouble when they go into ego. We go into ego by allowing another's actions or inactions to wound us. We go into ego when we can list out the ways another has "wronged us." We go into ego when we think we have been disrespected. Consider how this is true. What is ego? It is the individualized representation of self. What happens when that layer dissolves? We come out of that lower level of awareness and recognize ourselves in the "other." We

The Self Beyond

behave, and perceive reality, very differently when coming from the place *beyond the ego*.

We can review all personal situations to verify the presence of an ego sabotage. If you have recently felt resentful, blameful, or angry toward another ask yourself where that feeling came from; a sense of being attacked, a sense of not feeling recognized, a sense of being harmed in a way that must be acknowledged for what it has done to you perhaps? Can you see how all of these feelings, the many branches of their manifestation, all come from the root of ego? What if there is no you in the fierce sense we so often defend, but instead a seamless *us*, which only hurts or heals?

What are we doing when we come from ego? We are allowing our ego to cash in on our life at the expense of our happiness. The only way to rein in the ego, is to recognize when it is present. This can disempower anything it wants to sell you, or get you all riled up about. It works the same way as when you realize someone has been lying to you. Now, whatever they say, you will question. They will not have the same power to manipulate you they once did. You can no longer be a victim to them. Now you see from a greater perspective. In this same way, the ego cannot control you when you see it for what it is.

I would like to go into one of the most common issues we each have likely experienced for a short bit. I am going out on a limb to assume most readers have experienced some version of Love and relationship. Here, I am talking about romantic Love (for lack of a better term). Falling is easy. It is coming back up that gets so many of us. Romance is one of the most misused connections we form with another. People are physically intimate all the time, but rarely emotionally intimate. Many people have not yet done the right work within themselves to be emotionally capable of truly Loving another. That is because so very many of us are unhealed, and therefore we are often projecting nearly every deep wound on another. Add in another unhealed person unconsciously doing this, as well, and you've got a recipe for disaster. This goes both ways, making us both perpetrators and victims, though, we know that we are not meant to be either of those things. I hope to provide some insight on the way a healed and whole individual connects in romantic Love.

Romantic relationships move in a cycles. There are five levels in general: going up, coming down, the "in between," endings (which is where so many gets stuck), and new beginnings. When a relationship ends, it is important to consider the, often, overlooked healing process which, when neglected, can lead right back into the same patterns experienced in previous relationships. That is why it is important to do your best to identify the lessons and how you are directly connected to the outcomes in any relationship. That is the fertile ground for some of our deepest self-realization and growth work.

To make a disclaimer: many of us have had heart wrenchingly awful relationships at some point. Many of us would prefer a good swift kick to the head than repeat them. Understand, all that whole crazy story was really about is what you need to heal within you. That is it. Whatever issues came up, whatever triggers were unveiled, don't make it personal, they simply showed you (in a highly interactive way) just exactly what those issues were. That is the point. The mirror of another can show us what we need to see within our self.

Going up is the good part. We say "falling in Love" which is an accurate description in many cases. Though, true Love does not "fall:" it *rises*. We will talk about that more in a bit. For now, I want to focus on what most people accomplish in our earlier relationships, which is a type of compulsory codependence, and an addiction to the feeling someone gives us. We, literally, act like drug addicts when we "fall in Love." In fact, the same areas of the brain responsible for pleasure and reward, light up in someone "in love" as in someone on cocaine. The worst part is, even after the fact, after losing and suffering to near self-destruction, many would do it again. Love becomes a high, a drug, a new form of escapism, for so many. The Love of another becomes a substitute for the Love we must find within ourselves.

The story which follows is a varying version of this basic template: our eyes met, we felt drawn to each other, we just knew in a moment, the first time we touched, we fell in "love." They said the right things, did the right things, and made you feel all the right things. The next few weeks or months may feel like a waking dream, filled with blissful abandonment beyond all sense of reason. As you explore one another, every moment is timeless; every touch, every kiss is out of this world. The mention of their name causes your heart to skip a beat. Their voice, in all its sweet intoxicating glory, elicits nothing less than a swell of dopamine akin to ecstasy. We are so enchanted, we cannot see beyond our own self-indulgence. We are living in a bubble which will eventually burst if not based on the right substance.

Coming down is the crash back to reality. It happens suddenly (and we are always surprised). After the weeks or months of a purely ecstatic (though often blindly delusional) vacation in paradise we realize: we don't really know this person. They now say the wrong things, do the wrong things, and make you feel all the wrong things. Some may invite this phase on purpose, whether consciously or not. Many people will self-sabotage reflexively because they are scared to open up and be hurt.

Maybe it begins as a little event which causes us to wonder if the charm we had perceived is really them. Often, the issue is, we have placed this person on a pedestal of some sort. We believed them to be the embodiment of everything we identify with, desire, and believe in. This sets a standard which no one could possibly live up to. We don't do this on purpose. It is subconscious. So, then, it is literally only a matter of time until the self-made aberration dissolves into a state of questioning motives, trespassing morals, power struggles and more. Pause here for a moment to consider what this reflection shows us about ourselves.

During this time period, we may feel shocked, disillusioned, destabilized, or disempowered, the opposite of the alluring sparkle and fluttering heart rushes in the beginning. Where there was once fullness, there is an empty hole. That hole only seems to grow as days go on. The root of the issue is generally this: we believed this person to be an idealized version of who they truly are. We did not fall in Love with their actuality, but the projection of who we wanted them to be (and who we wanted ourselves to be). This created unmet expectations. This allowed for unfulfilled wishes and, inevitable, disappointment. Everything we once cherished in them has a dark side, and now the very things we Loved, are the things that have become intolerable. Their seeming strength becomes hard headedness. Their seeming sensitivity becomes emotional instability. Their seeming depth becomes taking things too far. The root is always some manifestation of us not Loving ourselves better.

The Self Beyond

The "in between" is exactly what it sounds like, a kind of limbo place. Some relationships end nearly immediately after the "going up" phase fades, yet, some are able to overcome the deluge of the "coming down" period. Instead of coming completely down, this phase settles into a cool down. This is the result of commitment of both people, and usually a lot of conversations and compromises. It is a benchmark to make it to this in between point. It is here the next phase is decided, whether that will lead to an ending, or a lasting Love. This greatly depends on multiple factors. Are both parties emotionally mature enough to have an adult relationship? Are both people willing to accept all sides of the other? Are both people already whole and complete within themselves without seeking that wholeness (through power struggles or other devious manipulations) from their partner?

Endings are, for some, the best option from this point. Sometimes, this is the healthiest choice to make. When you have two damaged and disconnected people, they will only hurt one another, or form a mutually self-destructive codependence. We cannot build a stable foundation with broken pieces.

Some couples may find they are simply not compatible, and it is a mark of maturity to recognize that. We cannot be compatible with *anyone* if we are not compatible, first, with the wholeness of our self. After establishing a healthy relationship with ourselves, we will only be compatible with others who are also equally healed and whole within themselves. This is a rarity (which is why books like this are so necessary).

The crisis we see in ourselves is the major crisis of every relationship, and translates into the greater crisis of the world; we are not sufficiently self-aware and we are not Loving ourselves enough. We are not connected to ourselves in the way that is required to receive another's authentic self without projections, expectations, games, or idealizations. Do not feel discouraged on this point. Knowing where we need healing is the way that we heal something. We cannot go beyond this root issue until we go beyond it within ourselves.

To be a Lover, we have to first be a Lover of ourselves. To have emotional awareness, we must first have it within ourselves. To be a friend, we must first be a friend to ourselves. To have a healthy relationship, we must first be healed. Until we

The Self Beyond

are healed and whole within, we are best off working on the most important relationship, which is with ourselves.

New beginnings can be both frightening and exhilarating, especially when ending a longtime relationship in which we may have lost our individual identity. Rediscovering yourself can be one of the high points of your life, if you allow it to be. When you are newly emancipated, figuring out what you want to do, for you, can be challenging. I recommend following your passions; things you loved before the relationship, things you had wanted to do or try but felt you "couldn't" because of your partner. Finally taking the reins and indulging yourself in what makes *you* happy can be wholly cathartic. Don't be afraid to do things alone. Embrace your newfound freedom! Let it be a time of healing through self-discovery.

There is far too much pressure society places on us to pair up. There is a stigma that we need to be in a romantic relationship in order to be truly validated as a person. The truth is, many people are much happier, living fuller lives, pursuing dreams they would have never dared to, things they would have been restricted from, by focusing on the relationship with themselves. Don't rush it, take all the time you need for you. It is okay to Love yourself first, and from there, the skies the limit.

BREAK OPEN

> *"Your heart has to keep breaking until it opens."* ~Rumi

Getting over heartbreak is one of the hardest things we are faced with in life. Heartbreak comes from many circumstances. Usually from "losing" someone we dearly love, whether by choice or not. I want to interject here that Love, True Love, cannot be lost. It can never be severed, separated, damaged or diminished. Love is the very core and ground of your Being. Every fiber, every cell, every molecule of your existence is imbued with a Love so grand that should you ever truly perceive the enormity of it, your earthly form would shatter and you would go supernova.

Still, most of us have had our hearts broken at one time or another. How did we survive? Often sloppily, clawing our way back up from the ravine which for some can take weeks, months, or even years. But we do it. We start again. Recalling exactly how is like recalling how you, somehow, made it into your bed with all your clothes still on after a particularly drunken night. We are in survival mode, and that is tough to map, should we need to draw from those tools of wit and will once again.

I want to sidetrack for a moment and tell you a small sliver of my own story in Love. As I explained, my first relationship was not good and set the stage for problems over many years which followed. I did not yet Love myself or know what Love really was. I had not healed from the trauma of my childhood.

My first partner was sweet and kind in the beginning, then abusive and possessive for the better part of three years. She had isolated me from nearly everyone. I had been cut off from my family. I was just so naïve and did not know how to leave. When she cheated on me, I ran from that relationship the way someone would run from a captor, thankful for my freedom, but unsure of how to survive on my own. I figured it out piece by piece, like we all do when we are in a sink or swim situation. But after that kind of damage, without proper healing, I was doomed to repeat a very harsh and particularly interactive lesson over the next decade and a half following.

My first real Love came much more intentionally. We had (and to this day maintain) a kind of soul connection. I Loved her in innocence, the way a little kid Loves their best friend. We had fun together, the kind of fun you have where you don't need to be doing anything to have it. But, after nearly a year together, she said that she was pregnant and I knew it was not mine (queue drums and cymbal) and it crushed me. Being still young and resilient, I picked myself up and believed that somewhere, someone would Love me like I deserved. I went back out into Love the way a deer crosses a highway, timid but trusting, and never thinking that there are, actually, people who don't care, and they will hit you.

The next few years were a series of relationships which mainly ended in further heartbreak. The two most significant being the woman I felt I did not deserve (and who agreed with me), and the woman who proposed to me, and a few days later said she wanted to be with a man instead. The former was my deepest heartbreak during that time period. It took me nearly five years to stop wishing we were together again. I picked her wildflowers and left them on her windowsill for months the

The Self Beyond

summer we parted. I Loved her even after I came home early one night to the apartment we still shared (about two weeks after our breakup) to find a man in my bed with her. She had many reasons to doubt me and I don't blame her, in any way. To this day, I understand her heart and it helped me understand my own more deeply. I recognize my part in allowing these relationships to be what they were. No one forced me. I chose them. I had to learn this lesson so I could someday be ready to help others.

I moved to Rochester NY at the end of 2004 and met someone a few months later. We were in a relationship for over three years, yet, something was missing. How can someone Love you if you are not in Love with yourself? I Loved her with what I had, which was a beautiful artful Love, however I was still so undeveloped. She made me want to be better than I was (which was good for me in some ways), yet, I was never quite good enough. She announced multiple times that a break up was well overdue, only to retract that opinion a few days later. It became a rollercoaster. *Every* time I thought she meant it. Every time I fought for us to stay together. Finally, around the tenth occurrence of this pattern I decided the next time it happens, I will let it happen and walk away. It was the thirteenth time before I finally agreed with her. I remember going to a bar the next day, broken, lost, feeling like I was *done*, done with love, done with romance, done with being hurt. Of course, that is when a particularly charismatic and alluring woman approached me.

This new woman and I entered into a deeply emotional and physical relationship and I felt closer to her in a few months than I had to my recently departed partner in the full three years. She told me I was the Love of her life and I believed her. I thought *this* is what Love should be like. It was not long before a few peculiar events led to the discovery that she had been, in fact, sleeping with someone else for many weeks while we were together. This *destroyed* me. We had such a deep emotional connection that my heart could barely handle it. I felt this pain like nothing before it. This particular heartbreak was, not so much, about the length of time to recover, it was about the intensity of the pain. I felt like something had been taken from me. Though, now many years later, in reflection, I recognize it was the very thing I had denied myself.

The Self Beyond

The only thing that saved me from an ever deepening plunge into existential darkness was a chance event, a music festival, which somehow reminded me of everything I had forgotten. I had forgotten my connection with everything. I had lost the part of me that celebrated the Love and happiness available from within me. I began to remember that everything happens for a reason and after weeks of waking up and going to bed sobbing, in a 24 hour time period, I turned my entire perception around and never looked back.

Over the next few years, I had several other relationships. I had entered a time of truly questioning what "Love" was. Was it the passionate chemistry that is felt in the first few moments, or the slowly built foundation of trust? I wanted to give the latter a chance but, ultimately, found that after a year and a half, despite how amazing she treated me, I was still not in Love. What was wrong? I wasn't ready. Someone once said, "Everything is chemistry and timing, but the timing's a bitch."

I spent the year following that relationship alone. I didn't want to hurt anyone (or myself) anymore. I spent it working on healing myself and trying to get a handle on repeated themes in my past relationships. It was a difficult time, but, I felt I grew from it all. After this sojourn from Love (and period of self-reflection), I felt refreshed and ready to Love again. I took a chance on myself, feeling some semblance of confidence reemerge within me and got back "out there." This did not go well *at all*.

I had a wonderfully tragic few months with a lover who left me by texting me four hours before I went into surgery. She made sure I did not even get to see her face again for over a month. That was an awful experience, to be left when I felt the most vulnerable. I did my best to recover quickly but couldn't help but fault myself. It was the same pattern that had emerged, despite the work I had done on myself.

That summer, while attending a friend's wedding in Hunter Mountain (Catskills, NY), I had some time between the ceremony ending and the reception dinner. We were in a beautiful lodge resort and it was the peak of summer, with a blue sky and billowing clouds. I decided I would get a little bottle of vodka and go meet cute girls at the pool (I was still young enough to fancy drinking at leisure). There were no cute girls at the pool. There were old wrinkled people spritzing (which was not the same). I

The Self Beyond

still drank my little bottle and headed inside to get cleaned up and dressed for the dinner. As I walked in, I crossed paths with a few old friends and their group as they were checking in. I could not but notice the most gorgeous creature I had ever laid eyes on, and due to my enormously diminished inhibitions, I walked right up to her and introduced myself. She was somewhat charmed by this approach.

At dinner we ended up at the same table and I could not take my eyes off of her. I couldn't help but notice she kept staring at me, too, with a kind of intrigued gaze. After dinner as fireworks went off and music played, I had a chance to talk with her. There was a tangible gravitational pull between us. Something I had never experienced before. She was entrancing, elusive, and magical. I was captivated the way an astronaut might be upon entry into space. When she spoke, she spoke with eloquence, her words were poetry to ears that had heard so many cruel and careless things in my life. I could not deny myself, we ended up in an inescapable affair. We had plans to be together, to live together. We shared so many things in common. She had me, from the moment we met, she held every part of me and I had nothing within me that could have repudiated it. I had never been in Love this way, prior to that.

There was a problem though, a very big one. She had a boyfriend who she had explained she was leaving. She was not in Love with him (and saying this, now I understand just how naïve it was of me to believe it, along with how unfair it was of me to have engaged in this before that had occurred). After a very intimate weekend just a few days prior, she called me crying and said she could not talk to me anymore. I could hear him yelling in the background and it was an awful moment that stretched out in its tormenting replay for months after. A million questions filled my mind. Did she Love me? Did she lie? Did he make her feel ashamed? Nearly a month and a half later she called me. With a sing songy voice, she explained everything was fine. She could handle him, and she decided to stay with him. This was a moment in my life which I experienced something that I can only describe as emotionally cracking.

I tell this particular story with such detail to express several things; that I am a regular person, I have made huge mistakes, I have repaid my karma for them, and then some, over these many long years. I understand that karma is not so much about having bad things happen to you because you do bad things, but more about having bad things happen to you until you learn you are the one responsible for them, that you are the one creating the need for these lessons. After that experience, something in me snapped. It was a catalyst for the next phase of my life—rebuilding and healing.

I began to write my first book. I feverishly poured hours a day into it until it was ready. It took me three years. I felt changed through that process. I found my voice. I found my purpose. While in the midst of my newfound revolution, I made a few more attempts at relationships which did not work out. My theme continued to be one of abandonment.

I attempted a relationship which I trusted slowly, but surely. I truly tried to do everything right. I checked all the proactive emotional boxes. Still, once my trust was gained, the illusions I had taken all efforts to protect myself from, once again, shattered. My new partner had hidden some very toxic aspects of her unhealed self from me, which all were inevitably apparent after dozens of depleting arguments she instigated. I tried to stick it out, and fooled myself that I could help her heal. But, I was (again) left a few days after another surgery before my first book was published. I, again, took a break from Love and *again* made my best attempt at healing, yet another broken heart.

If you are getting tired of this story, so was I. After yet a few more cycles of love and despair, finally, I stopped myself. It always turned out some variation of the same patterns. I fell in love again each time, but every time my heart would get broken. Every time, it became harder to put myself back together. So I, finally, summoned up the courage to be truly alone.

In my solitude, I felt very successful in beginning to identify some of my biggest issues. I realized I was continually involved with partners who I viewed as strong, but failed to recognize they were emotionally unavailable. I then realized that I was unintentionally pairing myself with partners who could do nothing, but devastate me. I was not seeing who they were. I was seeing who *I* was. I expected them to be kind and Loving because I was kind and Loving. Realizing this helped me to pierce my own bubble. This allowed me to begin see with a more objective

The Self Beyond

insight. It was not a problem of them not loving me, I was not Loving myself enough. That was my biggest problem.

I was finally able to recognize this and change my pattern, therefore disempowering its hold on me. As I Loved myself more and more, anyone who did not have a deep connection within themselves became less attractive to me. Where I used to feel drawn, I felt repelled. I began to realize if someone is reckless and careless with themselves, just imagine what they would do to me. It was a strange and empowering time. I began to feel as though I was standing on a mountain, and anyone I met, I could see from birds eye view. All the potential threats they held to themselves, and inevitably me if I became involved, were clear. I finally found the willpower to respect myself. I knew my heart, like every heart, is Gold. I began to feel that the only one who would care for it the way I deserved was me.

I spent two full years of sincere and dedicated focus on Loving and bettering myself, on being whole within myself and ending the cycle of breaking my own heart. Then the test came… a bright Light shined on my life. She found me by my words which she said led her to me. I did not feel the immediate attraction I had associated with passionate Love for so long. But, I had long since abandoned that kind of false attraction. Instead, I felt a strong *reverence* for her being, I felt a mirror held up to me that reflected what I most Loved and looked to cultivate within myself. We entered into a long and deep "conversation," one which would inextricably alter the course of my world and my work.

I don't think I knew how very much I Loved her until I heard her voice. It is worth explaining, she lived 10,000 miles away in Portugal while I live in New York State. We had the entire Atlantic Ocean between us. Yet, I could feel her energy as if right beside me. When I first heard her voice, it was like listening to the most beautiful Zen master speak, like a meditation, in itself. It moved me to my very foundation. My heart felt illuminated, activated, and draped in the presence of her Being.

We shared nearly every aspect of ourselves with one another; our pasts, our dreams, our understanding of the universe. She spoke to me in philosophical poetry, the language of Light that resonated from the Deep Magic and beauty of all things. We talked for hours, days and weeks about Love, consciousness, reality, illusion, dreams, the cosmos and every magnificent

The Self Beyond

subject that made my mind expand infinitely. We shared dreams and, even, astral travelled together. A mystical and truly sacred testament to the spirit's ability to transcend time, space, and everything which we suppose separates us from each other. We were 10,000 miles apart, yet I could feel her right beside me. We seemed to awaken something within one another, amplifying the energy we already possessed, as if someone turned up the volume on a radio. We merged as one soul, one energy, one waveform in a sea of particles. It was a soul connection in every sense, *beyond words* and beyond worlds.

Trying to recount exactly how I lost this pinnacle of Love in my life is counterproductive. It took time to understand nothing was truly lost, but perhaps changing forms. What started as two people genuinely coming from a place of conscious mutual self-Love turned, for me, back into my old insecurities. I could not believe they came up, again, after all the work I had done! *I became scared.* Scared to lose her and in one moment, as if the universe had been waiting for my next command, I slowly, then all at once, did. She seemed to disappear like a magic trick, it would have astounded me had it not hurt. She was continuing new levels of her own journey, like a butterfly that does not stay. I knew I could not go where she was going.

At first I felt an otherworldly pain, the ethereal presence which had been so prevalent seemed to disappear. The relinquishing of that bright Light dimmed my world. This ache that obscured all aches before it came from deep inside me and took no respite in the dim hours of my many long nights. This was nearly completely due to the bottomless question of why and how this could be happening to me, *again*.

It is here I would like to explain, I thought very long and hard about sharing my most private grief with the world. All the rejection, betrayal, disbelief, and self-doubt I faced was something hardly anyone knew. I share it now *in trust* that something in my story might touch your own heart, that within it there is a shared connection between me, the author, and you, the reader, to relate in the sense that we all want to be Loved and that none of us want to be judged.

I had been abandoned again… but this time, something remained. I was left with the knowledge of the last piece that would truly heal me. I had healed a part of my recent past which was crucial to moving forward, but I had not healed my deeper past. So one more time, I dredged down into the swamps of my self-reflection to spend *many* uncomfortable and unbearable days reconciling with my own shadow. There, in my grief, I found the last hiding place of my ego, and with nothing else left to give. I put my hands up in the air, in faith and at complete loss, and *surrendered*. To return at last victorious over the only thing I could have ever mastered—myself.

What got me through this last great test was one thought that transposed itself as a glowing layer upon all my inner work. I knew if I could do this again, if I could heal myself completely again, after losing the Love I had sought for my whole life, I knew that I could help others heal too. I hoped that somehow, another lost soul would find healing in my wound. I sought not to eradicate heartbreak from my life, because we cannot promise that to ourselves, but to understand it. To say that we will never let ourselves be hurt again is a lie. We cannot live our lives with a wall around us, we are built to break open. I remembered words I wrote in my first book, the voice of Spirit which came to me and whispered, "*Your heart is not breaking, it is opening. Let it.*"

To heal from someone hurting you, there are many things to continually remind yourself of and come back to. Remember that everyone is doing the best they can. They are on their own journey with their own lessons to learn. Most people are not deliberately hurting other people. If they are, it is due to a deep sickness and disconnection inside of them. It rarely, if ever, has anything to do with you, in any kind of personal way. (Although it certainly feels personal to have your heart broken). It is almost always 100% about them and their reality filters which can only reflect back to them a projection of their own inner state of being. If they are hurting, they will project hurt and that is a double-sided truth, meaning, we are like that too. And sometimes, if you are hurting, you reflect that hurt onto yourself through another, to illuminate the places that still need healing.

Recognize that there is something you are meant to learn from your emotional injuries. *The deeper the wound, the higher the lesson.* There is something that will, ultimately, benefit you, wrapped up in the disguise of unpleasant or even tragic events.

The more quickly you learn what the lesson is and hear the message, the more quickly you will be able to heal and move on. The whole truth is, the healing is about *you*. Rectifying the motives or perceptions of another may be cathartic but you cannot rely on that, or you will risk giving away your power. Closure does not always come. So, it is up to us to go within and look at, not how someone hurt us, but how we allowed ourselves to be hurt. To look at, not how badly someone treated us, or disrespected us, but how we have disrespected ourselves. *That* is the message. That message talks of a needed change within *us*. If you are waiting for the change to happen in the other, you are disempowered. You cannot heal what you have not learned the message of. *You can only heal once your wound has been heard*, and the lesson you needed to learn is embraced.

My intention has not been to map out a way to go from point A to point B with little boxes we can check out on a list. Life does not work like that. *We* do not work like that. My most sincere intention here is to provide practical and meaningful methodology, supportive self-tools, and encouragement for those who are still trudging that long road. To recover from anything, including heartbreak, these tools you are developing, right now, will allow you to connect within, and help you *heal yourself* from the inside out.

There is no spiritual progression, no inner healing, no emotional growth without discomfort. Swelling and all-encompassing discomfort that lasts for lengths of time and to such a degree that it may make us wonder if we have gone backwards, not forwards. This is partly how you will know you are, in fact, making progress. Layers of issues will come to the Light, shadows to be dealt with, acknowledged, and healed, layers of you that have been neglected and repressed. Do not reject them, or in doing so, know that you're rejecting yourself. Do not judge this process or interfere. Just surrender and trust. Allow yourself to be fully present. Be there with yourself, completely.

Do not expect every moment to be blissful. The golden moments will come. Be patient. Commit to this. Doing this halfway will leave you half healed. Half healed doesn't do a whole job. Only in wholeness will you be righted. Only in your total acceptance and allowance of the most uncensored expression of your truest self, the good, the bad and every facet between, will you break through.

Make no mistake, it will be hard. You may spend days crying, inconsolable. You may feel anger and even rage. You might feel the need to let go of many of the relationships you had maintained prior to your spiritual immersion. As you heal and your energy vibrates higher, you may no longer resonate with those you did before. Just allow what comes with compassion for your journey. Express any emotions in a healthy way. Draw, paint, write a letter you will never send, sing, shout, but let it in and let it out.

What I know to provide comfort and navigational insight from this place is this: you owe it to yourself to try. You owe it to yourself to be there for yourself. You deserve to be healed, to have peace, to feel Love as endless and immense as the stars in the galaxy. May there be strength in your compassion and compassion in your strength. If this was easy, everyone would do it. It is the hard that breaks us open. You cannot heal a wound on the surface. You have to go to where it lives, you have to go deep. It is the discomfort that shakes us awake, that moves us to shed all we no longer need, and that is what ultimately transmits our deepest healing.

INFINITE LOVE

Creating lasting relationships can only happen from the inside out. You are "the One" in your life. It was fate from the moment you were born and opened your eyes. The Love of your life was placed as near to you as your heart. The greatest Love is already within you. The sooner you are capable of falling in Love with yourself, treating yourself with respect, setting healthy boundaries and fully accepting your unabridged self for all you are, the sooner you will be capable of that kind of Love with another.

We say "falling in love" but Love, true Love, will never make us fall. True love is considerably more gentle and steady. Love should not knock us off our feet, but complement our balance and our centering. True Love is not about taking our breath away, but holds the breath of life within us as sacred. True Love should amplify the Love and wholeness *already* present within us, and it cannot replace the Love we must cultivate from within.

We can only connect with another as deeply as we can connect within ourselves. I will say that again: we can only connect with another as deeply as we can connect within ourselves. We cannot meet someone where we have not met ourselves. We cannot listen to another where we do not hear ourselves. We cannot understand another where we fail to comprehend ourselves. We cannot embrace another when we fail to Love, accept, and fully embrace ourselves. *You are the key* to every relationship you have.

Heal yourself first, do your inner work, and then don't look for Love, *be* that Love. Shower yourself with that Love. Bathe in it. Submerse yourself in what makes you, *you*. Ceaselessly commit yourself to what makes you happy and makes you shine. Become the Love you have found from within and then extend it outward to the world.

When you can look around you and see wholeness and sacredness reflected back in others, when you can look at another with non-judgment, compassion and understanding, when you can look at yourself with acceptance, care, and kindness, then you will know you are in a very good place, a lush abundant oasis for someone who has found the same level of self-awareness and will be a match for you to begin your story together. Love does not expect, or project, or restrict, or own, or hide. Love is self-respect, self-awareness, and self-caring reflected out to another. When two people are capable of doing this and maintaining this, that is a Higher Love Union.

We cannot Love someone "if only;" if only they do things to please us, if only they change a little bit, if only they would listen better, or call more, or offer to pick up more chores, or do more romantic things. If you truly Love someone, you must Love in freedom. Love for the purest expression of their personal truth, even when they are doing things or acting ways you don't like, or don't understand. You cannot pick and choose who that person gets to be. That is not Love. That's extortion. That's bargaining. Love needs to be nurtured.

Nurturing Love doesn't need to announce that it is Love. It will be obvious. You should be able to omit the word "Love" and still retain the qualities of Love. Love can be described as patient, kind, present, accepting, supportive, trustworthy etc. Who can you say that about? "They are so supportive?" That is Love.

"They are always there for me." That is Love. It is being able to say these things to our self, about our self as well. Building that kind of Love with another is the ultimate goal in a relationship of any kind, romantic or otherwise. We, so often, wait for the other to initiate this, but these qualities have to be nurtured from within us, then extended outward.

Always, always remember that Infinite Love *already* exists within you. Tell yourself this truth often. Affirm this to yourself every day, "I am surrounded by Infinite Love!" We are already perfect, whole and complete. It is a matter of bringing the pieces of our shattered self into alignment with the whole self we have always been. Do not lose yourself to another. The Light within you is to be shared, not taken. This Light is to be considered sacred, not neglected. We do not have to feel unheard, misunderstood, or unloved. We are heard, we are understood, we are Loved. This is eternally true and cannot be destroyed. Beyond the ego (that becomes so easily bruised), you already know this, once we stop chasing things to gratify the lowest aspects of ourselves. Honor the highest aspect of who you are. Start with how you Love yourself.

LOVE LANGUAGE

I leave you with one last nugget of wisdom about Love: how Love sounds. What do you think Love should sound like when we speak to one another? Very few of us have ever heard true expressions of Love. Instead most of us have only heard romanticized confessions of possession "I'm yours forever", attachment "I'll never let you go", manipulation "I could never live without you", and false promises "You're the only one I'll ever love" all dressed up as our idealized template for love. Can you see the dark web underlying these expressions? This has really done a number on us.

We do not belong to another, nor another to us. This concept has damaged people and relationships for centuries. Real Love would say, "I belong to myself, and you to yourself. In our individual wholeness I do not come from a place of lack or seeking fulfillment. I come from a place that knows I am already overflowing with Love and happiness and I choose to share this with you."

Possession is rooted in ego, along with attachment. We should always be free to come and go. Real Love would never stifle that freedom. It would say, "I Love you in freedom, with no projections, no expectations, no games or conditions, I Love and accept the free being that you are in the fullest expression of your truth, in your own space and your own time."

Real Love loves our self, first, and in that can say, "I am living a rich full life and do not look to you for validation, acceptance, or to fill in any gap I have not already filled. I welcome all that you are for who you are, and anything you share is celebrated in my heart." There are no barriers in this. This is open-ended and creates trust.

Love is inevitably shared with many others throughout our life, be conscious of how that Love is expressed. Change your language, change your Love. Real Love doesn't sound like a movie, it says: I Love you without condition. I see the sacred being that you are. I honor and respect you, as I honor and respect myself. I extend compassion to you as I do to myself. I hear you, I feel you, we are connected. I hold you in my light. In this place of Love, you are free and you are home.

SENSITIVITY AND STRENGTH

Sensitivity and strength are synonymous. Compassion is not the opposite of strength. Compassion is a prerequisite of strength. It is an ally of it. Without it, strength is nothing but force with no guidance. Punch with no direction, no focus. Sensitivity takes courage. It is the strongest of us who are the most in touch with our emotions and the emotions of those surrounding us. Be brave.

GENTLE WARRIORS

To my gentle warriors, I must take a few paragraphs and dedicate them to you. Never be silent. Our strength is in our voices. Beware the traps set in society. You will know you've been subjugated by the flaws of a culture built on patriarchy when you begin to believe that your emotion is a liability. If you resist expressing sadness, empathy, or (dare you) anxiety out of fear of being taken as unstable or too emotional, you have fallen victim to a one sided conversation in which only the heavy handed should speak. We have been raised in a society that has banished temperate compassion from every place of business, every higher institution and political forum in which such perspective is so sorely needed.

We have been embedded with the dogma that sensitivity means you're weak and no one can trust or rely on this kind of weakness. Emotion could make emotional choices. What kind of world would that be? A world with wisdom that is derived from beyond linear and mathematical sensibility alone: one which consults with the heart.

So many who are out of touch with their emotion would consider the capacity to feel deeply a handicap in another. Emotion, sensitivity, empathy, vulnerability are the greatest strengths we have, not flaws, but superpowers. To be able to let yourself break down without breaking completely takes more wit and will than any credit could ever give it. Our ability to feel, the sympathetic energy we were born from, that is what makes us human. And that cannot be stricken from relationships or from the highest places and most important conversations. That can never be lost or we will lose what's most important, the heart of who we are.

To my empath sisters and brothers, warriors of wisdom, do not be scared to wield your power. In tears, in trembling voices, let your hearts be heard. If the many millions of us stop apologizing for our emotion, for our passion, and raise it up to be acknowledged and reckoned with, what a shift we would see in a war torn world. To cry, to break down barriers, to really truly feel, that is the real revolution.

"The meek shall inherit the earth." ~ Matthew 5:5

THE SONGLINES

What was within the very first spark of fire, is within you. The music that inspired the creation of the world, inspired the creation of you. You are connected to a greater body carrying a

The Self Beyond

long tradition of wisdom and power. Close your eyes and listen, there are drums in the near distance, pounding like a pulse. Put your ear to the earth, hear the heartbeat of the elders, the medicine men and women of the ages call you back. There was a time when we danced to honor the past and to remember our connection. We have forgotten our link with this deep history. The spirit of a common rhythm courses through your veins. All lineages contain the fingerprint of the master. The Song of the ancestors is within you.

The indigenous Aborigines spoke of the songlines (or dreaming tracks) which trace across the lands of Australia. They believe they were made in the beginning. They are the footprints and paths of the Creator which stretched across valleys, peaks and mountains, crossing deserts and even the sky. The tribe members know to listen to the song of the earth and they honor all land as sacred. The song is a tool of navigation in the footsteps of the Creator.

Can you come with me in this moment and transport beyond the bondage of earth's atmosphere, to view the infinite points of Light which burn like the gleam of an eye through the dark vastness of space? Our ancestors watched the stars with deep reverence. They took great note to their movements and understood our connection to these cosmic forces.

We think of space as silent, but the higher overtones are filled with music. There is a symphony representing our truest state of Being. You have never completely departed from this ancient and eternal realm, not really. We become so enchanted by the illusions of this modern matrix that we lose sight of what is beyond it. You are an eternal Love. You are an ancient Song. Everything you are was planned long before you took your first steps.

There was a time when we were close to the earth. When we prayed only for rain. When we watched the seasons and honored the land, the water and the sky. A time when we celebrated the first crop. The sunrise and sunset was the only clock. There was a deeper way, a shared wisdom. In dreamtime we spoke from the heart. The ancient ones, the Originals, they speak to us still if we listen. It is time to remember what we have so long forgotten. That our home is the land, the Great Spirit is

The Self Beyond

our higher influence, and our tribe is made up of every being and creature on this shared world.

Today, make a commitment to reconnect with this universal heritage. With gratitude and awe, celebrate what is ancient and eternal within you. Speak as if you are singing, sing as if your song can be heard across the Universe. Recognize what is discordant within you and allow it to be released. Come back to harmony with how simple life is.

Know that your troubles and fears are not you, any more than the clothes you wear or the food you eat. Draw from the warrior wisdom within you anytime you need. You are an instrument through which the old ways are remembered and the new ways are born. The ancient ones call down to us, "We hear your song, and we see your spirit. Honor us and make us proud."

Only when we embrace the source spark of our soul can we ignite the fire of our purpose. Our purpose is part of a great collaboration that has been built upon by many lives. You are a key player in this grand masterpiece of time. Recognize each day as a new verse in the song of your life. Every interaction, every pause, and every act is a part of this celebration. Honor your story and sing your song.

INTERVAL

Consider how a moment is elastic, stretching on a lazy day, and contracting in a moment of excitement which seems to pass too quickly. Consider how long the minutes drag by when we wait for another moment to come. Why do we wait until later, until some other circumstance arises, to be happy? All the happiness available "then" is available now. You are always the one that permits the happiness to come in. If you recognize this to be true, then why do you hoard it for later? Why do we deny ourselves this happiness here and now? Regardless of the perceived conditions, we can always allow ourselves that happiness. Every interval of time is crafted by our own higher hand. There is no interim segmented off. It is all one moment, stretching and elastic.

If time is an illusion then what do you think about speed? Why do we organize our time into events, stages, levels and periods? There is no before or after. There is no "there," only here, and we are always arriving, always in motion, even in our perceived stillness. Space is a veil as well. There is no outside, there is only within. Only One to which we all belong—the Intelligent Love (however you define it), which is timeless super-consciousness, constantly expanding and contracting like a great universal heart.

THE CIRCLE

Existence is a circle upon which we perceive only the point we are on, in a linear way, yet that circle is endless. There is no beginning or end. It is, simply, a matter of transcending that linear perception of our existence to perceive the whole of the circle, rather than the point we are currently on.

There is no barrier between you and the object you are perceiving to be in front of you. We only define it as separate, and draw lines around the edges, a barrier we create in between. There is no difference between past or future as it were. It is nothing more than what you are currently perceiving that is relevant. The present is only the present if you are here with it.

Opening up your awareness means a dissolution of that perception of barriers and linear thinking, and a convergence of all concepts of time and space into one total interconnected experience. The cycle, the circle, of life is never-ending, or beginning. Its mantra is "change."

THE MICROCOSM

Every aspect of the microcosm mirrors the macrocosm, and vice versa. Look at how the cosmic, when scaled out to the supercluster Laniakea (which holds our tiny spec of a galaxy like a grain of sand on an infinite beach within it), mirrors the neurons of the human brain or, even, the networks of tree roots. Look at how cells, and molecules on an atomic level, reflect the motion of galactic bodies in space. The birth of a cell looks exactly like the death of a star. From stars to seeds, from quarks to red giants, everything is an echo, an emulation of the same design. Is the Universe part of a larger Mind? Is the mind a Universe on its own?

The Self Beyond

We are effectively connected through a conscious network, a Greater Mind. The human mind (in its uncorrupted state) mirrors this greater cosmic mind. As you begin, or continue, on your personal path of self-discovery and awakening, you contribute to a higher degree of awareness in the greater macrocosm you are connected to. You shift one more node, which intersects with the pathways of all humanity. You fuse one more synapse of the collective mind. You plant a seed which grows into something much bigger than you. This is the most meaningful act of transformation.

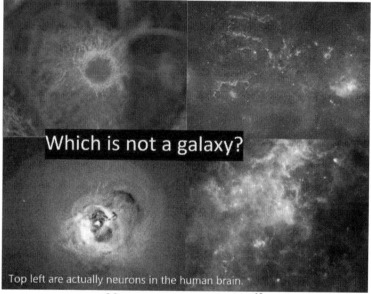

Neurons versus galaxies [65]

THE CUP

How we experience life greatly depends on how we view it. Our attitude determines a large part of our perception. We may look at our life and see the places it is empty, and, in turn, life feels empty for us. We may look at our life and see the fullness, and life, in turn, feels full and rich for us. Yet, neither point of view is

---

[65] Self-created using stock photos cleared for commercial use.

wrong, and neither are complete in their assessment, either. Life expresses, both, polarities of emptiness and fullness. The universe is not polar, it is unified field. Reality works in multidimensional potentials, and our impediment to experiencing that non-polarity, is that we are still looking at things filtered through a polarizing lens.

Every moment holds the possibility of misfortune and victory. Every day may hold pain and purpose, love and heartbreak. We have qualities both sacred and irreverent. We are living by both chaos and design. Water and fire are present in each of us. There are elements of this divine dichotomy in all moments and things and people. We define these aspects as good or bad. We think pain is bad, forgetting how often pain is a teacher in our lives. We think pleasure is good, often forgetting how often we lose ourselves in this state. Excelling past the limitations of labeling one negative and one positive, one dark and one light, allows us to become the wholeness that has been secretly and silently embedded in all creation. The ability to see the design in the chaos, the sacred in the irreverent, the purpose in the pain, can free us from polarization into unification. It can take us deeper into our own Totality.

Is the cup half empty or half full? Seeing one or the other is still half awareness. The cup is both full of emptiness and empty with fullness. Is fullness only substance? Is emptiness only absence? Is the ocean full and the sky empty? Both are breathing with the pulse of the Universe. So are you. And so is the cup you hold. Step into the whole truth.

MAGIC

Magic can only happen if you stop thinking of it as magic. It's not. It is reality. It is science, and you only have to think of it as possible. Consider that at this very moment, your entire life is engulfed in the miraculous. It is us who postpones the magic, the miracle. We hope and pray all day for miracles, yet we fail to see them happening all around us. Are you breathing? What a miracle! Are you fed? That is a magical gift! Are you alive? Can you comprehend the trillions of complex coordinated processes required to happen absolutely perfectly in order for life to exist? If you do not see life itself as magic, then nothing else will astound you. By all mathematical probability we should not be here, but we are.

    There, now you see that magic is happening all the time. We just have taken it for granted. Every moment is a miracle, all that comes and all that goes. Trust the Deep Magic of the Universe which bestowed you with that life, that food, that breath. It will always bring the magical to our doorstep, when we are ready to believe.

BECOMING LUCID

    One of our biggest obstacles in healing and mastering our own minds is actually *our own minds*. We are so ingrained with ideas about the laws of what is possible, that these sediments of impossibility have solidified like concrete in our psyche. The majority of us have been indoctrinated that we cannot heal ourselves. We think we need a medium to do the healing for us; a doctor or a priest, some surgery or medicine, or even some magical shaman or ritual. We personalize and identify with our diseases, or lower aspects of some self-created façade, and continually reinforce them. We say, "Well I just don't have that ability to stop being compulsive, that's just how I am," or "Well, that won't work for me because of my hormonal imbalance," or "Well it would be nice if I could do that, but I just don't have the strength." We make excuses to get ourselves out of having to do the work. I am not saying that these obstacles are not very real. I am saying we do ourselves no favors by underpinning those barriers to our progress.

    The problem is not the mind, it is how we have made an enemy of the mind. But the solution is, also, the mind if we can use its characteristic weaknesses to our advantage. How do we get around limitations transposed on our own perception using the tool which was damaged by this programming? If we don't believe something is possible, then it cannot be possible. We cannot mold those concrete opinions to become malleable, unless we can overcome this paradox.

A great way of bypassing this conundrum of the mind getting in the way of the mind is through the use of lucid dreams. Dreams, in themselves, are a multilayered abstraction of consciousness, whose very matrix is based on contradictory physics to what we experience in the waking world. In dreams, we may discover we can fly, or perform superhuman feats, we can travel great distances, and here, we can do incredibly effective and *deep* healing work. We can connect with our higher soul self to learn, and we can receive higher messages that our soul needs. Dreams function as dimensions that allow the psyche to express without the rigid boundaries of the waking mind.

Lucid dreams, in particular, allow us to take our healing further. Farther in that we are no longer passive bystanders to our subconscious, but active architects that can interact with and influence the dreamscape and our part within it. In a lucid dream, you might intend to do healing work through meditation within the dream. Or, by visualizing Healing Light around the physical area of discomfort which may, in a lucid dream, be visible. You might face characters or archetypes that have frightened you throughout your life and instead of running away, turn to face them, perhaps even embrace them and, in doing so, diminishing them to disempower their hold on you in waking life.

If you are someone who actively dreams and awakens with vivid dream recall, you already possess a strong aptitude for lucid dreaming. To "awaken" in a dream has many implications. If you can recognize that place of dreams while you are in it, you are essentially becoming superconscious. You are becoming aware of your awareness. That is a profoundly meaningful achievement, and the goal of many spiritual practices.

The methods of achieving lucid dreaming are many. I will outline a few that I find particularly user friendly and effective. One way to awaken in your dream is (obviously) to become aware that you are dreaming. This will take some prep work during waking hours. Try flipping on and off a light switch whenever you walk into a room in your home, make it a habit. You will note the light does, in fact, turn on and off. In dreams not everything works exactly that same way. The reality of the dreamscape can be incredibly vivid and realistic, but I've found lights will not turn on. Electronics don't seem to operate correctly, either. For instance, your cell phone may suddenly have futuristic technological capabilities, or malfunction. What you are doing when you check these real-world things is testing. You are asking yourself, am I dreaming or awake? The subtle irregularities or anomalies should act as a trigger to alert you of the dream state. So, when you go to turn on a light in a dream, and it does not turn on, you might say, "I must be dreaming."

Another way to achieve a lucid dream is by setting the intention. You can say, "Tonight I will have a lucid dream." You can even set the parameters by saying, "I will have a lucid dream and meet my soulmate in a field of wildflowers." Understand, this is not a skill you learn like others. It can happen spontaneously, so don't be discouraged. It might take many weeks or months. Leave the door open for this possibility.

When you do awaken in a dream for the first few times, you may be so excited, you will probably wake yourself up in real life. For me, many times, I would realize I was dreaming, but retained an awareness that the place I was in was real in some dimension, not exactly as a "made up" dreamscape. That was when I began to know I was astral traveling which is often experienced during "dream time" as well.

We do astral travel, meaning the essence of the spirit within us is not bound to this body, but sometimes travels while the body rests, if it so chooses. We can travel, not only, to earth based locations, but cosmic spaces and overtones. That is what is so incomprehensible about our psyche, it can connect with these multidimensional overtones which transcend space and time. We can visit times past, present and future. We can "real time" communicate with another individual across the globe. We can make contact with people and guides we have never physically met but who are very real. We can gain practical and objective insight into our lives through, what may seem, this highly impractical and subjective method.

I believe this to be one of the most under studied areas of the human mind. In dreams and astral travel, we can journey to other star systems and beyond. This is just another venue in which we can learn and consciously evolve. We can heal, or work on relationships. We can get closure that we never received. There are no limits in the place of dreams. We are tapping into the dream time of the ancients. The same place psychedelic explorers and shamans tap into through deep meditative states and visionary plants and brews. Our own mind is a powerful hallucinogenic—one which allows us to explore the very depths of our spiritual core.

Think of your consciousness as a tree. The higher consciousness acts as branches reaching out, capable of soaking up the energy of the cosmic intelligence. The practical day to day consciousness is the trunk, bridging the other layers of consciousness, but, also, acting as a gateway through which our awareness can pass. The subconscious acts as the roots underneath, plunging deep into the earth and stretching farther than the tree. There is, also, the collective consciousness, which can be thought of as the entire forest organism: the earth, the dirt, the mycelium, all connecting to the tree and every other tree.

That higher interval cosmic conscious space is where the core essential wisdom is. This is where we connect with our higher self and the Intelligent Field. The network connecting underneath is the deep, sacred wisdom of our time. The knowledge of our ancestors, which had only been reserved for the medicine men and women, is accessible to us, as well, from this octave of information. Everything is right there in that space just below the surface. All inspiration, creativity, insight and wisdom of the ages is available in these intervals of perception. The lovely thing is, there are many routes to this space. You can meditate your way there, dream your way there. You can enter these octaves in silence and stillness. It is not beyond you, it is a part of your spiritual heritage. So, play around to find what works best for your personal journey toward your own style of enlightenment.

TRAINING

To have a better handle on inner thoughts, it is helpful to recognize what thoughts are. Many automatic (or reactionary) thoughts are senses, just like touch, taste, hearing, smell, and sight. They are an internal reaction to an external stimuli, just like the feeling of cold when we touch snow. They operate as our sixth sense (you might say) in that they perceive what goes beyond our own body. Or to say this another way, this sense can perceive beyond the physical dimension, operating as intuition. We are not creating many of our own thoughts, we are perceiving them. The same way we are not creating many other external stimuli we observe, such as a bird flying or the warmth of the sunlight, we are experiencing them via our senses.

We often believe every thought we think, just like we believe every sense, but senses can be fooled and even subjective. For instance, someone could hold a banana up to your nose as you eat an apple and you would taste banana. It is not the truth, your senses have been hijacked.

We can observe our thoughts just like we can observe a piece of artwork. We might like it, we might not. Our sense of it is (and isn't) necessarily a reflection of us as a person. It is just a matter of taste. In this same way, we may like or dislike a particular interaction. We might have a negative thought in response to someone treating us poorly, for instance. This does not make you a bad person any more than observing a foul odor from a waste basket makes you a bad person.

Thoughts can act as a sense which allows us to "sense" ourselves. That is the fundamental point of it. Thoughts are like a differentiating mechanism that help us to put together the information obtained from all other senses. Thoughts can allow us to explore know ourselves, more deeply. However, our reactionary or automatic thoughts are not us anymore than our sense of smell is us.

Thoughts can be affected by energy pools of the collective field of information, for example: when we go somewhere where many other people have been perceiving a threat to their safety, like an old abandoned building rumored to be haunted. There, many people are leaving a vibration of fearful energy. So, when you enter that pathway your mind might coalesce with that vibrational field and you might take in those thoughts to perceive that you, too, are in some kind of danger. You might, uncharacteristically, begin to worry you will be attacked.

What this means is, some of the thoughts which we identify with are not our own. We do not have to claim them. We can observe them like any other sense, such as heat or cold, or beauty, or a bad smell. This means some of the fears and thoughts we have identified with could have been passed down from our parents and caregivers, or other external stimuli, such as ex-lovers who were insecure themselves. In some cases, we took on those anxieties and insecurities and believed them to be ours. Gaining this little understanding can greatly help you in managing your own thoughts, through knowing what is yours and what is not, and to discern what to allow versus what to release in non-attachment.

Higher thoughts come from a higher place, and those are not senses, but intuitions or insights. These are different than the more reactionary automatic thoughts which seem to spring up so often. Our thoughts are like our emotions, in that they are there to point us to something important we need to pay attention to, within us. They need compassion, recognition, and validation. Not the validation of being correct or incorrect, right or wrong, but the validation that they are present.

Any thoughts that arise can be traced back to an origin, an event or external factor that caused the chain of thoughts which, then, spiraled off of that original thought. Identifying that origin can help empower you to reverse the spiral and provide validation to your own beliefs and feelings about that thought.

You cannot change what your senses sense, you can only change what you offer them. That is why changing a thought is so hard. If you put a bag of trash up to your nose, it is going to smell rotten. You cannot just *will* yourself to smell something else. You can only change the response by changing the stimulus, by raising something up to your nose that smells good, like some flowers. The mind is the same way.

The best way to handle a damaging or unhealthy thought stream is to offer yourself something better to focus on. If you find yourself in a thought spiral downward, ask yourself what is it that started this chain? Allow yourself to identify that root and accept it, work through it, make sure you are listening to the message it is sending. Then, change your focus. Look at something beautiful that you like, notice it. Think about something funny that makes you laugh, focus on where that leads. Listen to something uplifting that can alter your current thought pattern to amplify the positives. Do this as often as you may need to. Understand, there is no bad thought or wrong thoughts. You can, simply, allow them to arise as do all the other things your senses sense. You can always change the scenery if it no longer suits your benefit.

BALANCE

Every area of our lives requires balance, from our relationships, to our jobs, to our personal lives. We need balance in order to be healthy. For instance, if we work all the time, without allowing ourselves a chance to rest and recharge, we will create an imbalance, and sooner or later, something has to give. Our minds may sound an alarm to let us know we need to relax, but we push back saying, "I have *no time* to relax!" At which point our emotions might kick in to let us know we *need* to relax. We become irritable, short, and over-emotional. If we do not take these queues, the body is the last alarm system we have which may try to force us to slow down by becoming sick. If we keep pushing through this, the sickness may become more and more serious. This is just one example of the harm imbalance causes.

What is needed for one person to gain balance, may result in imbalance for another. If you are someone who spends all your time relaxing, you might not need more relaxation. It may be more harmful than helpful for your balance. For another who can never sit still, this might be exactly what you need. No one can tell you what balance means for you, only you can see that. This can be seen by panning back a bit and looking at your life from just outside of it. Can you see what that person, who is you, in your life needs? What would you say to yourself if you were a friend of yours behaving this way for too long?

The majority of people I observe in my immediate world are extremely overworked. I know, in a practical way, that many people simply cannot afford to relax. Many truly do not have the time. That only emphasizes the shear necessity of *making* the time. How can we have balance or peace if we do not create it? Who or what else is possibly going to give us that? It is like waiting for a rainstorm to dry you up. It doesn't work like that. Balance is something we have to actively create. Peace is not something we find somewhere, it is something we tune into within ourselves.

To wait for outer circumstances or others to settle down for us to have peace and balance robs us of our chance. We cannot control what is going on around us or what others do. That is impossible. However, that is where most of us focus all our effort. We need to turn the focus inward and balance from within. Calm *yourself.*

Balance from the center where the true gravity of life rests. Balance between heart and mind. Balance between soul and body. Find balance between doing and being, between seeking and integrating what has been found. Balance what you are learning

The Self Beyond

with what you believe. Allow that to constantly evolve and grow with you, not against you. We have to both be and do. Both are necessary. We must allow ourselves rest and activity. Both are essential, but in balance. Seek to create *balance*.

Give yourself permission to be fully in the moment you are in. When you are resting, just rest. Do not shame yourself that you should be more productive. Immerse yourself in your time to recharge, replenish, rejuvenate and unplug. This will serve you well when you are able to come back to your to-do list refreshed, refocused, and reenergized.

When you are being productive, commit to it, work smarter not harder. Find ways to get organized with a goal of being efficient instead of overwhelmed. Allowing yourself to become overwhelmed costs you twice your time. It is not worth the investment. Give yourself a time limit for projects. Say, "I will work on this for two hours and then stop no matter where I am." Do not set impossible standards for yourself that will only stress you out. Prioritize and group together what you can. Leave free time scheduled into your day, even if it is only twenty minutes. It will pay off to give yourself that time.

My assessment is the busier you are, the more time you need for you. Real you-time is essential, not simply taking a break from working, just to shovel ramen noodles in your mouth, and looking over unopened mail while the kids run around the house screaming. That is not you-time. I understand the restrictions modern life imposes on our worlds. I am not immune to these obstructions, either. Consider inviting your children to take silent time with you. Share with them the art of meditation, which will be a lifelong skill they can draw from to help them be more peaceful, compassionate, and self-aware. Do yoga or artwork together. Any way we can, we have to prioritize ourselves.

Get yourself into nature. Get yourself someplace peaceful. Go into a space in which you can slip into your own silent stillness and actually recharge. If this means asking a friend or relative to take the kids for a few hours, then do it. If this means taking a few hours off of work, then do it. If this means the house does not get cleaned or laundry piles up a little, still do it. The house will get clean, the laundry will get done. It hurts nothing to allow yourself some time to reconnect with you and let that slide

The Self Beyond

when you can. One thing I can promise at the end of your life, you will never say, "I wish I had not left that laundry".

You are the most important person in your life. I do not mean that in a selfish way. Too often self-care and self-love is taken as selfish. But, who is going to take care of you if you do not do it? Who is going to offer you an extra few hours in your week, if you do not do it? Only you can give yourself these things. And to be the best we have to offer, this is what we need: balance.

HEART OPENING

Having an open heart is the most fundamental necessity for both healing, and personal alignment. The heart can become closed for many reasons; being hurt deeply, a learned sense of distrust, experiences of betrayal or emotional trauma. Each one of the reasons that can cause our heart to close can be helped, and even healed, through re-opening the heart. A heart that is open is one of your greatest tools.

I would like to provide a simple heart opening activation for you to make use of, as needed. Sit in a comfortable position. Try to center and align your body as best you can (without causing contortions that are not natural to you). Centering and aligning your physical body helps your energy channels flow much better to bring in that good healing and activating energy. Breathe a few deep breaths in and out. Close your eyes and enter a calm space within yourself.

From this place, you may state your intentions in creating an open heart. I invite you to create your own wording as it suits you. I will provide a template. You may say this out loud or from your inner voice. "Great Spirit that moves through all things, may my heart be filled with Love and Light. May my spirit find peace in the knowing that Love is all around me. May my heart be *open* to receiving this Love in all ways. May my heart be blessed and refined with the Infinite Love that is always available to me. Help me replace any hurt, anger, or sadness within me, with greater Love. May any wound within me heal deeply with Love, and may I now forgive myself and all others. May I release what is no longer needed into the Light to be healed. May I allow what is needed with the power and strength of Love. May I know in my heart that I am safe and I am Loved. May I know in my heart that there is nothing here to fear, I am carried by Love. May my heart *open:* to welcome Love and to trust in Love. May any barriers to Love dissolve into the Light. Let Love come fully into my open heart." Be grateful. Know that only in openness can we experience oneness, and only in oneness can we know Love.

From this place, allow yourself to come into forgiveness and be filled with Love. Visualize your heart as a ball of energy, a Light right at the center of your chest. Perhaps a deep emerald green Light which is pulsing with every breath. Can you feel the warmth that brings? Imagine Love entering this center of your heart as Light. From everywhere around you, Light pours in as Love and with every breath the Light of your heart becomes brighter. Can you imagine that any walls, any barriers you have carried are now released into this warm Light? Can you feel how much lighter you are beginning to feel?

From this place you may allow yourself to visualize letting go of someone who has hurt you. You may visualize letting go of a long held feeling which has been self-destructive. This may be an emotional experience. Cry if you need to cry. Do not repress your emotional cleansing. Think of each tear as a piece of a wall that is falling, and know that the wall was only keeping Love out. Be ready to allow this Love in, now. You can make this your intention. All we have to do is ask. Love is always ready to enter an open heart.

LIVING TEMPLE

In balance, in wholeness and in healing we may find ourselves tuning more deeply into the natural world. Nature is a living temple, a sanctuary with no walls and no ceiling. What could better support the nurturing of our growing spirit? Here, the divine energy of life is fully present, expanding in direct proportion to our own awareness. No priests or gurus, no go-between is needed, just solitude, just silence, just surrender and the ability to open yourself like a flower, unfolded petal by petal in the raw and wild wonder of discovery.

I invite you to set a date with yourself to do a little project this week. I invite you to spend time in nature with a tree. This is simple; go out to a local park or hiking path, leave your phone in the car, and find a secluded spot with a tree you feel drawn to. Sit there and ask nothing of yourself. Put away all distractions. Simply be in the presence of the tree. Look at it. Observe its trunk, the texture of its bark, observe the particular and unique direction of its many branches. Observe its leaves, their color, how the wind moves them, how the light interacts with them. Let yourself let go here. Allow yourself to go into a deep, almost trancelike, state of awareness. Wherever this takes you, it will be deeper into your own awakening. You are connecting with the pure energy and intelligence of the spirit and life within that tree. This is the same energy and intelligence within you, and it is a shared energy. When this conscious energy is exchanged, it is amplified.

> *"All arts lie in man, though not all are apparent. Awakening brings them out. To be taught is nothing; everything is in man waiting to be awakened."* ~ Paracelsus

Here, in this living temple, that energy moves through all things, and it does so with great purpose. Through diligent exercise, you will find the heightened awareness of a *living message*. When every sense is fulfilled: the colors of the flowers, the music of the birds, the scent of earth carried in the breeze, the soft coolness of the water, the warmth of the sun, the sweet taste of life in every breath, there you will find the translation. In a state of total reception, you become a direct line to the cosmic testament. No one needs to tell it to you or interpret the meaning. It is already in your own biological and spiritual vocabulary. This is the language you were born with.

No book, no carefully strung together words, could ever capture the secret truth waiting here. It is not to be explained but *experienced*. Its messages are written on the leaves, on the waves, on the wind, and on hearts that listen. We are nature. The whole of earth is a sacred site. We are also sacred. Here in nature, all you are is welcomed, as you are. Here, you are One with both Creator and Creation. Here, you are never alone.

TAPESTRY

The web of life is a tapestry made of people, plants, animals, little creatures, even the rocks, the water, and the sky. Humankind is, merely, a thread of that great web. This tapestry works just as any tapestry would: when one strand is pulled on it tugs at the whole. One strand added reinforces the whole. One strand weakened or one strand strengthened all affects the integrity of the web.

One strand as one life makes a difference. Every strand and every life is a part of this. Remember when you are in nature, we are in a sacred living space that is at the very cortex of this tapestry—we are held within this realm as the firmament holds the stars. Respect it. Care for it. Remember when you are in the world, every act affects the web you are connected to. Remember among people, every soul is another thread to which we are each inextricably bound. Every person, every act, every moment is connected to the tapestry. Know that all of this is a part of *all of us*.

---

[66] Obtained from Pexels under Creative Commons Zero (CC0) license

THE FROG

At one time, I was in a long distance relationship. It wasn't a London to New York kind of distance; she lived about an hour and twenty minutes away. So, most weekends after I got out of work, I could drive to see her and stay a day or two. At the time, I was working nights and got out around ten, after the sun had long set. There was, basically, one long road between us which hugs Lake Ontario. So, it was a straight shot to get there, which I would take on with a big cup of coffee. The road is not very busy, but it does become a single lane quite frequently, and for long stretches, so it was better driving at night then getting stuck behind someone (*actually* going the speed limit) in the day.

As I was driving there, one night in the fall, rain was pouring down. It was a little windy and there was a lot of newly shed leaves blowing around the road. As I got farther into the trip, I began noticing it looked like some of the leaves were bouncing. I kept rubbing my eyes, are those leaves, or are those frogs? I admittedly don't have the best night vision. It seemed ridiculous but more and more I saw what appeared to be bouncing frogs crossing the road. Hundreds of them! I wondered if I was hallucinating, honestly. I really wanted to pull over and get out to look closer, but I was afraid if a police officer saw me I would sound crazy trying to explain that I pulled over to check if the leaves were actually hundreds of frogs. So, I struck a compromise and slowed down greatly. I realized I was right! There were dozens and dozens of toads just trying to get from one forest line to the next. I let them know I meant them no harm and drove as carefully as I could. That doubled my trip time but that was alright with me.

A couple weeks later, there was an intense windstorm. Tree branches had fallen all over; lots of debris was strewn about. Nothing that stopped the world from turning, but that made for messy roads. I was on my way out for my weekend visit and it was another night, so dark it was almost black. Anything that fell outside the illumination of my headlights was a mystery. As I was driving, I noticed another bouncing thing in the road, so, I slowed down to almost a complete stop this time.

There he was, a beautiful little frog. I marveled at him as he seemed to look right at me, stilling my headway, for a long

The Self Beyond

moment. I said, "Hello, there, little guy." I decided there might be more so I slowed down to about ten miles an hour. Just a minute or so later, I came up on a tree that had fallen completely, impeding my single lane to which my instinct on a quiet road was to just go around it by passing in the oncoming lane. This observation was immediately clinched by a speeding tractor trailer truck coming my way, which, due to the slowdown from my little frog messenger, I was well out of the path of.

In that moment I knew, had the little emissary not come to tell me to watch out, and had my compassion for his precious life not compelled me to slow down, I could have hit that tree, or that truck. There are messengers everywhere. Nature speaks to us through animals, through trees, through the elements, if we pay attention, and if we pursue our lives with a sense of receptivity, appreciation for the message (even if we don't know why yet), and above all—Love.

67

SCULPTOR

You are the unparalleled expression of Divine experience that shapes worlds: the sculptor and the clay. You are the pulse of cosmic ecstatic motion collapsing then dilating. We are the vessel which the flow of life moves through. Not the blood, but the Life within the blood. Every season is possible when dreaming

---

[67] Self-drawn for this book

awakened. Just breathe and you have already become a creator. Oxygen breathes us too. It's not gravity that holds you to the earth; it is Love. *Know the Whole Self that you are.*

THE PATH

There are no coincidences, and in a cosmic world that speaks the language of synchronicity, it is not by chance you are reading these words. We are drawn to the people, places and experiences that offer us what we need in each phase of our life. That may be lessons, healing, insight, or gentle reminders that we are not, in fact, alone. Many people are experiencing "an Awakening." Realizing we are spiritual beings having a human experience feels as though we have awoken from deep sleep. Various factors through intentional seeking, tragedy, and ecstatic experience can all lead to awakening. There are many paths up the mountain. These subtle patterns of profound occurrences can more often not be explained by mere chance. The hope is that this sparks our attention and find our Path.

It is through our intuition realized that we find our way. There is a deeper purpose flowing through our lives like an underwater channel seeking an outlet. Many are no longer satisfied with the philosophies of outdated power structures. As our higher consciousness and spiritual nature unfold, we may recognize: this is not just about us. Seek alignment with something higher, seek to help others, to make a difference in the world, and to be of service to humanity. You, then, become something greater than just yourself; you become part of a connected global community activated to create transformation on earth, one which mirrors the internal transformation we are undergoing.

No matter the technological advancements we might make as a species, none of that will create a thriving world without a deep spiritual understanding at its bedrock. When we look around, we might recognize the suffering and destruction our abuse of energy and lack of spiritual awareness has caused. We cannot responsibly and consciously create a better world if we do not understand that energy and how we use it.

Delicate all-pervading energies infuse our lives and reality. These powerful energies must be understood to be correctly utilized with Love and respect. We use these energies daily, and when directed in misuse, turmoil is created. These energies are inextricably linked to our thoughts and our feelings. If we are continually negative, seeing the world as a difficult and hostile place, our life becomes challenging to navigate, because we have made ourselves incompatible with the flow. Equally, if we focus on the positive aspects, the deeper meaning and synchronicity, then we allow that energy to flow with us. Life is meant to flow. This flow is effortless and frees us to focus on healing ourselves and even to become healers in the world.

From birth, many of us were locked into a power struggle dynamic. Society teaches rivalry and revenge. But, the only relationship the energy of flow is compatible with is *partnership*. We cannot seek fulfillment from others. That is not partnership. We cannot wait for others to make us happy, to give us control, or to show us Love. This is, hands down, the root cause of every deteriorated relationship. When we are each coming from a place of depreciated energy, all we do is drain one another. The vessel runs dry. Love and fulfillment has to come from within.

There is no shortage of Love and joy in this universe. It is obtainable from within us and all around us. All we have to do is accept it. Create a space for this Love to pour into you. It can never diminish, inner Love will amplify and overflow. You can find it in the stillness of nature, in the warmth of the sunlight, the beauty of the trees, the pulse of the waves on the beach, in your very breath. You do not need to seek it, it is there with you, right now.

It is only through training ourselves to use our inner tools correctly, that we carve a pathway out for the flow to come through us. We cannot force control, it requires surrender. If we think too much about it, we tense up, we block it. Connecting with that divine flow, that ecstatic energy of Love and Light: *that* is the journey the mystics and sages have described throughout time. It is like plugging into a universal energy outlet which, once reconnected, restores our life. Through this we may experience a deep sense of bliss, well-being, contentment and peace.

We find through dedicated work on our deeper issues and patterns, a profound self-awareness, and the ability to *be* comes to fruit. It is within this full inner recognition of the wholeness that we are capable of, that we tap into a *greater state of Self*. This allows us to clear a path for the vision of our life mission and our divine purpose to be known. This is where we rekindle our soul inspiration!

When we are fully tuned in to the universe inside of us, we begin to not just exist, but Flow! When activated, we begin paying attention to everything around us, music, numbers, dreams, and personal insights, all which lead us further down our ever-evolving path. We begin to release our need to control. We recognize there is a more intuitive guidance available to us, as we become aware of our Higher Self. Intuition creates synchronicity and synchronicity feeds further intuition. This guidance is both practical and meaningful. It allows us to feel our way through problems and find solutions.

On my personal journey, all this has led me to appreciate in the deepest sense that we are all on the same journey, taking different paths. Everything we seek is available within us, we just have to see through our own crap. We have to go beyond our addictions, our projections, and our own illusions. We have a responsibility to find ourselves, and, when we can, uplift those around us who are still lost.

People are suffering from a lack of self-Love, and self-Love can begin seeding from the random act of compassion through another. We are drawn to some people and there is a reason. We feel repelled from some people, and there is a reason. We are meant to interact with one another in catalytic ways. We never know who may have a message for us, or us for them. Love and acknowledge these messengers in your life. Welcome and honor the many expressions of your whole self; with empathy, consideration, reverence and gratitude.

We are moving towards a spiritual revolution as a species. We are transforming as we heal, and as we become conscious and connected. Recognizing that this is just a step in *many journeys* brings acceptance that this life is not all there is. This life is transient, but there is something within us and beyond us, which is eternal. As we share in this higher awareness, with an advanced understanding of Love, it amplifies, it grows, and it transmutes the shadows that once lingered into a luminous comprehensive awareness.

Holding a deep vision, with our intention, is a powerful mechanism for creating a spiritual experience in a human existence. How do we implement these principles in our daily lives? Through intention, patience, constant compassion (for ourselves and others), and practice. We are only here for the blink of an eye. We are here to remember Love, share Love, and to come back to Love. This is what carries us into the higher levels beyond this life.

If nothing else, maintain faith in your *deeper-purpose*. Our intention, focused in meditation (reception), prayer (intention) and thoughts (direction) are *powerful*. Those intentions affect our lives and the world around us. The more Love, healing, and peace we create, the more we draw those people, places and experiences to us which further accelerate this energy. It is a positive feedback loop. That is the nature of the universe.

Deep within us there is a presence of something extraordinary. It is not out there in the clouds, or in another person. It is not on the pages of a book (except, in words may help you remember). It is not on your phone (I promise). It is *everywhere* and *nowhere*, and it is right within your heart. We might feel lost, disconnected, frustrated, and scared sometimes. But, that has its purpose, as well. Because you see, it is as we experience discomfort, that we begin to ask questions. We begin to seek, and we begin to look within. It is the discomfort that causes us to act on our own behalf.

We are, each, empowered with a connection to a Higher Insight, one which speaks within us. Just be quiet, be still, and listen. We are pieces of a greater whole, all part of a larger cosmic body. Recognize who you are. You are a free spirit. Do you know what that means? You are a divine being with a divine purpose, and you are not alone.

> "*The source of infinite wisdom in this infinite universe is that you are blessed with infinite love.*" ~Debasish Mridha

LOVE BEYOND

Our scars, our mistakes, our zig zagging pathways are the lines on a map that lead us back to the heart. Can you see that art is what happens on the way to making art? Love is what happens on the way back to Love. We are artifacts of the cosmic design, living organic material of a long-dimmed nebula. The Light that once glowed within those galactic clouds is still alive in you, even when no one is looking.

We are beyond sight. We are not our eyes or mouths, not our hand or our foot, we are not our mind or even our biological heart. We are the forces between stars and fragments of the Star itself. The gravity between souls drawing us back to the shore like waves upon the beach of the infinite ocean. Time is just a story; it is just what happens between covers. Close the book and look beyond the pages. There you are.

Look how the sunrise kisses the earth with her spirit before setting, how the rain falls down, then evaporates. We revolve in an unceasing orbit of boundless creation. Our emergence stretched out in every direction when we begin inwardly ascending. Our heart, mind and body are wrapped in skin but the depth of us is not contained by the same restrictions. We are, both, a masterpiece and a work in progress through self-reflection and self-improvement. Discard all illusions, preconceptions, and disguises. Throw out the masks, the doubts, and the fears. Embrace the fullest expression of who you are. Be naked, and allow yourself to see the Divine standing within you.

Nothing stays and nothing ever truly goes. We are, and were, and will, and do. When Love has traveled from so far, Light years from the nearest galaxy, space means nothing at all. Home is not a place, but a state of existence. We are forever: not on the edges, but in the Center of the Center; not fragments of a Whole, but the Whole. We are One Heart and One Soul that sees itself in pieces. There waits for you a Secret Garden that only you can know. It's a sky bound landscape of rich endless fields, after dawn. It is experienced as Love from Beyond.

PEACE

Going beyond Love means creating peace. If you can do one act of service toward the creation of peace in humanity, stop engaging in war. What I mean here by "war" are the little wars we are confronted with daily, in retrospect, too often, petty conflicts with various individuals. We feel disrespected, taken for granted. Whatever it is, it's usually driven by an unhealthy ego out of balance. Instead, choose peace. You have to actively choose it.

We go to war when we decide we will not let something go. We go to war when we cut someone off in traffic. We go to war when we say, "No I was here first!" We go to war when we are unkind to another because we don't like their attitude. We go to war when we overlook someone in need and pass by. Choose to make peace. If others want to make war, let them. We do not have to engage back. Nothing deflates hostility better than non-reaction. You will become a golden example of what peace looks like and that can inspire others to choose peace too.

Don't misunderstand, speaking up against true injustice is important. We cannot be complacent. However, even then, make it a point, not to act with ill will or to damage the offender, simply call out the poor behavior as what it is: poor behavior, poor attitude or ignorance, and recognize these individuals often are completely disconnected and without peace from within themselves.

Mother Theresa said, "If we have no peace, it is because we have forgotten we belong to each other." Make it a point to remember. And, at every opportunity, choose not to inflame the little acts of war. We change the world by changing *our* part in it. Everything happening "out there" is a reflection of what is happening "in here." We have to shift the narrative. We cannot reach every part of the world, but we can make a positive impact on the part within our reach. Love, random acts of peace, compassion, and acceptance can conquer every war, and by God, they are the only things that will.

Ending the war inside ourselves, could end all the wars of the world, because everything happening in the greater world, is just a reflection of our inner worlds. More than anything, we need people at peace within themselves, and there is no peace anywhere without peace first made from within.

FOLLOW YOUR HEART

Gaining peace is directly connected to tuning into your heart. Don't forget to come back to the heart often. Nothing we are doing here will have meant much if it is not about the heart. Your heart is your treasure, your greatest tool, your power, your guidance, and your key. Our heart can be our weakness, or our strength; use it well.

Every so often, when I have some spare hours, I like to do something I call "following my heart." This is not meant in the broad and general sense so many quotes allude to. Here, what I mean is more defined: to go towards whatever it is that makes you happy, without a specific agenda in mind. Not having an agenda is important because it allows the Flow to emerge unencumbered. The energy of life moves towards open spaces. Openness allows the quantum processes to unfold into unique and spontaneous experiences.

This process starts with an intuition, an instinct, as you may feel drawn to go to a specific restaurant, bookstore, or coffee shop. You might, initially, feel that it would make you very happy to visit a certain spot in nature. The place does not matter so much as the state of presence you bring into it. Allow yourself to be receptive and fluid. Start with the place that makes your heart smile. Go there and you will find you are beginning to follow your heart. If other locations catch your interest, go there too. You can move, and with each move, the momentum will build. This might sound like nonsense, but I invite you to try it.

I know it may seem too simple to, really, mean anything without us forcing meaning onto it, until you set this intention for yourself. Say, "Today I am going to follow my heart." Infuse that sole objective with positive energy and joy. Smile at this thought and be easygoing about where this takes you. This might mean making several stops wherever you feel led. This might mean pulling over on the side of the road for a particularly breathtaking scenic view. This might mean a hike all over an unexplored nature park.

You will find these are the times *bursting* with synchronicity. The timing will naturally align without effort, and your path will align with others you share connections with. You may meet important people who, just happen, to say exactly what you need to hear. You may see an old friend who you had not crossed paths with in a long time. You may have one of the most spiritual and unbridling experiences of your life; you never know!

How often do we really let our heart lead the way? My recommendation is to do this as often as your life allows. What have we done with our lives if we don't spend at least part of it following our hearts? You will find, when you do what makes you happy, things just line up for you that are both meaningful and purposeful. These are the days you will look back on and say, "That was a really great day." They are gifts and they allow for even more gifts to flow in.

Insight comes more easily when we come from our heart. Centering comes more easily when we allow the heart to drive. That is because we are in optimal alignment with our most natural state of being which is free, uncharted, and utterly wild.

LIGHTHOUSE

As we follow our heart we will let go of regret. Regret is just another way we take for granted what was meant to happen, as opposed to what we wished would have happened. The higher self in you comprehends the masterful design behind what happens and what is meant for you. Ground yourself into that higher aspect and your vision will greatly expand.

Every movement creates lines of Light outward, like ripples off a lily on a pond in the sunlight. Every stillness allows the Light to come in. Looking in a mirror is not an accurate representation of your beauty. How much money you make does not equate your value. What you own is not a direct representation of your worth. You are not the sum of your parts. You are a sum of the whole. Your beauty, your value, your worth is on the inside. Embrace the abundant you that is already present. Make the most of what you've got, worry more about what you're *giving*.

In all my life, what I most regret are all the chances to Love, listen, smile, or help, that slipped by in a moment while I did not take action. *Life happens in a moment*. Life is the art of taking action. Your talent is in making that action something beautiful. Every kindness, every caring word, every act of service to others makes a difference. We cannot fix the world. The world isn't broken. The problem is a human problem. It is a collective

The Self Beyond

crisis of the individual. But, if I fix and heal myself, and you fix and heal yourself, then the world will also heal. It will have to.

But it's hard isn't it? When life gets hard, *Love harder*, forgive more and look deeper. See from an open heart. Step back and appreciate the bigger picture. We have to make an internal shift, but one which can reach the outside world. That is what awakening means. With all the division, build connections. In a time of endless war, bring peace, carry it with you like a blanket everywhere you go. Be a *lighthouse*, an anchor, a life raft. Walk out every morning like a caretaker and do everything, I mean *everything*, you can.

[68]

---

[68] Obtained from Pexels under CC0 creative commons licence

The Self Beyond

Chapter 6: Beyond the Self

THE PLUNGE

I will tell you of a hidden history which has been disseminated through many channels and, even, eluded to in religious texts. Take this story, as perhaps, a parable of the individual and collective spirit-journey within you. What is reality but a dream, an allegory through which we can understand existence? To many, this can be taken as just a story, fiction if it suits you. I invite you to keep an open mind.

Several thousand universal years ago (or many billions of Earth years), a multitude of cosmic communities existed. Each in their own spheres, in their own worlds, in their own way. It went on this way for a time and was good.

Until, one particular group became infatuated by the illusion of separation—they entered into the hazardous terrain of the ego state. They chose to sever their connection from the Love of the All. They had a right to do this, being imbued with free will. However, this initiated a disease of the collective mind which spread like a virus and resulted in greed, apathy, disconnection and perpetual power struggle. This group of "fallen angels" wished to acquire the resources of various systems for themselves, forsaking the Universal Truth that we are all One. They sought control, supremacy, material securities, and deeper into the abyss of their dark dis-truth they plunged. Star Wars became a reality, a long time ago, in a galaxy not so far away…

Great battles went on for eons of time unknown, until an agreement was formed. Within this agreement, a crucial factor was set, which would inextricably alter the course and fate of a species just emerging on a planet in the vastest outskirts of the galaxy. As humankind began its journey on this little blue dot called "Earth," within the subtext of this agreement, the warring species was allowed to participate in the earth experiment. Their influence was no less than catastrophic.

Earth was meant to be an Eden, a garden of rare beauty, to which was found no equivalent in the many star systems across the galaxy. Earth, instead, became something else, a school and a kind of cosmic test. The original purpose shifted, making use of Earth's dense environment of low vibration, which as a consolation, can allow for a raising of vibration within the soul's consciousness by way of many unique opportunities earth, alone, can offer. One particular trait of this experience is the linear memory loss upon entry to the third dimension. Souls cannot consciously recall what came before this "singular life." This is coupled with a collective amnesia as a species, in that we have been cut off from our planet's history, save for a mere few thousand years.

Millions of earth years of human evolution and civilization have eluded us. Many times, empires rose to great heights and collapsed as supernovas under the weight of one simple flaw—an illusion which was injected so deeply into our past that it had become a kind of genetic epidemic in the very consciousness of humanity. The original "sin" occurred the moment we forgot that we are all connected.

The earth experience has been conducted in an inimitable polarized spectrum, these are the confines of the third dimensional reality as one of the harshest conditions of all the cosmic climates. Though, recently, (over the past few decades) the vibrational range available has expanded due to many higher frequency souls coming down and holding the Light.

Through this energy increase, now many are capable of connecting with higher dimensional levels through vibrating at a much higher frequency. What was once available, only, to dedicated masters and saints, is now accessible to any who would rise up from within. Here, in this now shifting dichromatic field, we are still capable of experiencing deep chords of darkness, but also the most radiant Octaves of Light. This journey allows for the Divine Spark within us to awaken, and to again come back to our wholeness.

Take this as you will. I hope you can appreciate the principle underlying the narrative. I discuss this, here, only to point to two things: one, that our cosmology contains within it a kind of "fall" in consciousness which allowed for the illusion of separation, the root of the many symptoms of illness we now see. (This perpetual idea of separation has created the fundamental sickness of individuals and the world as a whole.) And two, we are here now for a higher purpose and the higher levels of awareness are accessible to you right now.

THE INNER OUTER

Why is it so important to be centered, grounded, connected within ourselves, and healed? Aside from all the benefits this has on our personal lives and who we will, then, be in the world as we affect so many others, these changes get us ready. They get us ready to be able to handle the many big issues which need our attention.

Self-alignment gives us the insight, courage, and compassion to be effective world changers. How can we handle the bigger issues if we have not handled our own? How can we contribute to healing in the world if we have not healed? We cannot create a world that is more peaceful, balanced, and compassionate if we have not created that first within ourselves. Our job is to Love ourselves that deeply, and then extend that Love and wisdom outward in a world that greatly needs it.

There are real global issues that urgently require our attention. We cannot deal with these huge issues if we are not coming from a strong place of solid self-awareness. We wouldn't be capable of accepting the unsettling truths that are surfacing now. We need everyone who is willing and able to become aware of these bigger issues and how we are connected to them, so we can effectively change how we interface ourselves with our world. The inner is connected to the outer. It is time to connect the dots.

The outer world we see is simply a reflection of our inner states as we are undergoing a change from the inside out. Collectively, we are still at war with ourselves, divided within ourselves. Collectively, there is also a ceaseless thread of hope to which the spirit of humanity clings. This moment, as we stand upon the precipice, is an allegory for this age. This moment holds both tragedy and triumph within it, pain that is not without purpose, Love within the vast despair. All of this exists in the world as it exists within us, as individuals. We are pushing and pulling within, so we see great forces pushing and pulling in the world around us.

Consider, that fire can either destroy or provide light. Water can either wash away or sustain life. This time is both a time of purging and rebuilding. This time holds up to us a giant mirror to show us the work we need to do from within. Who we are and how we are living, either, supports the destructive cycle or supports healing. As you heal, as you center, as you become aligned to the highest aspects of yourself, this all lays down the bedrock needed for a better world.

We need to look at the world issues as we would our own issues, as the result of what we have not taken responsibility for. We can only heal them by recognizing our part in creating them. When we see the problem being "out there," that is something we can never control. This viewpoint leaves us powerless and passive. When we see the problem from within, we empower ourselves, that is something well within our control. We can change our part, and that part we change is connected to the whole. It is unavoidable that this then will create a chain reaction. Whether that chain reaction is one of healing, wholeness, and peace is up to what *we* do.

The Self Beyond

DUAL-MIND

We point our blame to other people, other groups, and other nations. Ever dividing opinions to the solution, which always lies on the other side of the line we draw. We see our reality in the context of a stark polarity from a mind of discrimination. A mind that discriminates, defines all else by perceiving it as disconnected, and therefore different, from itself. This can be a counterproductive view which does not allow us to get at the source of the problem. There is no separation, except the separation which exists within us. When we see others as separate, whether better or worse, we feel justified in engaging in all kinds of distasteful and, even, violent behavior.

Our worldviews are painted through a mosaic of experiences we have built up throughout our lives. Our perspective is profoundly filtered (and littered) by what we were taught and what we think we now know. Our views can be greatly expanded on, by taking time to become familiar with storylines beyond our own sphere of experience. If we have not engaged beyond our sphere, we become rigid and ignorant.

What happens when so many have not looked beyond their own worldview, is that little bubbles begin to form, cells coagulate together, which then split away from the greater body. They no longer communicate with the body. They view the other cells as threats, instead of pieces of itself. Then, these cells begin to attack the other cells. When cells of a body begin to attack the body they belong to, it is called cancer. This cancer is what kills the collective body of our society.

We categorize, label, and rate to differentiate ourselves from everything we believe is not us, or not like us. This has its uses, but *only* in so far as distinguishing the rudimentary surroundings of a condensed reality, and even there it is still subjective. When we look to transcend duality and heal as a species, we have to recognize the deeper connections we share. In larger scale perspectives, discrimination serves, only, to diminish us from our collective strength and, therefore, becomes our greatest weakness. Our most paramount potential as a species come through *objective* Love. Connection, compassion, cooperation are all acts of non-discriminatory Love which build strength.

Love has no opposite, no competitor. It is only us who defines a contrasting side in a futile attempt to balance our own imbalance. Love is already balanced, standing unaided in its wholeness, just as we are when we release our attachments to an otherwise erroneous illusion. There is no enemy to Love; Love does not separate anything from itself. Love is the great equalizer. Within Love, there is only totality and interconnection. To know this is to gain awareness of your own deepest truth.

We look at the ignorance surrounding us, and, perhaps, you can appreciate, many who display such ignorance have forfeit the sovereignty of their own minds. Their thoughts are not their own. They have been programmed by a unilateral system designed to captivate them into willful oppression. I think, you might find, if you really ask questions, many people do not feel how they think they feel, they are just scared of what they don't understand.

It does not help to attack ill-informed individuals, but to turn focus on the root of the very system which created them: the origin of the indoctrination which fuels the divisive and hateful viewpoints. We must not, only, overcome that system, but the systems *within ourselves* which have perpetuated their existence. The real revolution is not, necessarily, millions of people standing in the streets, but *one individual standing within themselves*.

Stand in your own Light; recognize your own shadow. Unmask your *own* ignorance, your own preconceptions that do not serve the whole to which we each belong. Constantly challenge your own beliefs, your own opinions. Listen to other viewpoints without automatic rejection or judgement. That is how we expand our horizons. Division only weakens. A dual-mind sees the whole.

You do not need to believe everything you think, or everything you were taught. You do not need to stay with a popular opinion that does not feel right. In fact, we have a moral obligation to go against any false premise, no matter how widely accepted. Allow yourself to reconcile the dogmas within you that have been a disservice to you or the world.

Acknowledge that we are evolving, constantly. Accept yourself and others with compassion and know that *we have to change* or nothing will change. Many of the biggest global issues are caused by what millions of people continue to do the same way, and think the same way, every day. As we change our minds we change what we do. As we change what we do we change who

The Self Beyond

we are. As we change who we are we inevitably, and *powerfully*, change the world.

THE DARK SIDE

To shine a Light, we have to see the dark. Focusing on Love and Light are important, but that, alone, is not the total answer: it is a privilege to live in such circumstance that allows us to focus on simply goodness and happiness. Living in a blissful existence communing with nature, laughing, creating art, connecting with others is a beautiful reality. But, what about those who do not have the privilege of the circumstances that allow for this kind of existence? To tell those, who are suffering greatly in situations we cannot imagine, that we can't pay attention to them and prefer to "focus on the positive," is a slap in the face that robs them of the validity of what they face.

There are *millions* of individuals who are dealing with appalling situations; gross abuse, war, starvation, loss of their families, running for their lives, expelled from their homes; people who have buried their children, people who have watched their family members snatched in the night by military, people who live under fierce oppression, people *who pray every day for peace*, for some semblance of comfort, for basic things like food, water, and safety. My god, there are millions of refugees that are famished, freezing, that have nothing but the clothes on their back. Many carrying trauma so recent and extreme, that we cannot conceive of its emotional and psychological gravity. Members of our human family, who must feel so very alone right now. And as you read these words, I compel any sense of compassion within you to *see that* and to *be there* in any way you can afford to be, even beyond what you can afford to do. [69] As Light workers, healers,

---

[69] [I hope not only to create awareness of these issues, but empower you with tools to make a difference. I do not endorse any *one* organization. I will provide information for multiple organizations who are offering support and aid. I have vetted these organizations to the best of my abilities, any organization I submit to you is using 90% (or more) of its donation funds to go directly towards aid and supplies that save lives. More resources cited in the To Help Others section at the end of the book]. The IRC (International Rescue Committee) is dedicated to

Love warriors, we are here to bring reckoning for these injustices and injuries. We are here to see that pain and darkness, and shine our Light there, too.

Simply focusing on Love and Light is an unfair, dishonest, and, even, cruel injustice to those individuals who cannot ignore the very factual reality of their grim situation. The profound pain of others cannot be overlooked. Ignoring what we deem to be "negative," only empowers the suffering to grow. A valid sense of anger, sadness, and grief are very real for many people. These are expressions of the human condition, which must be allowed a place to be heard. We are asked to see this pain, to stop ignoring it, and offer the compassion and support to help heal it at its roots.

Individuals living in these unfathomable circumstances are a part of us. To embrace our own wholeness, we are also called to acknowledge and embrace our greater family with kindness, with empathy, and with urgent attentive care. Any version of spirituality that does not allow space for this, for the healing of this, for the acknowledgment of this, along with action to make this better, is nothing more than a glorified and selfish ideology.

Enlightenment, *true* enlightenment, comes with a cost. The cost is that true transcendent awareness will always reach a place that recognizes, we are not only an individual. We are intimately connected to something much bigger than ourselves. It is that larger collective body to which we are bound. We are responsible for ourselves, for our own personal transformation, and deeper healing, so that we can be something better in this world. We are, also, responsible for the state of the world we have collectively created through our individual actions and inactions.

Spiritual enlightenment, of any degree, comes with a moral imperative of action; peaceful but proactive activism for the social and environmental injustices, to speak for those who have

---

helping refugees worldwide. When the crisis in Yemen affected over 350,000 people with an outbreak of Cholera and 600,000 more were threatened, IRC was there. When over 370,000 Rohingya muslims fled for their lives as their homes were burned down and families were threatened, IRC has been there. For the Syrian refugees, for the children and families IRC has been a presence. More mainstream orgs often overlook these under-reported issues despite their massive scale.

The Self Beyond

no voice, to come to aid for those that need it, to fix the conditions which have created the unsuitable situation in which so many of our brothers and sisters live.

When Houston, TX was hit by hurricane Harvey in the summer of 2017, people from across the US and, even, Mexico (graciously overlooking political administration hostilities) sprang into action. Communities came together. People volunteered to help from all over. Firefighters, officers, and civilians, alike, worked long hours for many days in a row to save people and, even, pets who were stranded by the floods. The website for Red Cross nearly went down, overwhelmed by the amount of traffic from those trying to donate to help. That is what enlightened community is about, and that kind of not-a-second-thought compassionate action is what is needed every day across our shared world.

By contrast, when hurricane Maria made landfall in Puerto Rico (the same summer), the United States was grossly negligent to respond. Many people did not even recognize Puerto Rico as part of the U.S. (despite the fact that Puerto Ricans pay U.S. taxes, they can be drafted into war, yet they have no representation in congress). This has been an ongoing tragedy in which hundreds have now died, due to lack of basic supplies like food and water, as well as being denied the medicine and healthcare they need. Reports of surgeries by flashlights, and toxic mold have been a very real example of the tragedy of neglect.[70] P.R. has made progress, slowly, but the initial abandonment highlighted just how important it is to start asking ourselves a fundamental question; what would we hope others would do if this was our family?

We cannot ignore, or deny, the dark side that exists in the world, or within ourselves. All sides must be integrated to have full awareness, which includes both positive and negative. From there, Love is the answer, but a Love that incorporates a place for the pain, the grief, and the suffering along with all the joyful states of being. A Love which recognizes that enlightenment does not

---

[70] To help Puerto Rico, check out the GlobalGiving campaign, Unidos hurricane relief fund, and Save the Children (86.5% of donation go towards programs). [These organizations/ campaigns are easily searchable online by using their name as the keyword].

mean living in a bubble. It is the opposite. It means going beyond that sphere of comfort into the dark places. It means being with those who are hurting and in need. It is a state of total sentience, total recognition and total allowance of all expressions as neither good nor bad, but as the full spectrum of the human condition which allows for both. There is nothing more spiritual than compassionate non-discrimination in action.

SERVICE TO OTHERS

Service to others is the hallmark of an awakened being. Caring about something bigger than yourself gives meaning and purpose. We cannot call ourselves enlightened if all we care about is our own internal experience, our own little worlds. It is not, simply, about the journey we make for ourselves, that is only the beginning. It is about what you bring back from the mountain of enlightenment, how you use it to change the world, heal the world, uplift and encourage others. The insights we receive on our journey are a gift we are often meant to pay forward. The powerful, resonant energy of pure Love is not meant to stay in a static state held captive within us. It is meant to be shared.

Humans tend to see everything through a narrow aperture. Many never open the door of perception to allow a full view. We see everything around us in terms of how it will benefit us and what we can take for ourselves. We see the earth, the elements, the resources, and many creatures as if they exist for our own provision. Even as some individuals move into more holistic and spiritual appreciation for this great tapestry of life we are each connected to, still the earth is looked at as the healer. It is not the earth's job to heal us, even though she is quite capable and gives of herself so freely. To be truly conscious, we must begin to ask, what we are doing to heal the earth? To advocate for *her*? To protect and preserve her in balance?

The earth is not our commodity, not her lakes or rivers, not her fields or forests, not her crops or the many creatures she supports. Like anything else, every flower, every creature, every drop of water has its own purpose for existing, and it is not to serve as a collation of products and services for human exploitation. Of course, the true balance of nature is to have a relationship. A relationship is a two way street. It means making contribution, creating partnership, and maintaining symbiosis. It is both give and take. Humans do not yet know how to have this kind of relationship because we have not successfully had them with ourselves.

The very instinct of nature is generous knowing all things are bountiful. No element, organic growth, or creature that exists is existent solely for itself. Only humans have taken that stance of hoarding, dividing, and misbalancing the natural order. The homeostatic harmony of the universe is one of sharing, recycling, contributing what we have, and not taking more than is needed. Everything on this earth, our own bodies, and even the energy we expend is borrowed. We must honor and respect everything, every single thing, as the sacred interconnected facet of divinity it is. To go beyond yourself, *live* in service to others.

HOME WORK

To build a better world we need to go home and fix our families. Consider why this is so important: if our family is broken (and so many are) no matter what we create in our life, it will feel fragmented. I understand and sympathize *dearly* with every one of you, in feeling how much this may hit home. I hear all the impossible obstacles, the unforgivable things and I wish for you now to have *peace* and *strength*. For some, this may truly not be possible and that is ok. Some families are born beyond the bond of blood and that can be your focus. For those who have even the slightest window of hope, consider how much it could benefit your life to mend those broken bridges. Some of the deepest healing you will create will be by healing your home.

It takes deep listening, watching closely and speaking last. It takes time to resolve something as complex as a lifetime of issues. All relationships are broken at a communication level first. This means every relationship begins healing through conversations. Through really hearing another, not just with an intent to impose our viewpoint, but to actually understand. Through being capable of speaking our truth without attacking, through creating two-way communication with respect for the other's feelings, perspective and truth, we can heal our broken lines of communication. If we can heal our families and our

The Self Beyond

homes, then we can heal *anything* else in this world, I promise you that.

We need to, also, go outside our families and build stronger, more connected communities. Many of our communities are fractured, distrustful, and segregated. This creates hostile climates that diminish the collective instead of nurturing individuals. Maybe this sounds like too big of a job, but if we can't help restore our local communities, then how can we restore our global one? This can be done by talking to our neighbors, by being involved in local food drives, sharing what we can, creating networks, supporting locally owned businesses, helping those in need, donating items not being used, participating in community gardens, and visiting public markets for groceries. Most cities already have groups and organizations set up and welcome all help. Communities thrive when everyone has a purpose and part.

When there is a need, we should look for ways to support, not only our own families or communities, but others, just like the trees and mycelium network in the forests sends nutrients and resources to damaged trees. As we do this, we build an active grid, a living world-wide-web, which serves to strengthen our human connections. A community based on a service-to-others attitude is a strong community. This is how we can magnify the unique potential of one person and develop that into a resource web which can sustain millions.

EARTH

Earth is home to an enormous amount of life; 3.04 trillion trees, 7.6 billion people, and 8.7 million species. After many millions of years of evolution, 99.9% of all the species that have ever lived are now extinct, a trend which began with the emergence of one species alone. Look at just a few species that have fallen during the time of "modern man;" the majestic West African black rhinoceros, the sleek and graceful Pyrenean ibex, the glorious Eastern elk, *many* species of wolves, the gentle Baiji river dolphin, many species of tiger, the California grizzly bear, the Great Auk penguin, and the Passenger pigeon.

The Self Beyond

In 2015, one of the last rare White rhino's died in a Czech zoo, leaving only four alive on the planet. These species are not dying due to natural selection, they are being exterminated by human activity, habitat loss, hunting, logging, mining, and agricultural encroachment. The Tecopa pupfish was declared extinct due to a bathhouse. Yes, a bathhouse. This now long gone, once precious, creature survived Death Valley and had adapted to temperatures as high as 110 degrees with high salinity, but could not survive the extreme salinity of the water once the streams of its home Amaragos River were combined for a human bathhouse.

This plague of recklessness is not just affecting animals, but vegetation too. Trees and plants have also been tragically lost forever and many others are becoming critically endangered. Many fruits and vegetables are sadly disappearing as well. In the past 80 years, 93% of the seeds creating edible vegetation (cabbage, peas, tomatoes, cucumbers etc.) have gone extinct. [72] [I

---

[71] Obtained from Pexels under CCO creative commons licence
[72] Dr. Mercola. March 11, 2015. Dr. Mercola. The Extinction of Fruits and Vegetables in 80 Years. Retrieved from

know what you are thinking, "Damn," but *there is hope* and we will get there but, first, we have to accurately evaluate where we are at.]

  An endangered species is a species categorized as likely to become extinct. Just a few years ago, in 2012, the International Union for Conservation of Nature Red List featured 3,079 animal and 2,655 plant species listed as endangered, worldwide. In 2016, six species of bees (which play a critical role in pollinating 2/3 of all the food we consume), were placed on the endangered species list. Elephants have become an endangered species along with; polar bears, nearly all species of sea turtles, pandas, orangutans, blue whales and many others.

  When I was a child, I was fascinated by the majesty of sea turtles. They are like the eagles of the ocean. I dreamed of swimming with them, someday, in beautiful turquoise seas. I remember seeing my first elephant, looking in its eyes and deeply feeling the gentle spirit of the giant behind those eyes. I have cried many times watching television, seeing polar bears swim for days, so long their cubs cannot keep up, trying to find an ice drift to land on as the polar caps melt releasing frozen fields of toxic methane. Documentary filmmakers were in tears filming a polar bear in 2017 as it starved due to the food scarcity conditions of human caused climate change. It is one of the most tragic things I have witnessed in my life, as well. I do not want to live in a world without these magnificent animals that make our planet such a gift. I imagine you may share this appreciation for the imperative. *We have to fix this.*

  As an automatic defense mechanism, we like to talk ourselves out of believing any fact that threatens our current comfort. We would, much rather, deny the logical consequences this reality leads us towards, rather than be inconvenienced by changing something we are doing today. I ask every reader to just appreciate these facts and their gravity, and to be willing to be changed by this.

  Some might downplay the scale and urgency we are faced with, "Well, we still have cows and chickens, birds and fish. We still have cotton and corn. What else do we need?" What we often

---

https://articles.mercola.com/sites/articles/archive/2015/03/11/extinction-fruits-vegetables.aspx

fail to pay tribute to is the importance of *diversity*. Earth biodiversity is critical, because without a diverse system, we lose the strength that this great organic-biological tapestry provides. *Diversity* is what creates stability. A system with fewer links in the food chain is much more unstable, and much more susceptible when one link fails. This is what we see as the salmon shortage (due to overfishing and a slew of other human rooted sources) causes the orca whales to starve to the point of near extinction. Something so little impacts something not only giant, but immeasurable.

Biodiversity is *essential* for survival not just for humans, but for every creature and plant in the vast connected ecosystems of Earth. Consider how farming and agriculture depend on the soil. Crops are only as successful as the quality of their soil. Due to industrial single crop farming (sugar, corn, soy)[73], much of the land is ruined; soil is completely depleted of the nutrients necessary to grow. For soil to continually support growth and life, it requires diversity. This means many systems of species complementing and supporting one another.

In order for a business to be successful it needs to profitable. In seeking to increase profit, many businesses seek to decrease the bottom-line. Historically the cheapest way is not always the best for the planet, which is why regulations and standards through groups like the EPA (environmental protection agency) have been essential to protecting the environment. Yet over the past few years, many key regulations have eroded away.

Mega-corporations, from Big Oil to Monsanto,[74] spend *big* money lobbying in the capital to loosen regulations, and secure

---

[73] Industrial single crop farming is a huge contributor to red tide and the algae which is causing hundreds of sea turtles, manatee, dolphins and fish to wash up dead on the shores of places such as Florida creating a huge concern for the future health of our oceans and entire food chain.

[74] Monsanto [which was recently bought by Bayer] is the leading manufacturer of genetically modified "foods" and the pesticide linked to the massive bee decline, Roundup (glyphosate based herbicide) which has knowingly poisoned millions of people for over 35 years along with over 282 million acres of land worldwide in which GMO seeds are planted. March Against Monsanto is a grassroots movement opposing

the rights to hundreds of thousands of acres of land across the world. It has always astounded me, the audacity we have, to operate as if the earth belongs to the highest bidder. And with corruption abounding in politics (through conflicts of interest), national land appears to be auctioned off to the most profitable firms.

Oil pipelines have already leaked into a third of the world's fresh water sources. We do not have a backup plan for what we will do when this limited water runs out. [75] So this is where we are at: we have to recognize the scope of this issue, reexamine how we have supported a cycle of collapse (so that we can stop supporting it further), and repair the damage done. We have to understand the roots of how this began. And, in all fairness, we have to appreciate that this problem is not just created by cutthroat CEO's—it was created by us. All of us. We paid into this way of living with our own ignorance. But we are solving that equation *right now*.

The near extinction of the 25-million-year-old Great Barrier Reef is perhaps one of the most stirring grievances to comprehend. The reef is the world's *largest living structure*, and the only one visible from space. It rests at 1,400 miles long, with 2,900 individual reefs and 1,050 islands. In total area, larger than the United Kingdom, and containing more biodiversity than all of Europe combined. It harbors 1,625 species of fish, 3,000 species of mollusk, 450 species of coral, 220 species of birds, and 30 species of whales and dolphins. [76] The slim threshold that sustains the reef continues to be challenged by factors such as climate change and ocean acidification. Pollution and irresponsible human

---

their irresponsible actions. Organic Consumers Association is another grassroots non-profit public interest group campaigning for health, justice, and sustainability.

[75] Stand up to big oil, Oceana, Green Peace, CAOE (Committee Against Oil Exploration), Friends of Earth are all seeking to end offshore drilling and oil expansion along with promoting clean and sustainable energy.

[76] Jacobsen, Rowan. October 11, 2016. Outside. Obituary: Great Barrier Reef (25 Million BC-2016). Retrieved from https://www.outsideonline.com/2112086/obituary-great-barrier-reef-25-million-bc-2016

activity is the culprit. This may sound scary and it is, but since humans have caused this, that means humans can change this.

The intricately connected systems of life on earth are fragile in many ways, like a web: if one thread breaks, the whole structure is weakened. But these systems can be strengthened by humans building a new network, working with the good of all life, not only its own generation, in mind.

Seven generations and sustainability has been explained as a *"philosophy commonly credited to the Iroquois Confederacy but practiced by many Native nations. The Seventh Generation philosophy mandated that tribal decision makers consider the effects of their actions and decisions for descendants seven generations into the future. There was a clear understanding that everything we do has consequences for something and someone else, reminding us that we are all ultimately connected to creation."* Sustainable development is, *"Development that meets the needs of the present without compromising the ability of future generations to meet their own needs."* [77] The sustainability of earth is not only a matter of its present stewards, but all those who come after. That is why so many are, now, working to become educated about permaculture and eco-sustainability. [78]

THE VEINS OF OUR PLANET

Do you have a favorite lake or river, a place you happily flock to during the warm summer season? For me, some of my best memories are in the water. Rivers, streams, and waterways are vital to the survival of *every* species on earth. We need water to live, to grow food, to drink, to wash, and to support the many other species and ecosystems.

Due to the obsession with petroleum, sugar, pesticides, animal agriculture, irresponsible use of plastics (single use and excessive packaging) along with a slew of other environmental hazards, many of our once pristine lands and waterways have

---

[77] Gibson, Kelly. April 11, 2011. Partnership with Native Americans. Sustainability, a Seventh Generation Philosophy. Retrieved from http://blog.nativepartnership.org/sustainability/

[78] For more on understanding permaculture, see: https://permacultureprinciples.com/

been perpetually polluted and infested. This topic is complex and while becoming educated on how many of our personal activities contribute to largescale pollution, along with adjusting our own routines and activities can mitigate our impact: I would like to hone in on one of the facets that captures a latitude of issues, which remains to be oil extraction and use.

On the hunt to extract every drop of oil humans have resorted to drilling in oceans, in vital habitats, on sacred sites and national parks. Countries like the United States have also gotten their hands very dirty with proxy power grabs for oil resources in occupied countries, using military interests to politically bulldoze our way over beautiful beaches and cities which obviously causes more than just environmental concerns.

Perhaps, the most pernicious of all oil extraction practices, since the turn of the century, has been the calamitous practice of fracking. Fracking (hydraulic fracturing) for tar sands (bituminous sands with oil deposits), not only destroys the land and water on the extraction site, but also (and often more relevantly) during transport. Shipped by trains, barges, and *pipelines* that often leak or spill, creating catastrophes which the companies liable are rarely held responsible for, except to send a few cleanup crews. These toxic spills poison, and in some cases irreversibly contaminate; soil, water, and air in one shot. This is not just a worst case scenario and goes far beyond the (uniquely) publicized BP Oil Spill of 2010, which leaked 172 million gallons of oil into the Gulf causing $17.2 billion in damage. (I would argue you cannot put a price tag on something like this, since we honestly do not know the long term affects such an event will create). The majority of these great disasters are not reported, at all. Since 2010, during a 5 year band, there were over 3,300 incidents of crude oil and natural gas leaks in U.S. pipelines.[79]

In November of 2017 an estimated 200,000 gallons of oil spilled from the Keystone pipeline in South Dakota nearly at the one year anniversary of a standoff between water protectors and

---

[79] Starbuck, Amanda. June 22, 2015. Center for Effective Government. Map Displays Five Years of Oil Pipeline Spill. Retrieved from https://www.foreffectivegov.org/blog/map-displays-five-years-oil-pipeline-spills/

police in 2016. Native tribes at Standing Rock Reservation in South Dakota faced bitter cold weather conditions and punishing water cannons, tear gas canisters, and rubber bullets from police to protect the water and to protest the access pipeline that was being driven through their treaty lands to prevent ecological tragedies just like this. [80]

I will provide more ways to make a difference on these big issues in a section coming up, but if you can appreciate the negative impact that the oil industry has single handedly created, then the solution might become more obvious. Use less oil, less plastic, less energy—*and*—use sustainable resources. It all comes down to understanding our impact.

By 2050 there will be more plastic in the ocean than fish. 80% of marine litter originates on land. The great pacific garbage patch discovered in 1988 is a collection of plastic debris and chemical sludge floating between California and Hawaii. It covers 1.6 million square km. Food containers, packaging, plastic bags, and single use products not only make up the majority of this mess (about 31%), they also represent the use of unsustainable resources. [81] This pollution has impacted at least 267 species of marine life: nearly all species of sea turtle, sea birds, and nearly half of all marine mammal species who ingest these items and suffocate, starve, or become entangled and cannot escape. "It's just one bag", said 8 billion people.

THE LUNGS OF OUR PLANET

Imagine, if you can, a lush canopy of rainforest above you, the calls of the birds overhead, tree trunks tall as skyscrapers that seem to touch the sun, shading you from the humid heat of the day. Everywhere you look is green. This atmosphere summons something tribal from deep within you. The voices of ancient medicine men and women are there, beckoning you to listen.

---

[80] Gibbens, Sarah. Welch, Craig. November 16, 2017. Keystone Pipeline Spills 200,000 Gallons of Oil. National Geographic. Retrieved from https://news.nationalgeographic.com/2017/11/keystone-oil-spill-south-dakota-spd/

[81] Learn more about marine pollution here: https://www.cleanwater.org/problem-marine-plastic-pollution

The Self Beyond

There are flowers of every color, which your eyes could have never conceived, plants with leaves in shapes and sizes that pique your imagination to times long past. There is a spirit here, an energy, and a deep sense of healing and connection.

Tragically, this kind of rare and mystical landscape is being lost. Mega-industry's endless drive to generate profit spares no expense to our planet. Everything from animal agriculture to the relentless resourcing of cheap fibers for clothing, packaging, paper products, and wood have created a modern-day plague, known as deforestation. Deforestation is clearing forests on a massive scale, resulting in damage to the quality of the land (this is an understatement).

Deforestation may not seem like a big deal to many who may believe it will all grow back. This is false. Deforestation, essentially, means gone forever. It will never grow back on its own. This is, mainly, an irreversible process which only takes, and leaves nothing. Resourcing un-recycled toilet paper, alone, wipes out an estimated 27,000 trees a day, the product of a 55-million-year-old rainforest all to, quite literally, be flushed down the drain.

Palm oil is a huge culprit, and I challenge you to go to your cupboard and just see how many labels this appears on, and food products are just the start. Palm oil is used in everything from packaging to paper products, from cleaning products to fuels, and from face wash to French fries. Palm oil's tremendous overuse has been a heavy plight on the most vital ecosystems of our planet. Some of the most popular companies are big fans of exploiting this cheap resource at the cost of future generations. [82] The big problem is, palm oil is in such demand, that farmers across the world are cutting down, or clear burning, rich biodiverse tropical rainforests to make room for one crop palm oil plantations.

What are we losing? A mere four square mile patch of rainforest contains as many as 1,500 species of flowering plants, 750 species of trees, 125 mammal species, 400 species of birds, 100 species of reptiles, 60 species of amphibians, and 150 different species of butterflies. There are more fish species in the Amazon River system than the *entire* Atlantic Ocean. The Andean

---

[82] Palm Oil Scorecard shows best and worst companies for responsible sourcing, http://www.ucsusa.org/global-warming/stop-deforestation/palm-oil-scorecard-2015#.WguoW7pFzIU

The Self Beyond

Mountain range and Amazon jungle are home to more than half of the world's species of flora and fauna. At least 1/3 of the planet's bird species reside in the Amazon rainforest. 37% of all medicines prescribed in the U.S. have active ingredients derived from rainforest plants. At least 1,650 rainforest plants can be used as alternatives to our present fruit and vegetable staples. 70% of the plant species identified by the US National Cancer Institute as holding anti-cancer properties come from rainforests. One hectare (2.471 acres) of rainforest absorbs one ton of carbon dioxide per year, while the clearing and burning of the rainforests accounts for 20-25% of the CO_2 emitted into the atmosphere. [83]

Environmental issues are always connected to the political. In the U.S., many of us are battling a plethora of government administration initiatives so criminal and bizarre, it is difficult to know where to begin. Attacks on the Environmental Protection Agency (EPA), the defunding of National Park Services (in blatant efforts to open National Parks to drilling by Big Oil), even as obvious connections are held by administrators with companies such as Energy Transfer. (The same company responsible for the pipeline running through the Standing Rock Indian Reservation.)

As of April 2017, the EPA was forced to shut down one of its most significant climate safety programs which provided smart growth, regulatory innovation and climate preparedness due to steep administration budget cuts to funding which political administrators believed to be a "waste of money." When we have political leaders with such deeply imbedded conflicts of interest with big business, especially big oil, this is what we will see. Felonious administrations will deregulate laws that threaten to emasculate profit margins, selling off *public* land for their own *private* interest, while protected lands, ecosystems and biodiversity will pay the price. This is often justified with hordes

---

[83] The Rainforest Action Network is a non-profit organization whose mission statement is "RAN preserves forests, protects the climate and upholds human rights by challenging corporate power and systemic injustice through frontline partnerships and strategic campaigns."

of prestigious scientists sent in to convince people their fears of risk or loss are unfounded. [84]

HOW TO BE A CLIMATE WARRIOR

What can we do against something so big? Do you believe one person can make a difference? Because, you can! The problems we see in the world are created by what millions of individuals do each day. We all love steps. Here are ten easy steps that can make a significant impact right now. Today you can be a climate warrior, a pollution protector, in the comfort of your very own home.

1. **Reduce, Reuse, Recycle!** Recycling is easy. I have a lot of fun doing it at home. Many cities are now making it even easier by offering one combined recycling bin. Plastic, cardboard, and tin can all be recycled (just make sure to keep the plastic bags out because they clog up the system used to separate the materials.)
2. **Go reusable!** Please stop using disposable bags, silverware, and cups. Start there. Little things like coffee stirrers and straws, they end up in the bellies of sea turtles, birds, and fish who mistake them for food. Get a refillable water bottle and wash your silverware for reuse. The amount of energy and resources we spend to make these plastic items used for a few minutes, and the length of time they reap havoc on nature and wildlife should be a deep concern for all. Limit purchases of items with excessive packaging. Invest in reusable grocery bags and biodegradable trash bags made of plant based materials (not plastic). They are easy to find online and only cost pennies more.
3. **Use less, buy less**—*live simply*. For example, do you really need a new outfit? The fashion industry has created

---

[84] Find out more about how to stand up against corruption and get money out of politics through: Represent US at https://represent.us/ and Inequality for All (seeking to end Citizens United which is a huge factor in political corruption) at http://inequalityforall.com/take-action/get-money-out-of-politics/

multiple environmental concerns (it is actually the second dirtiest industry in the world). [85] Choose a second hand store, when you can. Research where what you buy is coming from, consider the earth resources that go into making it, the many sore hands it may have crossed, and how long it will actually be used. Ask yourself, is that all worth it?

4. **Start with where you are**: your communities. Start a cleanup effort with some friends in areas you like to bike, hike, and swim. Don't leave out the city areas. All that trash on the street goes somewhere too! If you go on a walk, devote ten minutes of that time to picking up trash. It *all* makes a difference.
5. **Read labels**—get to know the companies you buy from and reward your business to companies that are making sustainable, *ethical* and responsible choices. An unsettling amount of goods and products are coming at a great cost, made or gathered through forced labor or, even, child labor. [86]
6. **Be kind to animals**—you don't have to be a vegan to make conscientious choices that make a big difference to our animal friends. But, know that eating a plant based diet is one of the most impactful choices you can make for the environment (as the meat and dairy industries are a leading cause of carbon pollution), as well as for your health and the world. [87] A great place to start is by having, at least, one plant based meal each day and going from there.

---

[85] Sweeny, Glynis. August 17, 2015. Ecowatch. Fast Fashion Is the Second Dirtiest Industry in the World, Next to Big Oil. Retrieved from https://www.ecowatch.com/fast-fashion-is-the-second-dirtiest-industry-in-the-world-next-to-big--1882083445.html

[86] United States Department of Labor. List of Goods Produced by Child Labor or Forced Labor. Retrieved from https://www.dol.gov/ilab/reports/child-labor/list-of-goods/

[87] Falcon G, Lisa. October 19, 2017. Universal Hidden Insight. Is Veganism Doing More Harm Than Good? Retrieved from https://universalhiddeninsight.weebly.com/uhi-articles/is-veganism-doing-more-harm-than-good

7. **Boycott factory farming** and buy from farms vetted as engaging in *ethical* farming. Factory farming has an enormous negative impact on the environment.
8. **Plant fruit trees and pollinators:** trees reduce CO_2 buildup, and fruit trees provide food at the same time. Pollinators play a significant role in the food chain and by supporting their survival, we can support a wide network of life. Remember not to use pesticides that harm more than just the little bugs.
9. **Speak up!** Many people are, simply, unaware of the scope of the issues earth is facing. A polite and respectful conversation, or well placed, "Did you know?" can go a long way to plant seeds of knowledge.
10. **Be willing to change**. You cannot change anything until you are willing to change something you do daily. Start with one thing at a time, and don't give up.

This list is by no means all-inclusive. I want to promote a sense of hope, but I do not want to dilute the fact that at this point, moderate changes will not save the earth. We need drastic changes made on every level of resourcing, production, and consumption. We need to eliminate our delusional idea of disposal because there is no such thing. Everything goes somewhere, we can't bury our trash, and we can't sink it or burn it. We have to think fourth-dimensionally and live from this basic understanding. This is going to take massive action on a global level. What the logistics of that action looks like will take the intelligent and careful thought of many people working together.

Clean water, clean soil, clean air should be the goal of every member of the human race. Remember, we are borrowing this earth from the seven generations that come after us, our children and their children, and we cannot take that for granted. We cannot let them down. I want my niece's children to be able to meet an elephant and swim with the sea turtles in clean turquoise waters. I want your children to experience that, too.

CHANGES THAT MATTER

We all have a vision of a better world, and where we are now, compared to that end goal, may seem like quite a gap. But,

The Self Beyond

it is through our cooperative conscientious efforts that we get there. Little things can make a big difference, because it all adds up.

The Dalai Lama once said, "*If you think you are too small to make a difference, try sleeping with a mosquito.*" If you think one small action done many times can't change anything then do this: every time you make a piece of trash, keep it, don't throw it away. It's just one piece of trash, it doesn't cause much trouble. See how long it takes for those accumulated pieces of trash to add up and become a big nuisance. What if instead of this trash experiment, you tried something with impact, like *picking up* trash, eating healthy, or helping at a local mission? How quickly would that add up?

We are starting to appreciate that to change our life, or the world, we must start with what we do day-to-day. For one important example, consider that most of us buy a lot of stuff. Remember that when you buy something, you are promoting that company: that company's ideas of moral business practices, its political views and contributions, its resourcing and production methods. That company may be cutting manufacturing costs through exploiting workers in a distant country with sweat shop labor—this is the case, more often, than many people are aware of. That company might be a part of the destruction of rainforests or sacred land to offset the expense of packaging materials. [88] That company might be lobbying politicians in Washington to remove any legal barriers which could hold them accountable to making environmentally and socially responsible business decisions. Every dollar we spend is a vote, a vote for the world we want. That is why being an informed consumer, not just in what we buy, but in every facet of our lives, is absolutely critical at this time.

As we see the issues, as a whole, and understand our piece in all of this—we change, we evolve, because a changed mind is a changed *person*. Healing the earth is as important in our healing,

---

[88] Visit the Palm Oil Scorecard 2015: Fries, Face Wash, Forests (last year data on this particular site was available) to view a comprehensive list of top companies ranked by their commitment to end palm oil abuse. Union of Concerned Scientists. At http://www.ucsusa.org/global-warming/stop-deforestation/palm-oil-scorecard-2015#fast

as our own work on ourselves is. It will require critical thinking. It will require independent research into the truth beyond the political marketing of the mainstream media. Understand that the media is owned by the same corporations that, essentially, own the government (or at the least nearly completely influence it). That system is funded and sponsored by big oil, big advertising, big military, big agribusiness, big pharma, big insurance, and big healthcare. Therefore, the media and political spokesmen support the systems which keep it (literally) in business.

The media acts as one of the most effective weapons to date, in that it comes at the very root of us: our consciousness. The viewpoint offered, is the perspective that holds to the status quo of the current power systems bread and butter. It decides and choreographs what you buy and who you vote for. Social media engagements, online material "randomly" coming up on your newsfeed, and television programs are all placed to deliberately influence your opinion. Through this, popular belief is sculpted by corporations, instead of chosen by us as individuals. No one is immune to this. We are what we believe, and what we do is based on what we think. Therefore billions of dollars a year are spent on shaping that viewpoint to bolster the system that is doing just fine if we don't see the truth. The urgent and compelling reality is that, we will need to look beyond what we think we believe to see the truth.

Occupy your mind. We must broaden our perspective to change our lifestyle from the inside out. We cannot fix something if we do not understand the way it is broken. There is no need for fierce battles of will to display our autonomy, no need for standing in the streets and shouting. We, simply, have to see the truth—we are being used. Many aspects of how we live assist this perpetual state of affairs, from our tax money funding the military industrial machine, to our requisite endorsement of petroleum. It is all connected, one aspect to the other. All we need to do is change our daily actions and put pressure in the right political places.

What we watch on television, what we are perusing online, what we are told in the most prominent institutions of indoctrination, what we are led to believe by biased news sources and bought elected officials, is all *controlled*. It all validates a broken paradigm, and an often diseased and unilateral way of thinking. This problem has a simple resolution, are you ready? Unplug.

I know these are difficult truths to reflect on, but there is a solution hidden in the problem. Within what seems our powerlessness lies our power. Without our buy in, without our agreement to continue fighting and dividing against one another according to lies and propaganda, they will not be able to sell us more war or false peace. Without our continual fuel into inescapable debt and profit schemes that sold us lies in the name of the "American Dream", then the predatory banks will close down. Without our continued use of unsustainable energy sources, the companies will be forced to become sustainable, and responsible, or lose all business. Without our continued consumption of the toxic products and mindsets of this system we have fed into all our lives, we will become something different entirely: a critical thinking, responsible, and effective answer to the question of who is truly in power.

I do not claim to have the ultimate solvent for our world's issues. No one person does, and that is a safeguard, that it will take *many* people with our best ideas, working *together*, to fix it. I only hope to in this small section provide a glimpse of what we are facing, in the hopes that you may ask yourself, "What can I do to make this better?" Your ideas are needed. We can shift the dynamic of this seemingly insurmountable circumstance. And the changes we make together, will change the world.

THE HUMAN RACE

The human race is a curious species, part animal, part alien in our own world. We have the capacity for Love and hate, for peace and for war, for logic and for irrationality. We come from different backgrounds, different viewpoints, and different ways of living. Despite our many differences, we share a common experience and a common search for peace, connection, fulfillment, and perhaps, when looking deeply, for truth.

Stop for a moment and consider the endless ineffable beauty of this life, all the opportunities available allowing us to

The Self Beyond

grow, to learn, and to experience this wide spectrum of choices and chances. Equally consider the great responsibility a life such as this implies. To understand that responsibility, we must recognize just exactly how we are connected.

We have explored the reality of a connected universe. That connection is the greatest law of the cosmos, as much Zen as it is factual. Every living organic molecule is literally interrelated; atomically, chemically, biologically and yes, even spiritually. This type of a world is constantly moving, with trillions of working pieces, to which each facet (including you), contributes. This world is a shared world, a gift, not belonging to you or me, but belonging to something bigger than all of us.

There are many issues the family of humanity is globally facing, which must compel us to look deeper at what we can each do to return this gift in the condition which will secure a thriving future for those that have loaned it. There is war, poverty, hunger, suffering, destruction to the sacred ecosystems upon which the entire web of life relies. All of this begs us to, now, consider—what is truly important?

Humanity is more than just a category: it is a *quality*. It means Love, compassion, understanding, and the ability to act, when life would be harmed or neglected without our intervention. We are living in a time where being a part of the human race must mean we take our characteristic humanity as an imperative to care for the whole.

What will be our story? Will those beyond us look down on earth a few mere centuries from now and remark, "They had a small chance to change, and they did not take it." Or, can we change history, and reverse the path of destruction we have been on? We are the writers of that future story, and our collective destiny is painted into existence by the brush of millions of individuals.

THE THEATRE

I want to make it clear, I do not take the discussion of political or social issues lightly, nor do I take sides. [Don't tap out on me here, we have to dig through the dirt to reach the gold. My hope is you can go here with me and look at these important issues. The *best* part of this work leads up from here to the end.] I am a highly spiritual person and I have a deep appreciation for the value of life. I hold all life sacred. I see all human life as one family, along with all beings and life forms in this shared Universe. I am an avid opponent of all acts of violence, war, and aggression, including the kind of nationalism that breeds racism and xenophobia. That kind of thinking only serves to harm and imbalance the world we share. In all my years of research into many subjects, such as consciousness, ancient history, quantum physics and spirituality, I was inevitably led to a greater awareness of the urgent plight our world is facing: political, social and environmental issues abound and we as caretakers are tasked to be aware, speak up, and act. I could not stand in my truth and not speak to some of this in this work, which, I hope, reaches and awakens many minds.

I am not attempting to stir fear. Fear is the lowest vibration. Fear is exactly what the governing powers at play want. If we are in fear, we are easy to control. It is easy to sell us all kinds of things in fear (from new products to obscure promises of security). But we must have courage and refuse to be scared away from facing the reality and existence of any darker agendas. Remember to focus on staying centered, remain aware of the Divine Being you are, and the Infinite Space you came from. My goal is to create a higher awareness, to educate and *empower* people to recognize that every one of us has the power to make a difference. That power is in what we do and what we don't do, what we say and don't say, what we know and believe, and it all makes a difference. *Hold your Light.*

The elections are double rigged on both ends and have been for many decades. Politics became entertainment, a kind of theatre to divide opinions from reality and misdirect the masses. The illusion of choice unilaterally built to appear dualistic. While media focuses its attention on one big distracting story, another unscrupulous bill is passed through silently, even against the will of the people. The most basic premises of illusion are used successfully to fool millions every day. These are things which I sincerely wish could be just a "conspiracy theory," but they just aren't. Creating fear to secure profit by offering security from that fear is a mob tactic. The same countries pumping the media waves full of new threats are profiting greatly in arms deals and weapon manufacturing sales. Any magician knows to tell you to look at the right hand while the real trick is happening in the left.

This all equates to a kind of Theatre, a display of carefully spun narratives to contextualize the violent reality. The same tactics are employed to misguide and divide popular opinion. Once you are aware of the method, you will be able to see through the narrative.

I say this to sow the opposite of fear. I say this to ignite *conscience*. I say this to empower you to see through the fear that is being shoved down our throats. *I say this to give you back what has been taken*, to spark within you a knowing that can give you hope, strength, and resolve. We are together in this, together across the world. Despite the lines drawn and the disjointed storylines repeated at nauseam on the news, we are not being told the whole story. I understand how troubling many of these issues are to look at, but this is a trouble we cannot afford to neglect or deny. Whatever intuition within you drew you to this book, you were meant to read this. We are here to be the ones who will build something better.

WORLD ISSUES

Consider that an average of 20,000 people starve to death every single day. I will mince no words on these points. 45% of the world's children under the age of five die for no other reason, except that they live in a world so narcissistically imbalanced, so completely disconnected from the meaning of life, that nearly half the world's innocent children die of starvation. 2.6 million children a year are lost to hunger globally. [89] How can we ever answer for this? How can we continue on knowing *that*, without changing in some way? This is not about religion, or statistics, or a political party, or any belief. This is negligence at the most egregious levels. [90] This exemplifies a massive failure as a species, but we can change when we become aware.

---

[89] Zero Hunger, November 4, 2017, retrieved from http://www1.wfp.org/zero-hunger

[90] Organizations that are feeding the hungry: World Vision (they do not just hand out food, they go in and meet with communities they work with. They have a conversation about what they need, food, schools,

The Self Beyond

Consider the amount of money spent not to give life, but to take it. The United States has waged a "war on terror" for nearly two decades, killing *at least* 210,000 civilians (in Iraq, Afghanistan and Pakistan alone) [91] Even innocent women and children have died, along with creating thousands of destroyed families and livelihoods. People who had nothing to do with any of the backhanded political corruption, whose lives were stolen while in their homes, at the market, or on a roadway, all of this, while millions of people starve and face displacement. [92]

I know many would still defend what they are certain is the humanitarian interventionist act of U.S. liberation, citing how many children we are saving. I wish *so much* that was entirely true. That somewhere in this mess, we could say we had been the heroes of the world. However, when so much is at stake, and so many lives have been lost, we cannot cling to subjective half-truths in the name of blind faith or unflinching patriotism. I invite and compel you to look deeper at the counterpoint of the cost of war. [93] I ask you to consider here a bigger picture understanding.

---

farming etc. Together they create a plan to implement to help the community become self-sufficient). Food for the Poor is another org in which 95% of all proceeds go to feeding hungry people. Rise Against Hunger is another great org making a global impact by providing food and aid.

[91] Costs of War, March 2015, Civilians Killed and Wounded, Watson International and Public Affairs, Brown University. Retrieved from http://watson.brown.edu/costsofwar/costs/human/civilians

[92] Organizations supporting victims of war: Warchild.org.uk (their mission is to protect, educate, and stand up for the rights of children of war. They provide support when conflicts break out and stay on long after. From helping provide access to education for Syrian children, or rehabilitating ex-child soldiers from the Central African Republic.) Sunrise USA is a leading provider of humanitarian aid to Syria. Doctors without Borders and Mercy Corps are providing consistent support and lifesaving care as well.

[93] These points are made *not* as pro-anyone, or anti-anyone. I do hope the U.S. can regain its moral integrity. I hope the bombings will cease. A poll was taken in 2017 which showed 75% of the American population is most scared not of "terrorists" but of its own government. This is about pro-life, pro-truth, and anti-war. Period. All life is sacred.

24,287 bombs were dropped at the behest of the U.S. in 2016 while "fighting terrorism", with a high percentage (up to 90% in one five month period), [94] striking innocent people, even women and children. On March 20 of 2017, the U.S. bombed a school and two days later, a market in Syria. [95] This brought in investigators from both Human Rights Watch and the U.N., who remarked, "There has been a staggering loss of civilian life" regarding the offensive in Raqqa, Syria. So many children have been made casualties in Pakistan, that artists have begun posting huge pictures of children killed on the rooftops in an effort to strike empathy in the drone bomb operators. I know many soldiers are doing what they truly believed was right, but, unfortunately, the justification many are told, is not always true. If we want to save children, we have to stop dropping bombs and start bringing food, water, medicine, and listening to each other. Artist and musician Michael Franti once said, "*You cannot bomb the world into peace.*"

A question must be asked in this madness. How does war eradicate terrorism? Doesn't it create terror? War, itself, *is* terror. How can a war based on this premise ever end? The answer is, it can't, and it is not meant to.

Since the disastrous war campaign, launched by Bush nearly two decades ago, the U.S. has spent over $820 trillion dollars on the war in Iraq, over $14 trillion dollars on "fighting terror," and over $768 trillion dollars on the war in Afghanistan, equating to a spending total of 1.7 *quadrillion* dollars on war, and that number increases exponentially every day. [96] By contrast, it has been estimated that a trifling $30 billion a year would provide

---

[94] Zenko, Micah. Wilson, Jennifer. Counsel on Foreign Relations. January 5, 2017. How Many Bombs Did the US Drop in 2016? Retrieved from https://www.cfr.org/blog/how-many-bombs-did-united-states-drop-2016

[95] Hussein, Murtaza. The Intercept. September 25, 2017. Dozens of Civilians Killed When US Bombed a School and Market in Syria. Retrieved from https://theintercept.com/2017/09/25/syria-us-airstrike-civilian-death-hrw-tabqa/

[96] Cost of National Security. Fighting for a U.S. federal budget that prioritizes peace, economic security and shared prosperity. Retrieved from https://www.nationalpriorities.org/cost-of/

food and the most basic human essentials to *862 million hungry people*. To put this in perspective, in 2016 the United States spent over $622 *billion* on the Military alone (in one year).

War creates many issues worldwide. These political issues become social issues and are largely complex. Here I want to focus on the humanitarian needs created. Global conflicts, the relentless drive of corporate interests, security threats, and perhaps even climate change itself have created a dangerous and unstable social environment over the past decades in much of the Middle East, particularly so, in Syria. These issues are multifaceted in their roots, and the social issues created through this instability are multifaceted, themselves. The total number of Syrian refugees is at 5,344,184 people of concern (as of the date 11/14/2017) and climbing daily. [97]

[98]

The violence of war kills and destroys. It leaves nothing, and as awakened beings, how can we overlook the toll on innocent life at such a scale as we become aware of the sacredness of life within ourselves? That becomes a double standard and a hypocrisy. The civilian casualties of the Iraq war (to which there can be no accurate count on this scale) have been an estimated

---

[97] Syrian Regional Refugee Response. Retrieved from: http://data.unhcr.org/syrianrefugees/regional.php
[98] Puskechina, March 11, 2017, under CC license retrieved from Wikicommons

193,702 people [99], the war in Afghanistan has brought 3,498 civilian casualties (as of 2016) [100], including over 1,500 children [101]. In Syria more than 1 in 10 Syrians have been wounded or killed since 2011, and a staggering 470,000 deaths have been caused by the conflict. [102] These were, mainly, non-combatant people killed while they were praying, while they were fetching water, while they were sleeping. This is the true cost of war, and no matter which "side" is right, or wrong, there is no *right* reason for children or innocent people to die.

In April of 2017, Donald Trump's stock in defense contractor Raytheon soared when he barraged the coast of Syria with over $60 million in Tomahawk Cruise missiles. A few days later, the U.S. dropped the largest bomb we have (next to a nuclear bomb) on what the media claimed was a "remote" area. This 22,000-pound GBU-43 bomb dubbed "the Mother of All Bombs" was dropped in Nangarhar province, an area home to roughly 1.44 million people who described the event as a "horror." We cannot allow ourselves to be so confused that we fail to see through the mass manipulation. The world begs us to recognize the conflicts of interest, to read the subtext, which all point to much less benevolent objectives then ending terror.

I ask every member of the armed forces (on all sides), who are actively participating in any hostilities, to seek within you the will to question what you are being told. To those who are acting in true humanitarian interest, building schools, bringing food and water, we do *thank you for your service*. For those who have been

---

[99] Iraq Body Count. Retrieved from https://www.iraqbodycount.org/
[100] AlJazeera. February 6, 2917. Afghan civilian casualties at record high in 2016: UN. Retrieved from http://www.aljazeera.com/news/2017/02/afghan-civilian-casualties-2016-170206062807210.html
[101] The Guardian. 'Alarming' number of child deaths push Afghan casualties to record high. Retrieved from https://www.theguardian.com/world/2016/jul/25/civilian-casualties-in-afghanistan-at-record-high-un-warns
[102] Boghani, Priyanka. Frontline. February 11, 2016. A Staggering New Death Toll for Syria's War — 470,000. Retrieved from http://www.pbs.org/wgbh/frontline/article/a-staggering-new-death-toll-for-syrias-war-470000/

fighting, you are being called to understand the deeper implications of these fights, and to do your own critical research on these occupations and offensive strikes. You are being called on to oppose any order given which violates the sacred spirit of humanity within you. Many may believe strongly that killing is sometimes necessary. I challenge that politically charged narrative and ask you to *search deeply within yourself*, to see others beyond the political barriers, beyond nationality or creed, and see the human being. We have more in common with those we fight than those who order these strikes.

In any other context, we might be able to sit and find out about this person's children, or how very scared they are for their own family. Please recognize the tremendous cost of war: to you, your families, and other families, as well. Please recognize how often blood is spilled to fill the coffers of career pack politicians. If you feel the will within you, many will stand with you, as you *stand down*. You do not have to fight in conjured confrontations for old mixed up millionaires who do not morn your loss. Refuse to be the muscle for their war dog, refuse to be a man or woman made into a weapon. A warrior fights against no other, *but recognizes himself in all*. Be a soldier in other ways, there are walls being erected that need to be stood against, homes that need to be rebuilt, wells that need to be dug to bring clean water to thousands. There are many ways to fight without fists. You do not need to wound yourself any longer. Come and be a soldier of healing. [103]

Many people worldwide are facing extreme humanitarian crisis due to conflicts of all kinds. Most of which, we are just not aware of, such as the crisis in Yemen where hundreds of thousands of people are at risk of deadly disease, due to large scale cholera outbreaks, the Rohingya refugee crisis which has been barely made visible through media and has affected nearly half a million people, the plight of the people of West Papua who have become modern day slaves (and those in Libya), the millions displaced on the Gaza Strip and the West Bank in the world's largest open air prison, while the West has turned away for over 60 years. This accounts for *millions* of people who are suffering and in need of

---

[103] To provide support for wounded warriors, visit the Disabled American Veterans site at https://www.dav.org/

basic human compassion and essential elements of survival, like food, water, medicine, shelter and freedom. (See the "To Help Others" section at the end of this book to find out more about these urgent issues and how you can help.)

This is heavy stuff, but we are now developing the strength to bear witness, and, hopefully, change our own perspective. Through healing, we are fortifying our spirits to be of better service in a world that needs it. We are now becoming awakened enough within ourselves to see how very much these global pains are felt within our own hearts.

This is a *shared* tragedy. That is a part of going beyond the self, and that is one of the ultimate message of The Self Beyond. We are here to heal ourselves, and extend that healing to each other. We are here to hold the Light and to carry Love like a lantern in dark places. This awareness empowers us into action. This, right now, is our chance to make a meaningful global impact and change.

THE ORDER

Look around at what happens when we lose our greater awareness. Wars are waged with public consent and no one questions the rhetoric of, even, the most blatant propaganda. Not all wars are waged with violence. Some are subtle. Some are mere ideas.

Walls are built while we forget how long we fought to tear them down. Raids and hostilities on innocent people, in the 21st century, so eerily reminiscent of WWII era Germany that, now, I do wonder if we can say with any integrity, that we would have stood up against Hitler and the rise of the Nazis. That rise did not happen in one day, it came on in layers building slow momentum, capitalizing on the weaknesses of people who just wanted to stay comfortable. That corrupt movement continued to push the boundaries of what people would allow as long as it meant they were still safe, even if their neighbors were not. We are watching the mechanism of this play out today. We have to be willing to be uncomfortable and unpopular if we want to truly stand on the right side of history.

Big media continues to wield weapons of mass deception to scare the masses into forfeit of not only rights, but forfeit of moral decency and, worse, common sense. Corruption painted so boldly, people, no longer averse to its presence, remark, "but is it art?" Collusion, outright lies and deception at the highest level of government, even where it affects millions, doesn't seem to trigger any real stirring for change. We are so tamed, they could open the gates, and we won't spook. They could kick us and we won't run.

We are facing a global agenda which seeks to control and corrupt, not only the social body, but the deeper spirit of man. There is a war on human consciousness. Do not be panicked, just by knowing this you are being inoculated from its effects. This battle is maintained by devices of social engineering, at nearly every institutional level, delivering willing submission to the bidding of corporate gluttony so deep, that not even the blood of millions could quench its thirst. So clearly defined are the parameters of status quo, and so forcibly imposed are the conditions of this submission, that any critical thinking "doubter", never needs to be destroyed by the system. The people will do it for them. Plays are carefully orchestrated to inflame every perceived value system, which is, then, used to manipulate our actions, our inactions, our reactions. Before the shock wears off, we are told how to feel about every next big event. Every incident is another "terror attack" linked to a constellation of defensive ideologies. What is *really* terrorizing us?

Ever weaving greater ambiguous and provocative threats, so built into the fabric of our lives, it has become commercialized, used to sell security like they would sell hygiene products. Entertainment and politics, so interwoven, viewing the "news" is like watching a reality show whose ratings are boosted by bad behavior. Concise and methodical psychological management, so effective that people are as programmed in what they think they believe, as they are in what they think they need to buy to survive. This apparatus of delusion has come at such a pace and frenzy, from so many directions, it has successfully fractured nearly every tribe of humankind to divide from our shared roots. It has shattered and fragmented us from the very core of who we are.

Understand the complex, yet, profoundly simple and effective systems, being used to maintain this strangle hold. We have to become aware to transcend these systems. Otherwise, we are no more than blind sheep, easily led by contrivances of the lost, led by the *least* and the *lowest* among us, compelled by the urgency of our lowest instincts; fear, scarcity, competition, and obliviousness. We must know, only the highest character and steadfast integrity we have within us, can deliver us into our most urgent moral imperative now. We know, deep down, that fear creates more fear. Fear acts to defend itself. Reason seeks truth. What is right?

Wake up and gently rage against the machine. Go in peaceful revolution, in sympathetic action. Go in with arms up, barely breathing, and show the presence of our strength has not vanished, but grown. We have not been divided, but the unbreakable common thread has been exposed.

Speak for the voiceless. Stand for the fallen. Seek those who have lost everything and heal what you can. Listen to their stories. Cry with the broken. Hold true to this connection of life that we share. Lift up your Light like a lantern in the darkness. *Do not be afraid*. Hold fast in your heart. Let us now show that despite over a thousand years of extortion and slavery, after decades of brutal tactical onslaught on the spirit of man, we are still here. We have not been quelled. We are the undying spirit of humankind, ignited.

> *I am a member of humanity. I believe we are all a part of a connected web of life. I value all life and earth itself to be sacred. I believe in freedom, respect, peace, and above all, Love. I refuse to be used as a mechanism of the perpetual violence, war, greed, and hate. I object to the acts of aggression and destruction made at will of those in power. I consider all acts which harm life, disturb the balance on this planet, or poison the spirit of humankind to be crimes against humanity. I believe life is precious, that Love is the answer, that knowledge is power, that truth can conquer a thousand years of lies, and that we can transcend this broken system. I believe that as I change myself, I change the world. And I am not alone.* [104]

---

[104] Please feel free to share this quote anywhere you can on social media to voice your opposition to the onslaught of global issues made at the will of those in power.

WAKING UP

To become truly self-aware as a species, we will have to recognize that we are all connected; that any organism which destroys itself, will not survive. We will have to recognize the backwards ways we have been thinking and living, the innate self-destructive tenancies of modern society. We seek security through war. We seek to maintain ourselves through destruction of irreplaceable resources. We seek improved quality of life through a kind of perpetual slavery. We seek synthetic connection, while disconnecting from what is directly in front of us.

Some would resent a person receiving public aid services, thinking, "Why doesn't he just work like the rest of us," while surrendering to the invisible double standard, as wall-street bankers receive bailouts in the *billions*. We do not always see the swollen faces of those neglected in the wake of corporate autocracy. We do not always see the poisoned waters on the shores of once beautiful beaches, created by commercial and consumer driven greed. There is so much work to do, and *we, the people,* need to wake up.

That is why Love and understanding are some of the greatest tools we will ever employ to manifest real change. They are not impractical or superfluous principles. They are, in fact, fundamental. Love and understanding are required to move beyond the broken paradigm of division into a cooperative model that has a chance to heal, to fix what is broken, and thrive. Understanding means looking at the bigger picture and becoming educated on the world around us, to understand how it operates, and how we *each* contribute to its health or disharmony.

Consider the implications of one powerful positive action, or one negative one. Look at how the world has been changed by one voice, one life, over and over throughout history. We do not need to have the greatest profound thought, or become some martyr to the ages. We simply need to become self-aware and do the work to change how we are living our personal lives. What we do *today* can, literally, change *tomorrow*. The greatest catalyst for a meaningful revolution begins with the ones we make for ourselves, in our own daily activities. It is our personal revolutions that become collective ones.

That is why the great masters have said, "Be the change you wish to see in the world." When you become aware of your connection to a larger collective organism in this universe, you become self-aware. You become responsible for, not only you, but for all life. This *changes* you, from a bystander into a powerful director of the energies of your life, a co-creator empowered to orchestrate real transformation in an, otherwise, synthetic and disconnected world. We can make progress in the race that matters as a team, working together. That, my beloved friends, is the only way—together.

If there is one thing I want people to understand, it is that *you* are powerful beyond measure. All these issues we see in the world, the corruption of political systems used as tools of corporate greed, the environmental destruction we are too scared to think about, because the vast extent of it just makes us feel small, the social injustices and human rights abuse that we can barely stomach other than to look away; we feel defeated before we even begin. But, we do have the power, and we have had it all along. The power is in our awareness, and our choices. If it wasn't, not a dime would be spent on managing every minor detail of what we think. Download that.

THE RE-EVOLUTION

To remember Love in a place where Love is forgotten,
that is our highest and most important task.

What we do, feel, think, and put our energies toward, what we share, and what we withhold, our actions and opinions, what we use and what we throw away, in every sense, each choice we make affects the world. That influence is spiritual, in that it is not only a material effect. The world is directly affected by the subtle energetic currents which we each feed. We feed these powerful waves of energy with our Love, we feed them with our misunderstanding, with our judgement or our acceptance. We see this energy shift as more people realize, it is not ok to hurt someone else. This is a shift we can see as we evolve beyond the mentalities of prejudice of all kinds. This shift is the impact we make when we refuse to buy into the division.

Our influence is also highly practical, in a sense that physical effects are measurable, tangible, and visible in the environment and communities of life surrounding us. This is the kind of change we see when people begin to grow their own food, or refuse to buy products of irresponsible industry. As we become more aware, that awareness grows into all areas of our lives: we start using natural cleaning products, we start recycling, we start eating healthier, and we start connecting with those around us with Love and respect. These physical shifts are noticeable as we become active contributors in creating the world we want to see.

We might begin to realize, through our own self-awareness, that *it is us who will change the world,* whether we like it or not. So, we have to do the right thing, make the right choices and changes that will benefit not only us, but all the life which we are connected to in this tapestry of existence. The pinnacle of self-awareness is to achieve collective awareness, to live for something bigger than yourself. When we help others, we help ourselves. When we heal ourselves, we heal others. This principle is interchangeable both ways, and operates as a positive feedback loop. All it takes is a spark for the fire of change to ignite.

GLOBAL COMMUNITY

What is our presence in the world? We are a part of a global community which cannot withstand the barrage of self-destruction for many more decades. What will be our individual contribution to cultivating our own tremendous potential, to create sustainability, development, and growth in the world? We are capable of synergizing a complete network of shared resources, where ideas and technologies are not sold, but contributed, where we could end war, hunger, and environmental destruction for good. Collective innovation and individual discovery could be the new mandate: to explore and go beyond what we have learned so far and to better, not only humanity as a species, but our footprint on this planet. Hell, we could be travelling among the stars if everyone could stop fighting!

Many people are turning off the news. I am glad to see this trend. But, many are scared to even mention the word "politics." I cannot imagine a time when politics has been more important to talk about, then right now. Politics affects all 8.6 billion people across the world.

Politics determines regulations that drastically impact communities and nations. Politicians lead the deciding body for social and environmental directives. Politics are at the center of nearly every world issue, because when 20 million people are starving, while the media focuses on dividing people by race, while congressmen retire as millionaires, while cutting their own taxes, while millions of people are displaced and without clean water, while Puerto Rico is still waiting for aid, while people are forced to set up go-fund-me campaigns just to pay their health bills, while billions in taxpayer dollars are spent on weapons and missiles, to gain control over oil resources for dirty energy that has been the foremost major contributor to climate change, then we have just touched on nearly every big issue. *Have we not?*

Politics decides what bombs are dropped and what troops are sent out—this means it, literally, calls out, who lives and who dies, creating traumatized veterans, creating millions of victims of war who were unanimously peaceful in most cases. People like you and me who just want to live out their lives with their families, whose livelihoods and families have been taken from them, who live in terror, who are brutalized and devastated, who have no help on the way, and despite my sincerest and most rigorous research, I simply cannot find the benevolent justification for what countries like the U.S. and others have done. To those people affected across the world, I am sorry for the actions of my country that have harmed the life that I (and so many others) hold sacred.

The more I seek to understand politics, the more I uncover the thickly embedded financial affiliations and blatant partisanship, and the more I understand: the governments are not for the people. They are for the corporations, and big business. Those big businesses have usurped any sense of human decency for profit and power. I will ask you to consider doing this research for yourself. Look at what those from other countries are saying, what they are dealing with. Hear their stories. Only through that will you begin to see beyond our so often one-sided storyline. If you have actively done this already, and continue to do this, I commend you. Hold your Light.

The Self Beyond

There are times in history when you have to take an unpopular position at the risk of many ignorant, or even violent reprisals, but many of us know, in our hearts, it is that time and it is the right thing to do. I have read too many horror stories, too many people who did not deserve their lives to be ruined who need us to not only wake up, but stand up. I am asking every reader to look deeper and make use of your most independent and critical thinking. Beware that the media (online and otherwise) will hone in on your most private preconceptions, and use skillful emotional manipulation to persuade you into believing you understand the true story—*challenge that story.*

These systems will inflate irrelevant drama and mitigate (or erase) their own errors. Do not allow the media to justify what in all clear conscience are crimes against humanity and decency. Voice your emphatic opposition to the ongoing military initiatives, the neglect of those who need water and food, not bombs. Voice your opposition to the ever dividing line. Our power is in our awareness, our unity, and our peaceful, but purposeful action.

This is not meant to create controversy but to empower you with perspective. Many of us simply do not think about the global community we belong to every day. What you now know, you cannot un-know. We can ignore it, or neglect it, but in doing so, we neglect a part of our self. Here, during this moment of global realization we come into deeper self-realization. We are all called to value truth over comfort. Know that you are not alone in this knowing. We have a collective voice. That voice is our power. We have the ability to act, and our individual actions shape the world. Be brave and where you now go, bring the Light of a greater mindfulness with you to speak and to act as an emissary for the world, all people, and all life.

ALL WAYS

When a man of color cannot walk down the street in a hoodie without being seen as a threat, or drive an ambulance, or stand, or lay, or put up no resistance and still be choked to death by those tasked to protect the people and uphold *justice*; when a woman of color who dared to oppose the officer who pulled her over and ask why, is found dead a few days later in jail; these stories chill me to the bone and they are occurring more and more often, especially under the current administration that seems to not only rally, but endorse it.

Out of nearly 1,200 people, 574 minorities (people of color) were killed by police in the U.S. in 2015. [105] This is just around half of the total deaths, yet black African-American or non-Hispanic people make up only around 12% of the population (as of U.S. consensus data from 2011). So many injustices are swept under the blue line, only to fasten political agendas on the backs of those whose lives were stolen.

If you or someone close to you is a member of the police, please, I compel you to promote the urgency of adhering to moral codes, to assess all courses of action with tenacious integrity, and provide a safeguard like the heroes we want to believe in. To those officers who are doing the right thing and acting as true protectors, we do *thank you*, and we rely on you to continue to do the right thing and stand strong.

Racism is not just deadly when it kills. It is deadly in all forms. In the form of discrimination, in lack of opportunity, and in challenges faced unique to marginalized communities. [106] Racism has not only operated as an ignorant opinion, but has also been used as a device of class warfare.

Racism is not just action, but inaction. It is not just what is said, but what is not said, the indirect judgements, biases, and preconceptions. These acts of "othering" are just as vicious as physical violence and just as damaging. This is where each of us must deeply examine, within ourselves to eradicate all signs of unreasonable assumption and social illiteracy to be replaced with *knowledge*.

Since 2001, in the craze of misplaced anger, anti-Muslim attacks skyrocketed. These were threats, acts of violence, verbal

---

[105] RT. January 2, 2016. RT. Almost 1,200 people, mostly minorities, killed by US cops in 2015. Retrieved from https://www.rt.com/usa/327740-killed-by-us-police/

[106] I offer my most vigilant sincerity in doing justice to this most relevant and imperative topic and to bring visibility, and even healing, to so many who have gone unheard, invalidated, and the many who still are, suffering and oppressed. Anything less than equal is not enough.

The Self Beyond

and physical assaults, and, even, murder. [107] These have continued as attacks on the mere *assumption* of a religious affiliation based on appearance alone, just as much as attacks on the religion itself. This wave has escalated, and it has not mattered whether someone identifies as Muslim or not, having brown complexion has been enough to usher vicious verdicts from the xenophobic.

For any reader who personally identifies with any of these traits or stories, I want you to know, I write this here for *you*, to be a voice of fierce opposition to the hateful, ignorant, and barbarous acts. *I hold you in my Light.* You are not alone in this stand. You have many allies who are with you now. I cannot know what you know, but I seek to be there and bear witness. I seek to stand directly in the path as an obstruction to injustice, along with many others.

I want every reader who is not facing these issues directly to please imagine what this reality must feel like. Have you considered the implications of this state? To have to fear walking down the street for the color of your skin, for your religion, to have to actually fear *calling* the police, to have to fear driving to the store or to your church, to have to fear for your home, your business, for your personal safety and the wellbeing of your family, your children? Can you imagine the gravity of this, of seeing these appalling realities play out on the news while you watch your daughter play, or while you send your son off to school? What would you tell them? What does that conversation sound like?

When thousands of members of white hate groups can, literally, march with torches, incite violence, and be called "fine young men;" while those of color march in peace with their arms up, saying, "Don't shoot" to protest the injustice of another life taken, only to be met with military audio weapons, sound bombs, smoke bombs, and rubber bullets, police armed with machine guns

---

[107] Please see: Kishi, Katayoun. November 21, 2016. Pew Research Center. Anti-Muslim assaults reach 9/11-era levels, FBI data show. http://www.pewresearch.org/fact-tank/2016/11/21/anti-muslim-assaults-reach-911-era-levels-fbi-data-show/ and SPLC. March 29, 2011. Southern Poverty Law Center. Anti-Muslim Incidents Since Sept. 11, 2001. https://www.splcenter.org/news/2011/03/29/anti-muslim-incidents-sept-11-2001

The Self Beyond

and snipers pointing riffles at them; peaceful protests intentionally sabotaged and infiltrated by planted cons to incite violence and demonize the protest as a whole—this is not just a marginal issue, but a red flag planted at the very roots of society. We make up that society, this is on us too. Indifference is tolerance, the kind of tolerance that maintains inequality and discrimination. The iniquitousness that exists draws its power from passive consent. It is not enough to disagree, or shake our heads at the violence we see. We are being called to stand up and speak out to rectify this imbalance.

Poverty and an ever increasing income disparity is a huge issue not just in third world countries but developed nations like the U.S. as well. 43 million people live below the poverty line in the U.S. alone as of 2015. [108] Poverty affects individuals and families across all lines, while minorities are disproportionately affected at a much higher percentage. I bring this up here, while it may seem misplaced in the context of this book, to bring greater understanding to what has prevented large groups of people from living their best life.

Dr. Martin Luther King was an avid voice for the poor to the end of his life because this issue is not just about money, but also, about oppression. The imbalance in poverty is, largely, due to many layers of an institutionalized system that profits at the expense of the poor. The impediments created are often not just tough to get beyond, overcome with a little hard work, but can be nearly impossible. Misperception number one to understand is that poor does *not* mean lazy. Poverty is not caused by careless people at the bottom, but careless people at the top. Some of the hardest working people just barely meet the poverty line.

"Imagine supporting your family on just $14,500 a year. That's what a full-time, minimum-wage job pays. According to the U.S. Census Bureau, a family of four needs to earn approximately $23,000 a year to live above the poverty line. Working full time, year-round at a minimum-wage job doesn't get you even close to that figure. We're talking about millions of

---

[108] What is the current poverty rate in the United States? Poverty Research Center, University of California. Retrieve from: https://poverty.ucdavis.edu/faq/what-current-poverty-rate-united-states

people—8.9 million working adults, in fact—who work full time but are unable to keep their families out of poverty. More and more, the face of the poor is that of mothers and fathers struggling to feed, house, clothe, and educate their children—parents who are doing their best but still aren't getting by." [109] In 2017 over 7.6 million Americans were working more than one full-time job and still in poverty.

Eight families, just eight, have more wealth than 50% of the bottom half of the entire world's wealth combined. It does not take a degree in social or political science to see, this is the mark of a deeply broken system.

Poverty, itself, creates cycles of more poverty, it is an ironic and sad fact that it is much more expensive to be poor. Poverty has also been used as a systemic weapon intentionally directed toward, largely, minority communities. Financial scarcity creates conditions for crime, and crime creates conditions for more poverty. [110] All of these factors stack up to greatly antagonize already challenging environments for survival. Lacking adequate resources, professional and educational opportunities becomes a huge deciding factor leading to one parent households, substance abuse, early pregnancy, and mass incarceration. There is a causal loop which must be solved and it begins and ends with recurrent social systems of prejudice and privilege. These systems are made possible through the sustained non-conversant judgements and justifications of those who quite simply, do not relate.

I am going to ask you each to do something of service, something of healing. Reach out and have conversations with your

---

[109] Steenland, Sally, Working Full Time and Still Poor, February 20, 2013, Center for American Progress, Retrieved from: https://www.americanprogress.org/issues/religion/news/2013/02/20/53929/working-full-time-and-still-poor/

[110] Please see: Samenow Ph.D, Stanton E. December 24,2014. Psychology Today. Crime Causes Poverty. https://www.psychologytoday.com/blog/inside-the-criminal-mind/201412/crime-causes-poverty and
Ward, Maurice. Feburary 1, 2015. National Dialogue Network. Poverty and Crime. http://www.nationaldialoguenetwork.org/poverty-and-crime/

neighbors and co-workers, understand their issues, their challenges, and their pain. If someone makes an ignorant or damaging comment, do not allow this to be acceptable or comfortable for them anymore. *Say something.* If you bear witness to someone being attacked verbally, or harassed, do not let the offender be supported by inaction. Say something. I'm not asking anyone to put themselves in harm's way. What I am asking is, to refuse to do nothing. When it is too dangerous call on help, but do not ignore it. We are tasked to make the presence of such ignorant, divisive, and hateful acts so intolerable, so repugnant and unwelcomed, that they are no longer accepted as punchlines, that they are banished from every place of reason. We need to educate and empower one another with such literateness that these divisive systems of violence are dismantled at their very roots.

UNCERTAINTY

Step back, there is some uncertainty here. It's a perspective shift, but on a personal level, uncertainty can be freeing. Uncertainty means an unwritten future, and the possibility of something better. Looking at the state of the world, none of us knows what will happen, how it will end, but each of us play a part in how this all plays out, do we not?

Things are falling apart, and breaking down. It is frightening. *But*, we each have a role in if this will be catastrophic or cathartic. Do you see it? We each have a place to bring healing, to build bridges over every wall, to stand up for those who are being oppressed, to do the right thing at the right time.

Uncertainty means the dark has not yet overcome the Light. The good has not been beaten out of us. Don't ever forget that. Within this uncertainty lives our chance to tip the scales back toward harmony, and the possibilities of co-creating a conscious, caring, and connected world. From a place of centered stillness within, you will know, peace is not only possible, it is *present*.

THE PARADOX OF THIS PARADIGM

One of the most useful insights I can offer is that the world we see around us mirrors the world within. When we reject the negative aspects of the world, ignore and deny it, it can be more damaging to the world. Just as it is within us, when we leave our sadness or pain no outlet to be acknowledged or expressed. When we accept the darkness as part of the wholeness, we can deal with the reality of that darkness as an unabridged part of our whole truth. We can look at the opportunities we have to grow, and, instead of neglecting the pain, we can heal it.

Many distractions have been placed as obstacles between you and your True Self. A world of healed connected people is bad for business, that's the bottom line. Because that is a world in which we need very little, aside from the basic essentials and the company of our tribe. That is also a world of individuals who are not easily fooled or exploited of by those who seek to dominate the faculties of man. Breaking free of this paradigm will not happen in a moment. It has been in the making for many decades now. Slowly and silently, people have been awakening into themselves. This momentum has been building as an insurgence of self-empowered, self-sufficient, self-liberated, and self-aware game changers.

There is an inherent paradox within the current paradigm. This is the ultimate puzzle, to which I believe there is an answer, but I leave it to you, the reader, to solve. Our current paradigm has acted like a smoke screen laid over our perceived reality. We have been conditioned to view our reality as one of competition, fear, separation, and duality. This has kept us sick, helpless, and submissive. The truth is that we each contribute to our world through our very awareness of it. Both individually and collectively, we are responsible for the manifestation of the reality we are experiencing. We know now, this is not a metaphysical concept. This is science and one of the longest understood components of ancient spirituality. This truth creates a paradox and I will describe it here:

On one hand, we must be aware of the truth, and we have done much of that work already. We know we cannot be ignorant of the inconvenient aspects of reality. Otherwise, we risk inaction in times when our action is imperative. On the other hand, we cannot focus on fear and negativity, either. Otherwise, we risk perpetuating the same destructive narrative of greed, conflict, and inequality. Therefore, there must be balance between what we know and what we feed into. This is where focus versus awareness comes back into play.

We cannot be afraid. We will not heal ourselves, or the world, by focusing on fear. Fear strengthens the momentum of the undertow like a self-fulfilling prophecy. Yet, there is a fine line between focusing on positivity, and living in denial. This is a very important contradiction to comprehend. Think of how we have been habituated, for many thousands of years, to expect an end devastation. All of our current global affairs seem to be fulfilling some kind of predestined end, to which we will, therefore, offer little resistance. Through prophecies, environmental predictions, and various other apparently well-meaning sources, many people have conceded to what they believe is part of "the plan", or inevitable.

With all respect due to every unique reader, I do not wish to disservice anyone or any belief system, I ask for this small consideration. Consider that we may have long past the "end times," many scholars of religion have proposed this, which would mean we are prepped to now move into a Golden Age of Light. Consider, further, that (maybe, just maybe) the rapture may mean, not a physical ascension, but a *spiritual* one. Consider that the return of the Spirit may mean the return of the Spirit within us. The Mayan calendar year reset on December of 2012. This did not mark an end, as many predicted, but a beginning of a new time cycle, a reset. In the Hindu calendar, we entered the Kali Yuga in 2012, as well. This cycle signifies an upward movement towards a time of awakening out of a deep sleep. Anyone familiar with Kali, understand destruction and creation are inextricably linked with this archetype. We are seeing both aspects unfolding worldwide today.

The future is written by the lives of many authors. We each usher in these changes. Utter destruction may have already occurred, many times, with us now on the other side of it emerging and tasked to rebuild.

Many of us have been implanted with this concept of an apocalypse, that all will end in some final epic battle of good and evil, the earth swallowed by fire and water. But, the word "revelation," itself, means disclosure, a surprising and previously unknown fact, especially one that has been held secret. Sometimes the beginning looks a lot like the end. Perhaps this time is a call to wake up and become our Golden Selves once more. To allow the King to return, *within* us.

I only know fear is the antithesis of Love. We cannot be afraid. Love, itself, must be backed by action, and our action cannot be based on fear. We must transcend this underlying loop.

We are powerful creators, too. We are dynamic, adaptable, and resilient beings. We must awaken, in whatever route the awakening takes form, whether by the notions of environmental concerns, political instability, social inequality, economic disparity, spiritual suffocation, or the need for deep personal healing. All of these can lead to a very necessary awakening for the whole of humanity, and, perhaps, that is the point.

We are now reconnecting with our healed selves and our wholeness. We can see beyond what has eluded so many before us. This is our time to come forward as healers, as medicine people, as Love warriors, as awakened ones, and to exemplify the Light of the world. [111]

> *"The difference between what we are doing and what we are capable of doing would suffice to change the world."*
> ~Mahatma Gandhi

---

[111] Some excerpts taken from: Falcon G., Lisa. (2013) Universal Hidden Insight: The Connection Between Love, Existence and Reality. Rochester, NY. Next Level Publishing. [I go much deeper into these global issues, the connection to our past, and the multilayered root causes in the first book, please do research these with this extraordinary, and vigilantly researched, publication.]

THE LIGHT SIDE

I do not want to reinforce the grim vision of a world gone mad, without highlighting the good news. The darker realities are very much present, but there is always a stream of Light shining down. We live in a time where many incredible things are possible. Diseases that were once death sentences are on the verge of being cured, like Polio and Smallpox. Doctors at LSU Health, New Orleans, and the University of North Dakota, have been able to reverse brain damage with hyperbolic oxygen therapy in a two-year-old girl. MIT Scientists have targeted an enzyme that may be responsible for the memory loss of Alzheimer's disease. Scientists are beginning to understand how we can repair spinal cord injuries to reverse paralysis. We are beginning to go beyond the limits of the body!

Astrophysicists can now actually "listen" to the universe, and the universe has responded! Yes, responded: in gravitational waves. There was the popular wave recorded in 2015, but there have been two more since 2017. [112] NASA and ESA are sending more detectors into space by 2034, known as LISA (Laser Interferometer Space Antenna), to study gravitational waves further. A team of scientists working on SpaceX with Elon Musk are planning to send rockets to Mars, and have already sent and returned a rocket to a small platform in the ocean. We are going farther than we have ever gone before!

For those born in the 1980's and earlier, you may remember the dark ages, in which only the rich could afford to buy encyclopedias to gain information about a vast array of subjects, either that, or spend many long hours in a public library. Now we live in an age of information, where much is available right at our fingertips. Sites like Wikipedia offer the largest information-based service in the world, for free. This underpins why measures protecting a free and open internet are so critical.

Political parties are becoming passé. As many people on both "sides" can now see the corruption present in the system as a

---

[112] Mcrae, Mike. Science Alert. June 1, 2017. It's Happening: LIGO Just Detected Gravitational Waves For The THIRD Time. Retrieved from: https://sciencealert.com/ligo-discovers-backwards-spinning-black-holes-in-yet-another-set-of-gravitational-waves

whole. The "system" is not working, and there is no hiding it now. On the surface, that may appear to be a bad thing, however, consider how this offers a new viewpoint, one which can transcend rigid party lines. This creates a new wave of possibility to build something better, to be truly independent.

Goals set by the World Summit in 1996, were set to halve the percentage of malnourished and hungry people by 2015. While there are still some 800 million hungry people with a long way to go to eradicate this humanitarian issue, 72 out of 129 countries included in the summit have come close to meeting this target within a small margin. [113] We are making progress, and this progress gives hope, and life, to millions more each year.

Despite what the news would have us believe, with new shootings, terror attacks, fires and floods every day: we are living in the safest time in history. Max Roser, an economist from Oxford University, is the creator of the website "Our World in Data." When examining global trends, such as violence, health and food access, his data shows evidence of positive trends. When looking at the bigger picture, long term changes, which can take decades to emerge, are showing a very different picture than the sensationalized singular events we see through the media. We are seeing, this is actually one of the most peaceful and inclusive times in history. This may be hard to believe, but the data shows deaths in every country decreasing dramatically since the early and mid-1900's. [114]

Across the world, great acts of compassion are made by regular people, every day. The media, often, ignores the good stories; stories showing the strength, the resilience, the kind-heartedness and the true power of humanity in action, but they are present when we really look. In one story a man in India has replanted an entire forest, by himself. Since 1979 Jadev Payeng has been replanting trees and today, the forest is lush, rich, and

---

[113] Food and Agriculture Report of the United Nations. World hunger falls to under 800 million, eradication is next goal. Retrieved from: http://www.fao.org/news/story/en/item/288229/icode/

[114] Raphael, T.J., October 23, 2014. PRI. The world is actually safer than ever. And here's the data to prove that. Retrieved from: https://www.pri.org/stories/2014-10-23/world-actually-safer-ever-and-heres-data-prove

thriving. In another story, at least 30 people came together to form a human chain and save a drowning family on the Panama City Beach in Florida in 2017. Look at what we can do when we come together. In Australia in 2014, at the Perth Train Station, dozens of onlookers came together to push a train off of a man whose leg was trapped.

More people, every day, are choosing to live a cruelty free life, centered around a healthy plant based diet. The number of vegans has increased 500% worldwide since 2014. You don't have to be vegan to see this is good news for the animals saved (more than 300 million animals were spared in 2017), the environment (80% of rainforest destruction is caused by clearing lands for factory farming, which is also the largest cause of carbon pollution), and the health of the individual (many diseases such as diabetes, heart disease, cancer and infections are directly connected to the consumption of animal products). [115]

There are more good stories than bad, when we really pay attention. In 2017, more than 200 nations promised to stop ocean plastic waste. On average, parents now spend twice as much time with their children than they did 50 years ago. A homeless veteran made news when he gave $20 to a woman who was stranded, and in turn, she helped raise enough money to buy his own home. There is still Light in the world, and we are each a part of that.

Police officers responding to a shoplifting call, decided not to make an arrest, and instead bought groceries for the struggling single mother who just wanted to feed her children. One women who found herself cooking too much food after all her children left home, decided to package up the excess and deliver it to homeless people in her area. When she arrived, she found a woman with three young children. The woman told her she had just been praying that God would feed not her, but her children. This one woman, literally, answered someone's prayers.

When I was at a local beach this summer (2017) at the peak of racial hostilities fueled by the media, I witnessed a beautiful thing: people of all races cooking up food with signs saying, "Hugs for Free." They offered food and bright smiles.

---

[115] Nemec M.D., Keith. All-Creatures.org. How Meat Can Destroy Your Health and Cause Heart Disease, Cancer, and Infection. Retrieved from: http://www.all-creatures.org/health/howmeatcan.html

They showed that our Love *can* dissolve all barriers. Over and over, grassroots community efforts to make a difference *work*. Feeding people, finding resources for those in need, growing and building projects, all of it matters.

> *"We still have a long way to go…If only we can overcome cruelty, to human and animal, with love and compassion we shall stand at the threshold of a new Hope In Action era in human moral and spiritual evolution—and realize, at last, our most unique quality: humanity."* Dr. Jane Goodall

THE CHOICE

We all have a choice, for the life we want to live, the person we want to be, and the world we want to help create. We choose each of these things every day. Each of these aspects are inseparable from the choice. They are affected with every decision we make. To do, is a choice. Not to do, is a choice. We are empowered.

We see the bigger problems as beyond us. We believe there are millions of people existing out there as some separate entity of otherness, but that is not truth. It is, instead, the million expressions and choices of one whole spirit force in many different bodies. We are connected with every expression, with every choice. If you want to heal the brokenness in the world, heal all the broken pieces within yourself.

No one has to settle. We can be anything we want to be. It's about believing we are capable of change and healing, in ourselves and in the world, and then taking the steps. It's simple. We want it to be more complicated, perhaps to keep it just beyond our reach because that makes it easier to refuse to change, but it is as easy as the choice you make right now. We do not choose to breathe, it is autonomic. We do not choose for our hearts to beat but they do. We have one moment, and we are in it. The only choice we have to make is to commit to that breathe, that beat, and the moment we are in.

We can change the world or let the world change us. Change is inevitable but you, Navigator, *you* steer the direction of that change. Your choices are your power. Every choice we make is important. Look at what you are doing today to make your life better, healthier, more balanced for you. Look at what you can do today to help heal yourself and those you make contact with. Choose from the moment you are in and keep moving forward. It gets easier and easier to make the choices that change everything for the better.

THE GARDEN

There is a garden within you. A garden that only you can tend. Like any wild thing, this garden contains beautiful flowers, precious blooms that come up to drink the Light, and weeds, here and there, that may choke the blossoms of what you want to grow. The weeds are our fears, our guilt, our over exaggeration of the perceived problems which obstruct what is good. The blooms are our dreams, the places we are growing that benefit our wholeness. The flowers are our capacity to Love, to enjoy our life, to make another's world better and brighter.

Tend to your thoughts, your emotional needs, your body and your spirit like a garden. Water your needs, nurture your growth, connect with your inner beauty and pull up anything that does not serve the garden within. Have a relationship with this garden inside of you. It is not silly or sentimental. This is your inner world. Your own personal temple. You do not need to go anywhere to seek it; it has been inside you all along. This is the most beautiful place you will ever connect with. As you tend your garden, you show others how to do the same. The world does not need warriors; it needs gardeners.

THE ROOT

So then, what is the biggest problem in the world right now? It is illusion. What is the biggest problem in the world right now? It is division. What is the biggest problem in the world right now? The failure to recognize every living being, every creature, every animal, every tree, every plant, every river, every ocean, and

The Self Beyond

every breath as a part of us—it is all connected. Do you get it? Can you see that this has been our ultimate self-destruction?

What is the biggest problem in the world, then? A lack of, not just Love, but a lack of self-Love. It is an entire species, segregating out pieces of itself it does not agree with, or does not understand. It is a lack of embracing and accepting the whole of who we are. Everything we reject is just another way we push away a piece of our own self.

This is the fundamental problem, not only in the world, but in ourselves. The solution, then, can only be a *revolution of Love*, greater than any revolution that ever came before it. A revolution of connection, of unity, of truth. The greatest problem in the world is directly connected to the only solution. And that solution is within you, right now. Be empowered. Love yourself, *every piece of you.*

The Self Beyond

Chapter 7: Activation and Ascension

ALCHEMY

Alchemy is not about just changing forms. True Alchemy requires disassembling every element to the fundamental level. Then, before putting it all back together, every aspect is purified—that is the key. This is the template for the greatest transformation of the spirit, to learn the mastery of taking apart, purifying and then transmuting the lead of the soul into the golden state, which is Love.

There is nothing that cannot be transformed into a higher state of being. There is nothing which cannot be enriched, mended, and revived by Love. As we stand within our truth, with open hearts, with a greater awareness, we are changed. We are capable of creating a meaningful transformation in ourselves, in our families, in our communities, and in the world. We are capable of transmuting heartbreak, pain, fear, and shame into an ultimate, and unconditional Love.

THE CRUX

Right now is the most important time in recorded history, and we are a part of that. We, collectively, get to decide if this will be the end, or the beginning. Yes, leaders are making reckless decisions that leave millions without protection for their most basic needs. Yes, corporations have overtaken the political stadium with their influence, which has turned democracy into a silent auction. Yes, violence is clear and present, we bear witness to genocides and mass subjugation in modern day, we see exploitation at the highest level affecting people and the planet, all pushed to the darkest corner of neglect. Yes, we still have our personal work to do in healing, and in becoming whole again. All of this is still present. What has now changed? *You have*.

We now see what has fooled us before: the roots of this getaway train. We see through the con of big money embedded in politics until the voice of one person seems all but dissolved. We are no longer ignorant to the corruption of corporate interests so intermingled with the overseeing powers that one has become indistinguishable from the other. We can now protect against the misdirection of big media to blame petty scapegoats so we ignore the real issues. We are aware that those in power want us conquered and divided; by color, by gender, by belief systems, and by every contrived faction. We are, perhaps now, aware that the very mechanics of this institution drives us to be disconnected and unhealed from within ourselves. But now, we have taken back our power: the power of choice, the power of individual awareness and action. Enlightenment in this sense means to become a spiritual revolutionary. We were once asleep, but now, we are awake.

To some, this time may appear to be the expiration of all that was good. I see a different outlook. I see this time, right now, to be a great unveiling of the sickness that humanity has harbored for generations. I see *right now*, as a time of uncovering the deep-rooted pain at the bedrock of our collective and individual identities. The wounds are being exposed. The need for healing has never been more apparent. This time right now, creates an unavoidable precipice from which we all must make a choice. Will we be better? Will we take responsibility? Will we feed the furious animosity and division of unconscious ego, or become something greater than we once were: as a healed, whole, connected and conscious contributor to collective change?

There is something bigger than you and me. There exists (if nothing else) a rich and diverse network of life, and we are *each* an intimate and central part of that network. We affect every level of that network as we progress and develop, as we heal and gain greater awareness. What happens out there starts in here. It all begins within us.

Our level of awareness, consciousness itself, is one of the greatest keys to making the shifts we need. Not only, to thrive as individuals, but to collectively heal this planet. To heal the root issues humanity faces, we have to evolve to a level of human consciousness that supports the web we are each connected to, meaning all life, every person, every creature, and every ecosystem which we rely upon. That is what it means to evolve as a species.

We change the world through becoming self-aware and socially aware. Be educated about the issues that matter, you can never learn too much. Be aware of the links between us, our families, our communities, our nations, and our world. Recognize and honor the vital contributions you can make and do not be afraid to rock the boat.

In a cohesive living network, every action has a consequence. This is a daunting obligation and an empowering mechanism for transformation. Every day, we are given the gift of a hundred new chances to choose what kind of change we will create. Through making those important choices we can begin to transcend the broken paradigms and create a new model, one in which we actively contribute to making the world better, through making ourselves better participants within it. As you heal yourself, you heal the world. As you wake up, the world awakens.

We have scaled this out big, but let's take this back home. *Start with where you are, right now*. Start with what you have, today. Start with broken pieces, start with questions, start with hands trembling and voice shaking. Start with the first thought upon waking, if you think of nothing else, say, "Thank you." Start there. Start with how you listen, start with how you speak, start with yourself and work your way out. Start with how you buy groceries and how you talk to your children, start with how you drive and in the smiles you give away. Start with any moment as a brand new opportunity; to be there, to be you, and to give yourself completely.

We wait until we can be more, but there is nothing more you need to be. There is no later time, no bigger reason, no greater cause to devote yourself to. It is happening now, in the seeming trivial interactions. It is happening right now, in between the lines we don't read. We do not have to do something world shaking to shake the world. Be kind, offer your gifts, and don't ever feel that's not enough. We cannot do everything the world needs, but the world needs everything we can do.

DRIVING FORCE

The driving force must be Love, especially Love for something bigger than ourselves. We are all connected: one organism, connected by Love. Love is a Lighthouse to guide us Home. Love is the mountaintop which allows us to see beyond our imagined limitations. Love is a bridge from one heart to another. Love is the tool that unlatches the traps of division. There is so much suffering, injustice, destruction, greed, abuse of power, and millions of unhealed people with whom we share this world. It seems the scale of mad delusion is unconquerable and may never be righted. Yet, every cruel action, every ignorant opinion that bolsters division, every injury delivered, is a sign of someone reaching out to know Love, to be healed, to be whole.

We will change the world whether we want to or not, I promise you this. You are changing the world every day you walk out of the house, with every conversation you have, with every person you interact with, with every product you buy, with every caring or uncaring contribution you make. Every time we hurt our self or another, we fuel the wave of hurt. And more powerfully, every time we support healing in ourselves or for another, we fuel waves of healing that *cannot be measured*. These waves ripple out in ways you cannot possibly imagine the impact of.

Why are we afraid, when we are empowered in such a way to be capable of manifesting, not only change, but groundbreaking change? We see so many scary stories everywhere we look. Those that are harming this planet, harming the people, desecrating the sacredness of life, are on their last legs. They are making one, last, desperate power grab to try and maintain what is crumbling of their wretched endings. They cannot win. There is still good in this world, and if you really pay attention, you might observe that people are overwhelmingly generous, caring, and kind. The Light will overcome.

Anchor the Light within you. Meditate on that Light surrounding you. Visualize that Light, literally, encompassing you, your space, your home, your Loved ones, and all beings which share our earth. Pray or meditate for *all* beings to be protected, to be at peace, to heal, to become whole, and to remember the Great Spirit that connects us (however we define it).

In these troubled times, ground yourself in Love. With such intense forces of destruction waging reckless war on the very spirit of humanity, meet and match that force in equal intensity with Love in everything you do.

Be good to everyone around you. I cannot stress this enough. *Be good to everyone around you*, every path you cross, as often as you can. It is ok to feel anger. You should be angry if you're paying attention, but use that as a tool, not a weapon. Let that embolden your sense of utter necessity in embodying and extending radical Love and acceptance. There is nothing in this world that cannot be made better and brighter through Love. Love will have the final victory. That is the only part of the story that has always been set in stone.

YOUR CALLING

Do not become infatuated with the extraordinary. The world doesn't need extraordinary people. There's enough of the extraordinary, already. The world is in need of the ordinary things by regular people, people who show compassion, feed the hungry, help grow gardens, rebuild homes, and share in basic kindness and connection. We don't have to be amazing to do amazing things. All we have to do is care. All we have to do is see we are part of something much bigger than ourselves.

You are being called to rise. You are being called to heal. You are being called to act, to speak, and to kindle the fire from within. It is Time. The time to liberate all that has been suppressed. This is not a mistake or a generic anthem meant to be taken lightly. You are One among an ever-growing body of awareness. You are being asked, now, to raise up with your highest intentions, to summon every gift within you and play your part. You are being called to use your heart as a beacon. You are being called to make Love your greatest art. You are now being asked to bring back what was forgotten, to share it, to embody it, to ground it to our plane of existence so deeply, that its roots cannot be upended.

If Love is your calling, then Love with all your heart. If building is your calling, then build bridges, not walls. If medicine is your calling, then bring good medicine, bring healing. If writing is your calling then write a message that will change the world. If music is your calling then let your instrument carry the Song. If you are a visionary, then envision a better world and seek to create that. Whatever path you choose, go where your gift is most needed. Go as if you are bringing water to the thirsty. Whatever you do, whatever your passion, there is a reason for it. It is a gift not to be wasted, but shared. Now is the time you are called to cash it in. Use it to make the world a better place.

Know your purpose; know your mission. Get quiet enough to become clear in your hours of self-connection. We are not here on accident. We chose to do this. We have come to change the world. As we have healed what was broken in ourselves, we know *there is wisdom in our wounds*. There is revolution in our blood. We all have one task: to align with our highest self, open our heart and represent Love in every aspect of our existence. Let this Love stir within you to surge, like a wave that will transform the very face of our world. Return to read these words as often as you need them, and know, you are Loved. You are deeply, truly, Loved.

ATLAS

Take a deep breathe. Are you ready? You have now carved a pathway back to your heart. You will continue in your healing, as your awareness increases, your connection will fuse even deeper. You are strong. You are important. You are worthy. You are free. You are safe. You are cared for. You are supported and guided with Love.

Every action is a choice. If we made more choices from a place of Love that recognizes the me in you, and the you in all things, I am certain this would be a great change in the world, from

The Self Beyond

what we eat to how we drive, from what we say to how we listen, from what we do for others to how we Love ourselves. That is our power, the power to change, and it is the only real power there is.

What is the centerpiece of the new life you are entering into? What, now, will be the focus in the life you want to lead? Do not get lost in the complexity of human drama or the seduction of self-limitations. Do not get swept away by the overcast projections of dreary days to come.

You are the Atlas, the map is within you. The Sun on the horizon, the stars above you. You are the Captain of your ship. You can steer toward the storms that have overturned you so many times before, or set sail for better shores having learned to read the skies. You get to decide the meaning your life will, ultimately, have. You are the director of your sails, you are even, in the wind that moves them. Head north.

ACTIVATE

What does it mean to activate, to make something active, or operative? To activate is to become, or, rather, to come into being what we have always been, but had lost sight of for so long. We came into this world activated. We came in shining as Lights with full Love. The ultimate takeaway is that you *already* have it within you; you just need to turn it on. Connect within yourself. Light up your own sky. This is not just about what we know we should do, but what we are actively doing, not just who we want ourselves to be, but who we are actually *being*. The world is made by the activity of many lives. Our lives are crafted by the level of our actions and self-awareness. Higher awareness means higher actions, higher actions mean higher impact.

There is nothing in this universe that is not already whole and complete. One already with the Universe/ God/ Source (however this resonates with you personally). The Divine Intelligent Love of all Creation that flows through worlds, also flows through you. Flowing even now, through your veins, through your breath, through every word, and, every silent moment of reverent awe. Make sure you are listening.

Make sure you can now understand how to come here to this place, deep within yourself, where all the tools, insight, guidance, healing and higher wisdom is always available. Take all measures to restore your highest right state of consciousness in Love and full activation. Take every next step you must to come into a deeper personal evolution.

We have been like a person lost in a thick woods of darkness, stumbling around through impassible bushes and twisted vines. No light could reach us from this place. But, as we have sought our way over many dark nights, now we have found a path to take us onward, a path back to the Light. Follow your pathway and know that, this path, *your path*, will lead you Home.

We are not here together in ego. We come as representatives of the Universal collective. We have a divine directive and soul purpose. We are tasked to transform ourselves and the world through our very existence. We are meant to coexist and co-create in Love. We can, now, act as a reflection of the higher Light we are meant to embody. We can now be an emissary of the most sacred message, which is *Love*.

We are the change the world needs, if we would just step up. We activate through our own healing, through alignment from within extended outward. We activate by becoming part of a culture of intelligent compassion, intentional creation, and cooperative partnership, through initiating meaningful connections and engaging in open and honest dialogues. We activate through restoration projects, through cleanup efforts, through education and empowerment of others.

We share all this with dignity, honor and courage. Someone once said, "Imagine that every person in the world is enlightened by you" (a quote often misattributed to Buddha). Imagine, instead, that *you* are enlightened by every person in the world.

CROSSING OVER

Find the place where the Light envelopes you. Feel it breathing through you, pulsating, like a great heart. There is a bridge within you, between here and there, crossing over this world and the next. You will find, even as you have been waiting, that you have *already* crossed over. Ground this higher energy of

The Self Beyond

Light and Love so deeply into the earth that it *sings*. Sing to the lost, the hungry, the homeless. Sing to those that are suffering in need. Let your heart sing and be there for those who need hope. Peace be in Palestine, Syria, and the Middle East. Peace for the people who have lost everything. Peace for all races. Peace for all beings. Compassion and action for Yemen, Somalia, Sudan, the horn of Africa and *all* who need humankind to reach out. Peace and comfort for all coming home. Peace for all those who are now passing through.

You are on your most sacred journey and you have come so very far. This journey continues long after the pages end. Remember these lessons and stay devoted in your own practice, seek with your heart *in Love*, and you will not lose your way.

May we hold this shift, this cosmic charge, in who we now *are*. May we resonate with the spirit of the earth and Love her fiercely, gently, with respect, and honor her every tree, rock and river. May we take only that which we need. May we know nothing is ours. All is borrowed, even this body, even this soul.

May we be utterly grateful in every now moment. May we heal in our healing and spread kindness like wildfire. May we master our emotions and thoughts in what we now co-create. May Unconditional Love and deep understanding grace everything we do. May we live up to the Light of the Masters, by being the Light of the world which we share. Beyond belief, dogma, ideology, or limitation, this is what we make it: a shared dream of a better world. This is how we become, and hold, the greater Self Beyond.

THE UNCONQUERED

  Warriors of Light, there were, who fought back the onslaught for endless Ages, standing against greed and misplaced power that embittered so many men. Great illusions had projected onto their minds by the shadows, but held there the Awakened onto the Highest Truth, walking the Way, and keeping their Balance, in tune with the Cosmic Tides and the Eternal forces beyond. Opening their heart space, they tapped into the Sacred Wisdom. Felt they, within them, a deep connection to the Soul of the Source, took up Compassion to bear as the Sun, and blaze through the veil that stayed many men in their sleep. All with a wick to bear flame were watched over by the Knowing, until too grew within them a Fire of Light. Kept clear the vigilant Message of Love from the All Loving Spirit, and never were they conquered by the fierceness of Night.

  One by one, the Light Within kindled and sparked into a Divine and Unbroken Flame. Every Fire, lighting up hundreds of others to Rise, like a Star, past the Darkness of Night. Vibrating higher, rising and lifting, until the shackles were broken and thrown to the earth. Glowing and shining as Children of the Sun, having remembered the rights of their birth. The Water of Life pierced through all barriers until, at last, they were Freed from the shadow of night. Expanding and seeing with pure inner vision, crystalized within them the Light of the All, the Heart at the Center, the great Soul of Creation, ready to be joined Together with the many as One.

  Stay on your Path and Walk in your Truth. Know you already the answers of the Heart. You, my Beloved, will be carried homeward, there to be celebrated and welcomed as a child and a Champion, of Light, one with the All, One in your Wholeness, back into the Eternal Embrace beyond the self, within the Great Beyond.

The Self Beyond

Once the river has met the ocean, there is no way
of going back.
~Swami Rama

The Self Beyond

Affirmations for a New Beginning, starting Today!

- Today, I am making a change! Today is a beautiful new day!
- I have energy and focus to make the most of this time!
- I Love and accept myself! Everything I need is within me and available to me!
- I am safe. I am protected! I allow the flow of life without resistance.
- If I have a chance to help someone today I will do it!
- I will show kindness and offer my service as often as I am able!
- I have faith that all is well and moving towards my greatest joy!
- In the infinity of life where I am, all is perfect, whole and complete! (Louise Hay)
- I am worthy of Love, respect, and compassion!
- I have a boundless well of Love, deep at the center of my being that is always available to me!
- Life is simple and meaningful! I do not have to worry, I have what I need.
- I am doing what I Love and Love permeates all that I do!
- All my relationships are harmonious, Loving, and peaceful!!
- I am divinely supported and constantly guided through my journey!
- I release all expectation and I Trust that all I need will come to me!
- I release all negative conditions, thought patterns and emotions that have created situations, relationships, and illness that no longer serve me!
- I forgive the past and let it go.
- I allow myself to learn the lessons I needed to learn, I bless them, and let them go, as well.
- I allow the space for True Love, well-being, joy, and prosperity to come into my life!

- I have aligned with the right energy and created the conditions in my life to manifest and maintain a life of enjoyment, abundance, and Love!
- I am worthy and deserving of kindness and respect!
- I am in sync with the divine flow. I am always in the right place at the right time.
- I am in balance and harmony. I have peace in my heart. I have Light in my heart.
- I am connected to the Source of Love at all times! I trust the Source and the Source within me.
- I am connected to my higher self! I am aligned and balanced in all energy centers.
- I am conscious of the energy I feed into. I only feed Love!
- I do not allow anyone to take from my energy or attach negative impressions to my energy field. I vibrate on Love.
- I am a constantly overflowing vessel receiving, amplifying, and radiating Universal Love.
- I am the creator of my reality. I am confident! I have faith! I allow! I receive!
- Miracles happen every day, miracles happen to me!
- Everything is possible today!
- The Universe is filled with Magic and that Magic flows through me.
- I surrender to the Highest Divine plan!
- I extend Love, compassion and blessings to ALL beings, I hold all others as a part of me.
- I am blessed! My life is blessed! All I experience is blessed!!
- I am connected to the Loving Intelligence of All things.

The Self Beyond

To Help Others:

Understanding world issues and the many humanitarian crisis can enable us to effectively take action. I believe education is empowerment. Here are just a few issues in which we can make a huge difference if we can extend our Love and support to our world family that needs us. For every purchase of this book a significant portion of the proceeds will be used to support refugees, as well as environmental and wildlife conservation. [116]

[117]

---

[116] 1/3 of all proceeds from this publication to be donated to the International Rescue Committee (IRC), animal conservation (Defenders of Wildlife and Edgar's Mission), and rainforest preservation through the Rainforest Action Network (RAN).
[117] Obtained from Pexels photos under CC0 creative commons license

Cholera Crisis in Yemen,

Thousands of civilians have died since the start of a brutal conflict in Yemen (2011-2012), and millions more have been displaced inside the country. 60% of the country is food insecure and over half the population is unable to access safe drinking water. Many areas in Yemen are just one step away from a famine situation.

The war in Yemen has caused more than 8,000 deaths - mostly of civilians - according to the World Health Organization (WHO). More than 44,500 people are estimated to have been wounded. The situation in the country of some 27 million has been worsened by a massive outbreak of the bacterial infection cholera. More than 600,000 people are expected to contract cholera in Yemen (2017). More than 370,000 people have fallen ill and 1,800 have died since late April in Yemen's second cholera outbreak in less than a year, according to the ICRC and WHO. According to the WHO, 5,000 new suspected cases of cholera are registered every day in Yemen, which is facing the world's largest outbreak of the disease. A Child dies every 10 minutes in Yemen.

Radhya Almutawakel, Chairperson of Yemeni NGO Mwatana Organization for Human Rights, said, "As the bombs rain down on civilians and the blockade imposed by the Saudi regime stop goods coming in, time is running out for people in Yemen. More than 10,000 have been killed, 20 million people are living in desperate need, including those affected by the world's worst ever outbreak of cholera, and a child dies every ten minutes of disease and hunger. The sale of weapons to Saudi Arabia for use in Yemen must stop immediately."

How to help:
- For more on how to support the children and people in Yemen through Doctors without Borders, you can go online to:
  http://www.doctorswithoutborders.org/country-region/yemen
- The International Rescue Committee (IRC) is also a pivotal organization providing aid, supplies, and support to refugees worldwide. See more at:
  https://www.rescue.org/

Help for the People of West Papua,

In West Papua over 500,000 civilians have been killed in genocide against the indigenous population of West Papua in Indonesia. Thousands more have been raped, tortured, imprisoned or 'disappeared' after being detained. Entire villages have been demolished, entire generations wiped out. Basic human rights such as freedom of speech are denied and Papuans live in a constant state of fear. The world needs to know what is happening in West Papua, but the government of Indonesia is blocking human rights investigators.
    Learn about more ways to help the people of West Papua at https://www.freewestpapua.org/

"I am a West Papuan independence leader. When I was a child my village was bombed by the Indonesian military and many of my family were killed. Later, I began to campaign peacefully to free my country from Indonesian occupation. For this 'crime' I was arrested, tortured and threatened with death. I managed to escape to the UK, where I now live in exile. My people are still suffering. Hundreds of thousands have been killed, raped and tortured. All we want is to live without fear and for West Papua to become a free and independent country."~ Benny Wenda

Human trafficking is a form of modern slavery—a multi-billion dollar criminal industry that denies freedom to an estimated 40.3 million people around the world. This was recently unmasked by the media in places such as Libya, but the sad reality is that this is occurring around the world and most often targets the already disadvantaged and poor communities. From the girl forced into prostitution at a truck stop, to the man who is kidnapped, stripped of his passport and held against his will while his family is demanded to pay bribery. All trafficking victims share one essential experience: the loss of freedom.

Who is affected? Men forced to work in fields, mines, or shops, held against their will and kept in inhumane conditions, women forced into prostitution or day labor, people forced to work in agriculture, domestic work and factories, children in sweatshops producing goods sold globally, entire families forced to work for nothing to pay off generational debts, young girls forced to marry older men.

There are estimated 40.3 million people in modern slavery around the world, including:

- 10 million children
- 24.9 million people in forced labour
- 15.4 million people in forced marriage
- 4.8 million people in forced sexual exploitation

How to help:

- **Antislavery.org** www.antislavery.org/
- **End Child Trafficking** www.savethechildren.org/
- **Coalition Against the Trafficking of Women** http://www.catwinternational.org/
- **Global Alliance Against Trafficking of Women** www.gaatw.org/
- **End Slavery Now- Volunteer to help** www.endslaverynow.org/act/volunteer

Peace for Palestinians

The situation in the Gaza strip and West Bank has come to a head at the tail end of 2017 and with interference from foreign leaders enraging an already inflamed situation. Since the Palestine war in 1948, a line was literally drawn to divide Israel and Palestine which ran through homes, neighborhoods and communities, displacing millions. Without taking a political or theological stance on this (and with great respect for those seeking peace on both sides), I hope to bring awareness to the humanitarian crisis; today.

"Nearly one-third of the registered Palestine refugees, more than 1.5 million individuals, live in 58 recognized Palestine refugee camps in Jordan, Lebanon, the Syrian Arab Republic, the Gaza Strip and the West Bank, including East Jerusalem" (cited from UNRWA). The United Nations Relief Works Organization for Palestine refugees in Near East Global News reports that the staff of UNRWA, which runs 82 schools, provides food, and shelter to over 200,000 displaced Palestinians, are at a "breaking point" trying to deal with this humanitarian crisis.

There is a clear highly repressive military occupation present, which has defined the Palestinian and Israeli political relationship. Many activists and scholars have criticized the violence, both within Israel borders and occupied territories. As awareness grows of this issue, the Palestinian situation only worsens.

The attacks on Palestinian children:

On December 19th, 2017, 16 year old Ahed Tamimi was arrested by Israeli occupation forces and taken from her home and parents in the middle of the night. Ahed has been charged with 12 crimes which sees her facing a jail term of up to 12 years for resisting Israeli soldiers. This is not an isolated event, young children often arrested and detained, accused of "throwing stones."

Israel's occupation routinely targets children: Israel systematically detains and prosecutes children through military courts, lacking basic due process. According to Defense for Children International-Palestine, Israel prosecutes 500-700 Palestinian children in military courts, annually. At this moment

450 Palestinian children are kept in military prisons by Israel, waiting extensive periods for trial; denied access to their parents, intimidated, interrogated, often abused and harassed. Some as young as 12, and holds on average more than 200 Palestinian children in detention at any given time. With a 99% conviction rate, it is a terrifying situation for many families. Child-detention is a violation of child rights, human rights and international law. Investigations by United Nations agencies (including UNICEF), Human Rights Watch, Bt'selem, Amnesty International and Defense for Children International – Palestine, have found evidence that:

- 3 out of 4 Palestinian children arrested experience physical violence during arrest or interrogation.

- 85% of Palestinian children arrested were blindfolded and 95% were hand-tied, denied access to lawyers and their parents during interrogation and are coerced into signing confessions.

- Palestinian children are often held in 'administrative detention'–children can be detained for many months without charge or trial.

How to Help:

- One of the very best things you can do, right now, is to write your representatives to urge Israeli authorities to release immediately and unconditionally all political (child) prisoners.
- The Palestine Children's Relief Fund has an urgent Gaza fund. "PCRF is responding to this ongoing crisis by identifying injured kids and providing them with critical medical care, as well as providing poor, displaced families with the urgent humanitarian aid that is needed." http://www.pcrf.net/

Rohingya Refugee Crisis,

Since August 25th of 2017, over half a million Rohingya refugees have fled the Myanmar's Rakhine region. Myanmar has a dominant Buddhist community and the Rohingyas are a Muslim minority. They have been the targets of violence by both the state and nationalist groups. Sadly, the Myanmar government refuses to recognize the Rohingyas as citizens and, as a result, they have been denied basic rights and employment opportunities. They have faced persecution and have been told to follow Buddhism. The clash between Rohingya and Myanmar forces have led to entire Rohingya villages being burnt to the ground, causing widespread destruction for thousands of residents in the area.

Rohingya refugees in Bangladesh told Human Rights Watch that Burmese government security forces had carried out armed attacks on villagers, inflicting bullet and shrapnel injuries, and burned down their homes. Exact numbers of displaced people are unknown and hard to determine, but an estimated 370,000 people have crossed the border into Bangladesh and more are coming every day. Urgent needs include food, water, sanitation, shelter, medical and trauma care.

To provide help,

- International Refugee Committee (IRC) The International Rescue Committee responds to the world's worst humanitarian crises, helping to restore health, safety, education, economic wellbeing and power to people devastated by conflict and disaster. https://www.rescue.org/
- Khalsa Aid is an international NGO with the aim to provide humanitarian aid in disaster areas and civil conflict zones around the world. The organization is based upon the Sikh principle of 'Recognize the whole human race as one'. https://www.khalsaaid.org/
- UNHCR, the UN Refugee Agency, is a global organization dedicated to saving lives, protecting rights and building a better future for refugees, forcibly displaced communities and stateless people. http://www.unhcr.org/

**Go beyond ego and step into being,
go beyond being and step into Love.**

The Self Beyond

Lisa Falcon G. grew up in the Finger Lakes Region of New York State. She took an active interest, at a young age in spirituality, creative arts, and the great mysteries of life, constantly seeking to expand her understanding of the universe, existence, and love. She spent several years in the Adirondack Region of NYS, which was a pivotal time in her spiritual growth, her appreciation for the deeper meaning of life, and developing her higher awareness. This foundation continued onward in the work she began almost a decade later. Lisa has spent two decades researching and studying many subjects related to spirituality, science, and the human condition. In 2014, she published her first book, Universal Hidden Insight, The Connection Between Love, Existence and Reality, and The Self Beyond in 2018.

She continues to do work through her writing, research and website to raise awareness about global issues, to educate and empower individuals to be a part of the change the world needs, and, ultimately, to look within themselves to create a greater awakening of Love.

"The Self Beyond is a response to a greater need for spiritual perspective, insight, and deeper healing in humanity, and the call for global action at an individual level." ~Lisa Falcon G

Universalhiddeninsight.weebly.com

The Self Beyond

Dedicated to Playa 2004-2016~

A Special Soul: thank you to the spiritual team that worked through me for this amazing book. I felt many masters speaking to me, guiding and supporting me as this process of creative expression unfolded. To my soul team present here on earth, and to those on the other side, to the Bright Light which inspired this, I am filled with gratitude and infinite immense Love for all you have shared. This belongs to you All. May it fulfill the mission of raising the vibration on earth, and instill within many the awakening within.~

Made in the USA
San Bernardino, CA
23 October 2018